We Call Our Daddy "Mister"

We Call Our Daddy "Mister"

James E. Schell

In Defiance of Convention

Life and Times at the Rose Hill Plantation

Grateful acknowledgment is made to the following for permission to reprint previously published material:

Chattahoochee Valley Historical Society for its Bulletin entitled Pinewood Cemetery and other documents hereafter mentioned.

The Troup County Historical Society for documentation and photographs recounted herein.

ISBN: 978-1-4276-0692-1

Alfred Lee Harrell,

Patriarch

(1808-1866)

List of Illustrations and Photographs

Illustrations

Photographs

- Miss Mary Bessie as "Miss Tenth Street High School" with attendants (l-r, Mary Alice Hunter, Dorothy Wright, Minnie Tatum, Hettie Lou Canady)
- Class of 1945 (Alfred at right, top row),
- Class of 1947 (Mary at left, 2nd row, et al)
  -Mary and Jim Fannings highlighted
- Glee Club, 1946 (Mary and Gaines at center, 3d row, et al),
- Jim and Mary
- Wedding scene, Elbert Fields, Nanny Fields, bride Patsy Fields and groom Jim Fannings Jr., Mary and Jim Ernest Fannings, Sr.
- CME Church Scene (Jim and Mary flanking members)
- MSgt Gaines Tyrone Winston-Harrell
- Gaines and Friends at Ft. Jackson, SC, 1951

Back Cover (MSgt Gaines T. Winston-Harrell)

Contents

Foreword

The impetus for the story you are about to read came from the gathering of former students and graduates at the Tenth Street High School Reunion in West Point, Georgia. In 1999, attendees at the high school from the 1930's until its close in 1957 were welcomed at the Lafayette Inn in LaGrange, Georgia. West Point no longer had a facility large enough to accommodate such a large gathering.

As is common at reunions, a great deal of time was spent trying to recognize one another. Some had not seen each other since graduation day whenever. Some who attended were never known to have gone to that school at all yet somehow were welcome. It was just amazing to witness all of the camaraderie, goodwill, and joy experienced. Most had married and dragged their spouses along with them. There were more than two hundred attendees. Most of the celebrants were relatively mature as it had been 43 years since the school closed and was demolished for highway construction associated with Interstate 85. Some were in their eighties but partied along with their sons and daughters and grandchildren, no less.

The air was festive. Auld acquaintances had been renewed and long running feuds had been forgotten. It was not realized that so much fun could be had particularly when one recognized that the education received was at best substandard and for all of the deprivations that had been experienced, it really didn't matter anymore. For the most part, a great many of them had succeeded in overcoming many of these obstacles and pitfalls so as to be proud of their accomplishments of family and of careers in later life.

It was banquet time. The ladies arrived in all of their splendor and finery looking as exquisitely fine as they did on graduation day eons ago. A few of the past faculty members were there, including a couple of principals arriving, in surprise, to receive their students of long ago. They, too, had come from all over the United States. And to the person, each was recognizable after a while although a bit stooped, bespectacled, and with an accompanying hearing aid, a cane, here and there.

The food was sumptuous. All of the vittles that were the staples back when were served up and piled high and bountifully so that one could gorge oneself, if desired. Then came the promised short speeches but many were so long winded that anticipating the end was tiring.

There was dancing and table hopping, slide showing, backslapping and the expected farewells in case on Sunday, the next day, not everyone could say goodbye at the church of choice. It was the slide show which produced a photo showing a "white boy" in dead center of the picture among of all others being "colored" except one other who was his sister. That center shot was a trompe l'oeil that inspired this story. The lights were turned up brightly so there was a full view of the massive banquet hall. There were two tables off to one side of the room. A sea of white persons occupied these two tables. Now Tenth Street High School was segregated throughout its existence, so what gives? Did integration take place after the Supreme Court decree in 1954 and this was the result of compliance? Not a chance! These were the Winstons and their families. A rare sight in the South of such mixing of the races even to this day. They were being fawned over as usual and the Winstons reciprocated such as well. They were these kind of people. The first notion that came to mind when seeing this intermingling is why the Winstons, as they were black, not cross over to escape the harsh treatment and deprivations of the society? Some of their spouses were actually white but one didn't know that and truly didn't seem to care. Here was a family as comfortable in its "blackness" as its "whiteness." If one knew no better, one would think that there is a story in this. Just think of all of the situations that did and could arise. Relocating away from the black community forever as many did never to see their loved ones again. The isolation that would have to take place to protect their secret life to be lived would be foreboding. The denial of one's being behind the mask of another. The pretense that must be maintained to hide this "imitation of life" spectacle would be a daunting life indeed. The fear of being exposed or "outed" would be ever present to the point of one's becoming a sheer basket case. Life would be a living hell.

x

Acknowledgments

This story relates the life of the Winstons and their relatives coursing through a world of uncertainty and still surviving standing up. The story could not be told unless there was the involvement and some accommodation by John Will Johnson, Jr. of the white side of the family, Chairman Emeritus of the CharterBank of West Point Georgia, and maintains his practice of law as well. His knowledge of the family's history and being was invaluable in getting a "male point of view" of the certain happenings although he allowed that he didn't learn of "Uncle Burrell's family" until he, "Bubber," was 35 years old (1955). It was his insight and his occasional association with his Uncle Burrell that revealed so much of the character of Burrell Floyd Harrell, heretofore, somewhat of an enigma to the author and many others. All five of Burrell Harrell's sons had passed on at the initiation of this project.

Sincere appreciation is extended to Frank Colville Harrell, the son of another nephew (Roy Harrell, Sr.) of Burrell Floyd Harrell, for insights, recall, and his extensive knowledge of the affairs of his Uncle for over a century and a half as well as his analytical skills in conveying it to the author. It is Colville who today governs and manages much of the property acquired by his Uncle Burrell and later his father, Roy W. Harrell Sr. Colville is further complimented for his review of the manuscript for perception and accuracy from his family's point-of-view. Some of the assertions made herein may not necessarily be considered favorable to the image of the family itself.

Acknowledgment is extended to Pearson Parker's contribution, which provided some in-depth male insight into the lives of his five uncles, only one of whom was ever married. Pearson is the eldest grandson of Rosa Winston and Burrell Floyd Harrell and is the first born of Rosa Belle (Harrell) Winston Parker.

Tribute is extended to Ardell Davidson Winston, widow of John Thomas Winston, regarding her association with the Winston family and of course her husband, the only one of the Winston boys to marry. Mrs. Winston's information was invaluable, as she provided details not

xi

voiced by anyone else with the author's assumption that she was speaking through her husband, John Thomas, himself. John Thomas died in 2002 at the age of 80.

Acknowledgment is also made of the contribution of Roy Harrell, Junior, nephew of Burrell Harrell and older brother of Colville, in rounding out some of the stories that could only be alluded to by others as he played as a child with the colored kids.

Special acknowledgment is extended to Jeannette Fichter Frandsen, a granddaughter of Ethel Harrell Whitten, sister of Burrell Harrell. Mrs. Frandsen is the "Keeper of the Records" of the Harrells and more appropriately the consummate archivist of all of the ten generations of families to whom she is related. Nearly complete genealogical information was placed at the author's disposal as well as bits of historical data of essence not heretofore made available. She is a significant contributor to the archives of historical societies in the region regarding her extensive pioneer family connections as well as to the Archives of Auburn University, the family's college. The author has been privileged to consult the unpublished manuscript, _The Story of a House_ by May (Mae) Jimmie Harrell Duncan, the eldest sibling of Burrell Floyd Harrell, to glean an abundance of information some of which is used in this book. Mrs. Duncan's book could have been entitled: "The Story of the House of Harrell." There was no mention of brother Burrell's family though their association was not meager.

Appreciation is extended to Archivists Kay Minchew, Director, of the Troup County Historical Society, LaGrange, Georgia, and to Barry Jackson, and Diana Thomas for their assistance, support, and patience. This enabled the author to navigate and archive through more than a century of information from the stacks as well as their digital library, digitized renderings, many of their sponsored publications, and custodial files of the Superior Court of Troup County, Georgia as well as the Probate Court.

Acknowledgment is made as well to the Chambers County Circuit Court for opening its Records and Proceedings enabled by Charles Storey, Circuit Court Clerk, Lafayette, Alabama as well as to the Probate Court of Chambers County.

Many thanks to Mrs. Anne Alsobrooks, administrator, of the Cusseta Cemetery Association, who related the history of the cemetery and conducted a tour of the grounds.

The author is much obliged to Ms. Miriam Syler, Curator and Archivist of Cobb Memorial Archives, whose diligence and interest in the project gave impetus to the author's recounting so much of the essence of East Alabama and West Georgia. Thanks is offered to Ms. Mary Hamilton, Director of H. Grady Bradshaw Chambers County Library and Cobb Memorial Archives, Valley, Alabama, for her support in the use of the archival materials covering the historical data of Chambers County. Many references in the archives were used to establish the historical bearings of the area the many publications of the society to include the book *West Point on the Chattahoochee River*. The author was introduced to another book: WEST POINT: The Story of a Georgia Town by Mark E. Fretwell of which good use was made because of its incisiveness.

The author would be remiss in his not acknowledging the suggestions, assistance, and the compilation of bibliographic leads and materials by Dr. Michael A. Chromey, Humanities Librarian at the Robert W. Woodruff Library, Atlanta University Center, Clark Atlanta University in Atlanta, Georgia to better understand the American period of slavery. His annotated bibliographic leads enabled the author to refresh his own memory of the many stories told by his grandmother, Mary Heard Davis Schell (*b. 1879*), of issues in "slavery time," though she herself was emphatically never a slave.

The author was truly privileged to have worked with his own father, Nelson Henderson Schell, Senior, during his summer breaks from College in the late 1940's. He was a former employee of the Lafayette Lanier family household of West Point/Lanett and related his knowledge of the many prominent families in the region both White and Black in West Georgia and East Alabama through his association with them and of the events of note in the area.

The author has made references to the work of Margaret Anne Barnes in her telling the story of *"Murder in Coweta County"* to highlight attitudes and perceptions in the late 1940's as it may interrelate the story of the Harrell family. It was Colville Harrell who established the relationships of the Harrell family through the marriage of his grandfather, Tom Harrell, into the Wallace and Strickland families of Meriwether County, Georgia. The family genealogical records at the appendix display several generations of both families. *"Murder in Coweta County"* was made into a TV movie starring Johnny Cash.

Acknowledgment is made to Dr. Randall Kennedy, author of *"Interracial Intimacies"* to validate so many of the impressions voiced in the telling of the story of the atmosphere, attitudes, and times in which this story takes place. The author reviewed Carter G. Woodson's *"The Mis-Education of the Negro"* which was published in 1933. It was fascinating reading, as many issues appear not have not been appreciably resolved to this day. One other book has been invaluable to the author in relating genetic and sociological information pertinent to the story's being told; it is *"The Myth of Race in America"* by Dr. Joseph L. Graves, Jr. It is a must read for anyone interested in the vicissitudes of race in the family of Man. Three works of the author were consulted, namely, *"Human Sub-specific Variation"*, an independent study in Advanced Anthropology while studying at California State University, Northridge in 1979, *"Aunt Nora, The Life and Times of a Wise Woman"*, and an unpublished memoir, entitled *Moi*, 1994.

The author is indebted to the Troup County, Georgia Executive through the use of its good offices of The Hall of Records for tax rolls, wills, and deeds to research and study the court's archives for minutes of court proceedings for the record.

This story is also about land. To get it right insofar as land use, the author is indebted to Ms. Jane Smith, legal coordinator to the Georgia Department of Transportation, Region 6, for use of its opening of the files for recounting the construction of the Interchange at Interstate I-85 and Georgia SR-18 at West Point, Georgia. Mr. Jason McCook whose referral by Mr. Dennis Studstill, then Chief Engineer, coordinated these efforts. Ms. Britt Perry as the Legal Services Coordinator for the Georgia Department of Transportation, Atlanta, worked her magic in bringing aboard Mr. David Jennings who arranged for the lion's share of information which in turn enabled the author to research those areas pertaining to the construction of the "Montgomery, Alabama to Atlanta, Georgia Road."

There are many other contributors as well as those who listened to this story who may not have been heretofore acknowledged. Those contributions are indeed acknowledged here with appreciation and apologies for such omissions.

The author asked several friends and colleagues to review, edit, and just read the story for its soundness and cohesion. Thanks to Anthony Head for his initial editing and design of the body of the book. Thanks is also extended to Colonel (Ret. USMR) Mark Haiman for his prompt review and cogent comments. Many of the reviewers were Georgia residents during the times described in the book to include his wife, Doris E. Hunter, his sister, Juanita Schell Rutland, cousins Lamar and Yvonne Schell, and Oscar Malone. Their comments, suggestions as well as their first-hand knowledge of the events added value to the manuscript's preparation. Finally, much appreciation is extended to David Deal, celebrated artist, writer, and historian for his consummate knowledge in ushering the book to the publisher as well as to Apta B. Good for his expert rendering of the final manuscript to the printer.

Prologue

The aftermath of the "War Between the States" was as devastating to the general population of America as it is in every war, no matter the real reason for which the battles are fought. The real reason itself is never important. Ordinary and common folks always lose. Their lot, too, is almost never better but in the case of the American Civil War, as so many of the common people were slaves or indentured servants, or "poor whites;" they could only stand to gain. The slaves were Africans or descendants therefrom and the indentured persons or servants were almost always "poor whites" of European descent. The latter's lot was generally better off in public places, because they could publicly pass for landowners, overseer class, planters, and the like. The slave's lot and freedom was constrained by the color of his skin; however, if his skin color by virtue of his white ancestry enabled him to pass, it was at his peril should he be detected. He then became co-dependent and ward of his owner, who was as much dependent upon the slave as the slave upon himself. The slaves were considered simply chattel. The slave was sustained primarily for the value of his productive labor both in the big house and in the field. This meant that he was nurtured and in many cases endeared as a "member of the family." An agrarian society that was the economy at the time demanded that there always be liberty.

Slavery officially ended in 1865 with the enactment of the 13th Amendment although The Emancipation Proclamation freed only slaves in the rebellious states. President Abraham Lincoln signed it on January 1, 1863. Most slaves remained on the plantation after being "freed" as they were not prepared or sufficiently pacified to move into a "foreign" economy and society. They had neither the schooling nor the cultural wherewithal to survive beyond the plantation. Some plantations were benevolent; however, sanctuary was offered for those who dared remain a part of the "community" and presumably a part of the economy as well. They subsisted as sharecroppers or laborers for hire. The sharecropper system enabled the indentured whites to be "freed" as well from a kind of peonage that also beset so many of the ex-slaves.

As one looks over this landscape and its surrounding fields today, one can hear the voices harmonizing across the valleys and hills as the land was being tended. Songs rang out from one plantation over to another in the "call and response" technique so reminiscent of the songs of Mother Africa. The singer was trying desperately to locate a lost brother or sister or tribal member to share the burdens of his captivity, all longing to be free, longing to return to the place of their origin. As the farms prospered, more and more slaves were brought to the plantations to grow cotton, sorghum, ribbon cane and other staples for the marketplace. Oftentimes, the slaves outnumbered the planters, owners, and overseers and, of course, the gentry. Many of the gentry lived in northern climes such as Philadelphia and Boston and were of aristocratic bearing.

Large numbers of slaves could and did pose problems, as not all would accustom themselves to captivity and subjugation. The means of keeping them under control were harsh and brutal, such as floggings, canings, and even to the extent of killing the runaways or escapees and brutalizing the insurrectionists to make them examples for defying the established order. The effectiveness of the slave system was assured because the U. S. Federal Government was in sympathy with the owners, many who sat in the Congress. They had invested heavily in the slave enterprise, and a return on their investment was, in effect, guaranteed. The Church was a supporter of Slavery and cannot escape its culpability during this inhumane period of American history. From time-to-time, the slaves were allowed to organize themselves into small communities and set up family relationships, but under the guardianship of the owners or their overseers. Children would be born to these couplings, not necessarily with the benefit of marriage, but those who "took up" with each other. Many times the children born in slave families were those not of the husband or "father" but of the master or his planters or overseers. Too often, the real owners were absentee-landlords having residence in other states or countries as far away as Great Britain. They could not care less as long as the profits kept rolling in. This is not to say that there were not those who were in sympathy with the plight of the slave, and who tried mightily to lessen the slave's burden or even preach abolitionism. This intransigence eventually led to the great civil war that is still being waged on some political and economic fronts today – many if not all wars are spawned by economic uncertainty. Flags of division, such as the Confederate Stars and Bars still fly and are paraded. America's penchant for cheap labor still creates instability in the economic system. Songs of praise for the system are still being sung, as exemplified by the singing of the Battle Hymn of the Republic. Still being sung reminiscing the hardship of slavery is "John Brown's Body . . ." and so many of the Negro Spirituals lament the hardships of bondage.

The settling of the Indian lands in the area and subsequent ownership of properties was by lottery as proclaimed by the then Governor of Georgia, George M. Troup, for whom the County in which this story transpired was named. Eligibility to draw a lottery stake was confined to being white and supposedly a citizen of the United States, although many of the masters at a later time ceded land to their former slaves.

The story related in this book springs from such a background.

Disclaimer

This book in essence is a true story, that is, to the extent that the "truth" can best be known and perhaps told. The stories and the events contained herein were derived from interviews, archival accounts, old newspaper articles, court records, family records, general discussions, hearsay, memories of stories in the distant past by forebears in the oral tradition, and unknowingly to the author, many could very well have been only latent memories. Many of the events included herein were derived from interpretations to answers, which were either partial, marginal, non-responsive in the form of puzzlement or abject silence. But to a sincere person, it is likely that most of the answers given were the truth in the mind of the answerer and deemed credible by the author. The test of reason has been applied.

Much of the story is told in the idiom of the early to mid-twentieth century South. Many of the persons depicted in the story were not well educated and some were unlettered; all were real. The technique used to tell this story allowed those persons to tell their own story in the first person and in their own way. The author heard their stories as if he were really there. Sometimes situations and venues appeared to exist in his mind as if they were real. He could visualize in actuality what they were talking about. Such a technique brings to the mind Edmund Morris' treatment in his writing the biography of Ronald Reagan called _"Dutch."_ Most if not all of the events indicated herein more than likely happened. Those parts of the story where there were legal implications are well documented and in some instances are included as part of the text to bolster authentication of the event. The author injected himself invisibly into the periphery as if he were there witnessing the goings-on. This was transformational in nature for it allowed the realism of being present to come through although the recounting sometimes may reveal imagination.

Chapter 1. Rose Hill Plantation at the Long Cane Creek

The winter of 1882 laid waste to the farmlands in East Alabama, Cusseta, in Chambers County, was one of the areas already hit hard by fierce winter storms. Ice and a little dusting of snow covered much of the area. It was almost too late to batten down the barns and stables to protect the horses and other livestock for safekeeping and for their being fit for the early spring planting. The winters in the South were generally mild, and this kind of weather was unusual. It was one of those freaky winter storms that seemed to come out of nowhere.

One of the leading families whose properties were threatened was the Harrells. Alfred Lee Harrell, born in 1808, the son of Samuel Harrell, headed the family. The Harrells were members of a prosperous and pioneering bunch who had first come from Virginia and the Carolinas to settle in Alabama to seek their fortune. They came also in response to the Georgia Governor's invitation to settle and populate West Central Georgia. Like most of their new neighbors, they were farmers and artisans, but foremost they were pioneering settlers who braved the elements to exact the promise of a new venture and fortune in this, their great new land. Their path to riches was to be cotton farming.

In addition to their Alabama holdings, The Harrells also held large parcels of land in nearby Troup County, Georgia, where they were beneficiaries of the land lottery system that was practiced in Georgia at the time. Their holdings in Georgia spanned the Military Districts or civil communities of West Point, Long Cane, and Rose Hill. Other prominent families also held interests in that area, but were ready to sell off to the next buyer -- because times were still so hard, cash was always so scarce, and farm labor was a killer. Slavery, now illegal, was on the wane and the ex-slaves were not as productive as had been claimed. They were now free to work for whomever including themselves if they pleased but an overwhelmingly large number remained with their last masters.

The land in the area was perfect for cotton growing. It was fertile beyond belief, as the topsoil deposited from the annual spring flooding by the Chattahoochee River over the centuries left a deposit of silt or topsoil so rich and widespread that almost anything would grow bountifully. The landholders in West Georgia at the time were the Maulls, the Ealys, and the Erwins, the owners of Rose Hill and other outlying communities. Settlers coming into the region seeking opportunity were the ones most likely to buy or stake claim to any available land. A parcel or a Land Lot at the time consisted of 283 acres. Burrell Whatley Harrell was such a prospective buyer, and buy he did. He was the son of Alfred Lee and Mahala Whatley Harrell, born in 1847 in Alabama, and he was ready to take full control of the family's operations at Rose Hill and seeking adjoining parcels to expand beyond those already owned by his father.

The importance of Mr. Burrell Whatley Harrell's arrival was announced in the *LaGrange Reporter*, LaGrange, Georgia, on January 19, 1882. It read:

"Burrell (Whatley) Harrell has moved back to his plantation on the Long Cane Creek and has purchased from A. M. Eady & Co. the 'Rose Hill' place joining."

The existing plantation had previously been farmed by Burrell Whatley's father, Alfred, from his Alabama base in Cusseta, his having only 33 slaves to work the plantation. Cotton farming was anything if not labor intensive. To the "good" fortune of the Harrells, there was an abundant labor supply in the form of the freed slaves mostly still living on the old plantations. Their very presence there was due to the need for backbreaking labor in the cotton fields. This was the beginning of the sharecropper system, whereby subsistence and housing would be furnished in exchange for labor in the fields and a share of the profits, should there be any. The whole arrangement was just a notch away from slavery except now the freed slaves were citizens. (It can be said that the slaves were citizens before being freed even three fifths so, but the master was the keeper of the slaves' citizenship.) It, too, was the precursor to the system of legal segregation that was at the time in its inceptive stages. It was also the beginning of the period of palpable "separation" of the races, that is the "colored" were made to understand that they did not belong to the nation. The freedmen conducted

2

themselves as if they were of another nation and therefore became "invisible." This was also a sign that the farming communities were at long last beginning to recover from the devastation and disruption brought about by the "War Between the States." The battles fought locally had extended to the famous Fort Tyler area of West Point and spilled over into the Long Cane region. (See Troup County map.) Until now, even twenty years later, recovery had been slow. The families that populated the plantations had to be mollified and provided for, as most were ex-slaves and their descendants, who truly needed such pacification due to their former enslavement. There was also a sprinkling of indentured servants, whites, and their offspring. None owned property to speak of, and they certainly did not have an understanding of property rights. These poor souls were now citizens, having gained it through the defeat of the Confederacy, the abolition of slavery and had it guaranteed by the ratification of the 14th Amendment to the Constitution of the United States of America. Many had large families and for their survival, needed assistance in this new condition of freedom now so strange to them.

Burrell Whatley, showing his maturity, took a wife, whose name was Cordelia Alpha Combs. She was so named "Alpha" because she was the first child born to the family of James Evans Combs and Raney Rebecca Floyd Combs. Her sister, who was the last daughter born to the family, was equally aptly named "Omega." The Combs miscalculated in that there was a son born still later.

To Burrell Whatley and Cordelia Alpha were born ten children, five girls and five boys: May Jimmie (1870), Alfred Lee (1873), Thomas Gordon (1876), Robert Claude (1878), Ina Verne (1881), Burrell Floyd (1884), Ethel de Vere (1886), E. O. Evans (1889), Samuel Cheatham (1892), and Cordelia Combs (1896). The Harrells were fond of naming their children for some forebear. (A visit to the family tree at the Appendix shows for whom each of the children was named.)

The Harrells now had a vast plantation, not all of which was under cultivation. In all, it comprised more than fifteen hundred acres of land, some of which had been cleared by the previous owners, including the Choctaw and Cherokee Indian Nations that preceded them. Some Indians remained as stragglers on these properties even after the tribes had been driven off, and became renegades who on occasion disrupted

3

the tranquil life that was beginning to emerge on the plantations. Burrell Whatley intended to farm big time when he acquired all of this land with almost a hundred ex-slaves. Georgia Highway No. 1 or the Old Columbus Highway divided these properties. The Rose Hill Plantation was on the south side of the highway, where large parcels were allocated to cotton and corn growing with attending and surviving slave quarters. He dreamed not only of fame but also the fortune that would make him "King of the (Rose) Hill" or "King Cotton." It was known throughout the region that it was he who fashioned the very first successful bale of cotton. This whole enterprise was, to say the least, daunting, so much so that Burrell Whatley's untimely death in 1901 was most likely brought on by his unbounded ambition and his physical inability to handle the vagaries of the weather.

It was their fourth son, Burrell Floyd, just 17 when his father passed, inherited his father's high manner, cunning, prowess, and even his ruthlessness when called upon to deal with others while controlling the family's entire holdings and interests. Burrell Floyd in his power and glory was to become known as "Mister Burl." Notwithstanding his birth order, Burrell was recognized as "Big Brother" to May, the first born of his siblings, Alfred, the first born son, Robert, Evans, Verne, Thomas (Tom), Ethel, Sam, and Cordelia, the youngest and named for her mother. Each was unique in his or her way, setting each apart from the other. On his deathbed, Burrell Whatley had charged this seventeen year old lad with the responsibility to take care of his mother and sisters, brothers, if necessary, and any and all other female relatives from both sides of his family who may need the steady hand of a strong male. Women's rights were a fiction at the time. "Girls," daughters and women, did not in general inherit property, and were not entrusted with the management of the family businesses and outside concerns. This is not to say that they were not capable but it was just not done. Their affairs were "seen after" by the males in the family. Burrell Whatley left no will, but his widow Cordelia Alpha (otherwise known as Miss Cordie) was up to the task, and took a strong position on matters of the family as the administrator, with her son's (Burrell Floyd's) consent and approval, of course.

Burrell Floyd organized settlements on the properties, and built houses or renovated existing ones to house the field hands' families. Rose Hill

4

was his "pet" or special project. It was his headquarters. He erected or improved the barns, stables, and sheds to shelter the feed for the animals and farm implements needed to till the soil. Although cotton was truly his crop, he was planning to raise vast numbers of cattle later on. His further plans were to grow his own seed and raise his own feed for the cattle, not just his own herds. He aimed to become a commercial factor in the region, to be as independent as he could possibly be, while yet cornering the market, and being known for the best grain in the region. His ambition was, like his father's, unbounded.

No man, however, is worth his salt without a woman at his side, and Burrell was not one to waste time. He had already surveyed the field, and now he set out to find his bride-to-be. Many a mother in the area had already taken note of this young, handsome, industrious, and vigorous man, now all of 25 years old, and wanted to snare him for their eligible belles. Burrell realized that he could have the "pick of the litter" but found them all wanting. He had already made his choice a long time ago when she worked alongside her own mother in the Harrell's kitchen. But there was a "problem." Her race. In their youth, Burrell and Rosa Rutledge Winston had fallen passionately in love with one another, but they knew from the outset that theirs could never be. She was a beautiful young lass, now all of 18 years, and only seven years his junior. She wanted to run off with him, but Burrell, with such an immense sense of his responsibility, knew that he could never leave the farm and Rose Hill. His family and their stake were there in his hands and were always at risk.

He was constantly reminded that he was the chosen one to look after the family and the welfare of his mother, brothers, sisters, and others. Some special arrangements had to be made, for this burden was unwieldy. Later, two of the sisters would marry as well as two of the brothers; but the two other brothers had to be looked after, as they were not suited for family life or farm work, given the state of their physical and mental health and their having absolutely no desire for farm work of any kind.

Rosa was a mulatto, of sorts, meaning that she was not a first generation offspring of white and black parents, and not a "quadroon" whose parentage was three quarters white and one-quarter colored. Rosa looked so white early in her life that only the family members could tell otherwise. Like others "in the know," of course, they were accustomed

5

to the offspring of such pairings. Hers was a truly "mixed" family, as attested by her sisters of varying hues. Rosa's Mother, Miss Belle Rutledge, in her younger days had been "lily-white" herself. Belle's father was believed to have been the master slaveholder of Rosa's grandmother, Lillie – a slave house servant girl who was not even American born; she was a North African of Arab admixture. The white admixture in Lillie's children was also thought to be of the Rutledge Clan of pioneer stock and settlers from South Carolina, and signers of the Declaration of Independence. Belle had been born in a slave environment, just days after the signing of the Emancipation Proclamation in 1863, on the Rutledge Plantation, in fact, no less than in the kitchen of the Rutledge mansion when her mother was tending house duties. This mansion still stands today as a reconstructed Greek Revival edifice, which looms majestically on a knoll overlooking lush green forests just beyond the city limits of West Point, Georgia. Belle grew up on that plantation and remained there until she married Lovett Winston and moved on to the Rose Hill Plantation under the ownership of prior landholders. Lovett was her second husband and between her two husbands, she had 13 children.

Deeply in love, Burrell and Rosa decided that they would "live together" in effect becoming man and wife – a common law arrangement. The customs of the region did not allow for even a common law union or mixed race co-habitation or better put, a "marriage" between a white and a Negro. A person was defined as a Negro if he or she had just "one drop" of Negro blood. The so-called law had been already codified into Georgia law in 1856 under the Race Integrity Act.

"Who is to tell me what I can do?" Burrell exclaimed. "I am my own master! Rosa is the woman I love and she will be mine, forever!" His Uncle Roy warned him that this arrangement would never be tolerated in the South.

"I hear you, but watch me," Burrell retorted. "This is the woman I choose to be my wife and the mother of my children."

"Then you will have to leave the family and go on up North somewhere," said Alfred Lee, one of Burrell's three remaining brothers, speaking very gingerly as Burrell Floyd could limit his inheritance.

"Burrell Floyd, you don't seem to understand. You are just being pig-headed. That is not our way. Can't you understand that?"

"I control these properties, they are mine to do as I please," Burrell said, rather gently for a change. "If anybody's gonna leave, it's gonna be you and all of you other grubbing deadbeats who have not lifted a finger to help with any of this. I'll stay put. I will build a house for her and me and we will start a family. You can put that in your dadgum pipe and smoke it. And remember, I am a white man and I can do as I please, law notwithstanding. Get off my land, right now!"

"Do you realize, Burrell Floyd, that the Ku Klux Klan will come after you and burn you out, maybe even kill you?" persisted Alfred Lee, his oldest brother. "This will be the ruination of our family. Don't you understand that? This is crazy! Mama has tried so hard to keep the family's name upstanding. She's been trying to get all of the girls educated to make sure that they will be set for marriage. Don't ruin this!"

"Alfred Lee, I love all of y'all, but this is bigger than you, family, or anybody or anything else. That's it! Put the word out that I will arm my men here on the plantation, and we will fend off anybody and shoot to kill, if necessary, not to scare, any son-of-a-bitch that sets foot on my property if I don't give them permission that they can. I will go into town and get provisions whenever I want to and where necessary, I will bring her and any of the children if and when they come. I can't be no clearer. Do you understand me? And don't call me crazy! I will set up lookouts if need be."

"There's going to be a showdown, Burrell, you mark my word, y' hear?" warned his Uncle Roy as he drifted away.

"I won't lose not one drop of sleep. You mark **my** word!" Burrell bristled.

"Come on Rosa," Burrell called out. "We got to get moving."

"Mr. Burrell," as Rosa characteristically called him, "maybe we should think this through. Is this all worth it? I am so scared as you can see that I am trembling."

7

"Mister" or "Miss" was the handle or title attached to the first names of all whites that had reached their majority, and sometimes before, married or not. The custom required the colored to call the whites such as a matter of respect, to emphasize their low status, whether it was fitting or not. Sometimes, the whites would even call one another or refer to themselves as "Mister" or "Miss" in the presence of the colored, so they would never forget who was in charge.

"Nothing to worry about, Honeybun. It's all settled. I'll be your protector."

"There's one more thing I have to tell you, Mr. Burrell," sighed Rosa.

"What is it, Honey?" Mr. Burrell demanded.

"I just don't rightly know how to put this to you," she stammered.

"Aw, come on, what is it? Let it out!"

"I am with child, Mr. Burl," Rosa said, so fearful that this would rile his ire that it would mark the end of their relationship and he might abandon her. This had always been the case when the colored girl, mulatto or not, bore a baby for a white man, married or not.

"Hot damn!" he exclaimed. "I'm gonna to be a daddy! We really got to get on with it now, Rosa. No time to tarry. I will build us a house on the Rose Hill Plantation over here. We will start directly. We will stay together, you and me, you just wait and see."

He tenderly reached for her hand and helped her climb into the buggy. He snapped the reins and off they went. There was a long silence as they rode up to her mother's house. He did not realize how upset Rosa really was of her pregnancy, and especially out of wedlock, because of its disgrace in the eyes of her community. Worse yet, it would be disclosed that the father of her unborn child was a white man who would not or could never marry her.

They kissed their goodbyes as he slipped away driving the buggy ever so hard over to the Big House that was about a mile up the road on the north side of the Highway. This was the Harrell homestead. This was the house in which Burrell Floyd Harrell, himself, was born, as well as all of the other brothers and sisters for that matter. It had come into his family right after his Dad first moved back to Georgia from Alabama in 1882 after some land disputes within the family. This house was also considered of the Greek Revival period though it was not a grand house, per se, in the manner of the typical plantation 'big house" of the antebellum period, but it was fashionably appealing for the times. It was the most prominent house for miles around, perched on a knoll so that most of their Land Lots could be viewed from that high vantage point with the ever-present Long Cane Creek meandering through its landscape.

When word got out that Rosa was pregnant, the "natives became restless." The Winston family would be disgraced in the eyes of the community, no matter how solid it was considered to be up to this point. All knew that Mr. Burrell was sweet on Rosa Winston. His or her relationship was no secret to anybody on the plantation. It was thought that this was going to be like all of the other couplings, where the poor colored girl would be left holding the bag. As good as Mr. Burrell had been to them, nearly all of the tenants felt that he would be no different from the other white men who took advantage of the poor helpless colored women and girls, married or not. Such behavior made them either their mistresses or "bed warmers" without providing for them or the ensuing children. Rosa, herself, could be ostracized. She would be made to feel that she had betrayed her race regardless of what she felt for her lover.

After dinner was finished, Miss Belle called in her extended family, consisting of her own sisters as well as daughters, to sit down with her and Rosa to find some way to save the family's good name. They all came to realize that they had nothing to do with it, nor could they do anything without Mr. Burrell's say so. This was the first time that they had come to realize what freedom meant, that they were on their own, with nobody to tell them what to do or how to do it. Their actions could very well decide their fate. This was their first real experience with determining their own fate, because the slave master of the past had made all of the important decisions governing their lives.

"Why don't we make Alec Davidson marry her," suggested sister Caroline. "He's got light skin, too. Make him think he the baby Daddy.

9

We know Rosa done been sweet on him. He won't know no difference."

They all mulled the idea around and thought it would work.

"I won't do no such thing," Rosa said. "Mr. Burrell said that he would stay with me and the baby."

"They all say that until they get what they want and will leave you high and dry. Mark my word," Martha, another sister, said.

Mama Belle then spoke up, "That's what we'll do. Two of you, Lizzie and you, Martha, get the wagon hitched up. We going to get Alec and find that new preacher over at Mount New Harmony Church. We got to do a wedding tonight."

Rosa protested but to no avail. It was very dark that night, and treacherous to go the three to four miles to the parsonage, but they made it in good time. Caroline had found Alec, but gave him no idea what was about to happen, and delivered him to the scene.

Without questions being asked, the minister dutifully delivered the vows, they were exchanged, and the deed was done. He was accustomed to these shotgun weddings usually being accompanied by the father of the bride, never by the mother, but stranger things had happened.

One of the field hands, Manfield Harris, the Harrells' most trusted worker, sneaked over to Mr. Burrell's and squealed that the Winston family women were meeting trying to find some way to get rid of Rosa's baby. Mr. Burrell knew that men never got involved in matters of this kind, even though he was a party to the mess in which they found themselves. He stayed put. He thanked Manfield for keeping him informed of the goings-on around the plantation. Mr. Burl intuitively knew the happenings on and around the plantation, but he would never let on to any of his informants what he already knew for fear his sources would dry up. To remain in control, you had to have a "main mole" somewhere any the operation. Manfield was that character and was always considered to be the most reliable and useful of the tenants and servants, but he was roundly hated by every one of them.

"Burrell Floyd, what's the matter?" Miss Cordie, Burrell's mother asked. "What's going on out there? It's unusual for one of your nigrahs to come over here at this time of the evening unless there's real trouble over there on the plantation."

"It's nothing, Mama. Whatever it is, it'll be taken care of tomorrow. I promise you that."

Out of the blue, she mustered enough courage to confront Burrell about his bachelor status at the ripe old age of 25.

"Burrell Floyd?" she said. "Don't you think it's about time you start looking around again for some nice white girl to get married to? You still hanging 'round that mulatta gal over there on Rose Hill? You know what the situation is around here. How old are you, anyways?"

"Mama, you are 32 years older than I am. You know when I was born, so you shouldn't have any difficulty figuring that out."

"Burrell Floyd, you're sassing me. Did I ever! I won't have any of it. Can't a mother still look into her boy's life?"

"Momma, did you see that beautiful comet in the night sky. It has a mighty long and beautiful tail. You can even see it in the daytime if you know where to look." Miss Cordie just stopped and stared at Burrell in his feeble but unsuccessful attempt to change the subject.

"It's a wonder you ever saw anything in the night sky, Burrell, because you are always looking down when you are with that gal," Miss Cordie said rather caustically.

"I'm sorry, Mama. It's been a very hard day. I'm going to put in and say good night. See you bright and early in the morning."

Burrell tossed and turned all night wondering what in the world had he got himself into and what were they trying to pull over on him. Whatever it was, he was not going to let it happen. Even dismissing the situation like that still did not give him the peace of mind to fall asleep. But what could he do? His family's name was powerful and he would never do anything to tarnish it. Yet he knew that he was not like the rest

11

of "them night rovers and scoundrels" who pounced on any of the colored girls and women who dared let themselves be out alone or away from home at night. He would face his duty like a man and do the right thing toward Rosa, no matter what. He settled in and finally fell asleep, although fitfully.

"Burrell Floyd," Miss Cordie called out. Burrell was still in his room in the back of the house. "Better come over and get your breakfast while it's hot. Carrie's done fixed your favorite vittles, some hotcakes, eggs, streak-of-lean, sausages, big pot of coffee and all of that. If you don't want the hotcakes, there's a big pan of hot buttered biscuits. There's plenty of grits, too"

"Mister Burrell! Mister Burrell!" Manfield cried out as he bounded up the back steps almost out of breath. "I need to talk to you, Sir, Mr. Burrell, right away!"

"Manfield, dammit, can't this wait? Don't you see I'm having breakfast with my mother and my sisters? You know better than to break in on me like that," scolded Mr. Burl.

"I understand, Sir, and meaning no harm but I think you want to know this right now."

"All right, go on over to the carriage house and I'll be right out." Burrell was always very careful to keep the women folk out of his business.

"Burrell Floyd, what's going on?" Miss Cordie and each of his sisters demanded in unison.

"I'm not sure, but like I told you last night, it'll be taken care of. I know it's no use of keeping whatever it is from you, and I will tell you in time." Burrell always gave his mother an answer, even when it didn't make sense, for he was always the loving and respectful and dutiful son. Somehow, this satisfied her for the moment.

Manfield was the mechanic and handyman to take care of the several carriages and drays that the family used for going overtown, to church on Sundays, or just getting around the plantation. The carriage house

12

was Manfield's domain. Nobody, but nobody, except for Mr. Burrell ever ventured in there.

"OK, what is it, Manfield?"

"Mr. Burrell, them women done decided last night that Miss Rosa gonna marry that good-for-nothing nigger, Alec Davidson. And you know what? They even went and got that new preacher from that Mount New Harmony CME Church and he done married them just like that. They left for town late last night, but I really believe they went up to Gabbettville. Both of them got some relations up there, you know."

Gabbettville was nothing more than a hamlet or a way station with a general store and a Post Office to provide for the scattered families in the area. It was truly a "one-horse town."

"This makes no sense! I don't believe you. What's the meaning of this? Are you a part of this?"

"Oh, no sir, Mr. Burrell. I just told you what I overheard them boys say last night at the moonshine still. They didn't know I was there. I kind of hid in the bushes. Everybody knows what's happening, Mr. Burrell. Even them po' white sharecroppers done got the word. Please don't be mad at me. I swear before God and hopes to die, I'm telling you the whole truth."

"All right, what else is going on over there on the plantation, Manfield?" asked Mr. Burrell patting Manfield on the back while trying to show some cool. Manfield was a snitch, an informant, and the best yet. Like all stoolies, anyone, and more never trusted him than likely he was avoided or kept in the dark by his fellows, lest the boss would learn their personal business or plans. He was ostracized and never allowed to be in the "secret" meetings that were necessary to be free of the boss' control. These little meetings were developed during slavery to plot escapes or revolts. So many of the desired actions never happened, because the boss was able to find out in time what was going on through likes of a Manfield, and to prevent any kind of insurrection.

"Sir, it's all so quiet, I don't rightly know. But I told you everything I know and I'll let you know more as soon as I can find out. Maybe you can help me, sir, what do you think got into her and made them do a thing like this?" Manfield, as good as he was, always missed a few of the essentials.

"Thank you, Manfield, you can go now. I got some hard thinking to do."

Burrell was flabbergasted. He moped around for days trying to come to terms with what had happened. He thought of nearly everything. Nothing would work. He had to get real. He finally hit upon what the Rutledge and Winston women were trying to do. Rosa would not have to have the baby out of wedlock, hence her marriage to Alec Davidson. Alec was also a mulatto of sorts himself, and therefore, the baby would most likely appear to be fair skinned, no guarantees, and nobody would know the difference that he was not the real father. But Burrell would be damned if he would allow anybody to have his woman and his child. He and Rosa had bonded. He felt that Rosa would be faithful to him in spite of her situation. He would find out where she was and would see her on occasion, even though he could not stand to be apart from her for even one more day. And at the right time, he would make his move.

A beautiful little girl was born to the couple. Both Rosa and Alec admired and marveled over her. She was blonde and blue-eyed, a veritable princess, so fair of skin. She was indeed the fairest of them all. This was May 11, 1911.

Alec was so deliriously happy that he called out, "Look at what I have done! My little girl. What we gonna to name her?"

"Let's call her Rosa Belle after her mother and grandmother. It's so fitting." Both agreed. Rosa knew that the baby's last name was going to be a problem. Should she be "Davidson" for her legal father? Should she be "Harrell" for her blood father? Should she be "Winston" that was Rosa's maiden name, as common law held it that the offspring of a mating between partners shall be known by the last name of the mother? Or should she be Winston, for it was never doubted that Lovett Winston was Rosa's father. What entanglements are woven when custom or law, common or otherwise, does not treat human beings as equals!

Rosa was a bit upset over Alec's words, as she knew that the baby was not his. Alec should have known as well, as their marriage had never been consummated; yet she would never allow Alec to come to terms with the true situation. In due time, Rosa believed that all would be well, and that she and the baby could return to Rose Hill and somehow, she could be with her family and the baby could unite with her real daddy.

Time wore on and the couple became more and more entrenched in Gabbettville. Rosa would not allow herself to accept the situation because it was living a lie and just plain wrong. She no longer wanted to continue this sham; she wanted to go home. In the meantime, Alec and the baby became inseparable. He adored every moment he could muster to spend with her and she with him. Alec threatened that he would put Rosa out and keep the baby for himself if she did not stop all of the trouble she was making for him and the baby.

Rosa couldn't take it any longer, so she returned to Rose Hill without her baby.

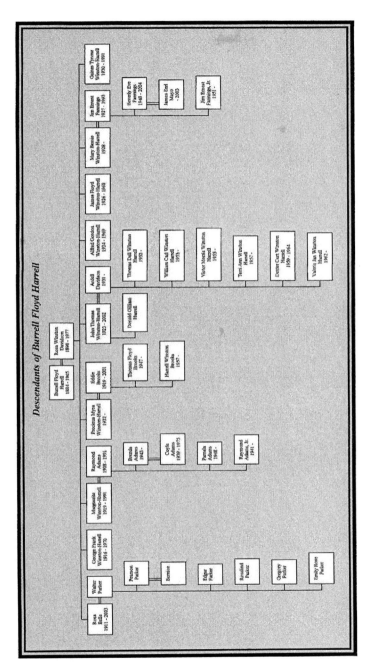

Descendants of Burrell Floyd Harrell

The Burrell Floyd Harrell Family Tree

16

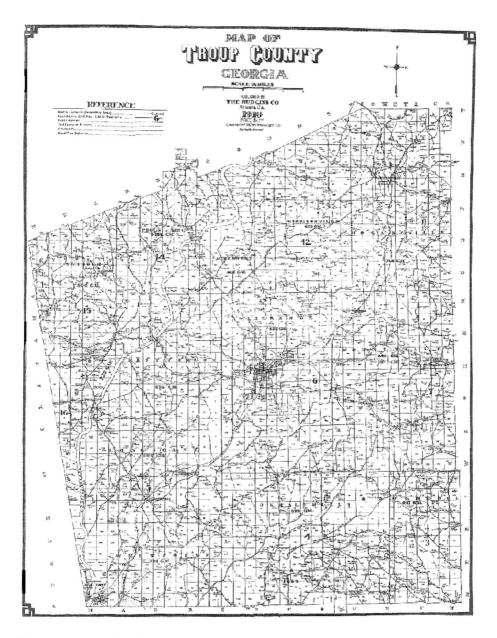

Troup County is situated on the western boundary of Georgia at the Alabama line. It has been the center of the textile industry in Georgia. Its principal cities are West Point and LaGrange, the county seat. West Point, seen at the lower left corner, is the location of the story. The Harrells owned significant acreage and were big time farmers.

17

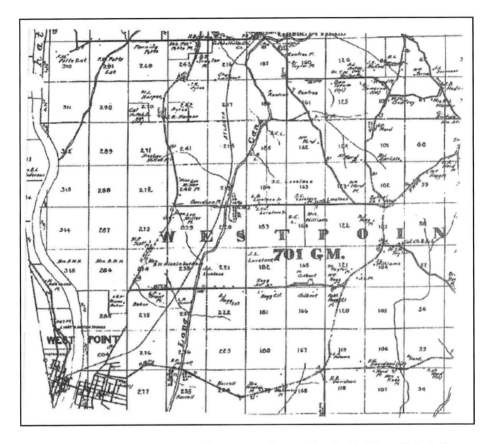

This excerpt from the proceeding map shows the B.F. Harrell holdings in 1910. The Rose Hill Plantation occupies Land Lots 235 and 234 and into 175. Acquisitions by B. F. Harrell and later by Nephew Roy extended north and beyond. The intersection of I-85 (not shown) and Georgia State Highway 18 is at a point east of the Long Cane Creek extending through Land Lots 165 and beyond. KIA Corp. has purchased more than 600 acres to the west of the Interstate with plans of acquiring more toward the east.

Chapter 2. The Common Law Marriage

Burrell heard that Rosa was back, Manfield made sure of that. Burrell decided that he had to see her right away, that very night, as his life had been a total wreck since she went away.

He dropped everything and immediately went over to the Winston Family house, and rapped on Belle's door. Miss Belle appeared as if she were in shock to see him. "Mr. Burrell, what in the world do we owe for this visit so late at night?"

"Belle, I'm here to see Rosa. I know she's here."

"Come right on in, Mr. Burrell, she's been expecting you."

They met face to face for the first time in nearly two years and immediately fell into each other's arms. It seemed that they would never let go. They kissed and sobbed, and sobbed and kissed. It had indeed been too long. They were speechless for a while, just staring into each other's eyes. They were together. They were right again.

"Where's the baby?" asked Mr. Burrell.

"I left her with her father and his aunt, but I do so want her back here with me. I am so miserable -- just a wreck! I think I just want to die. I can't live another minute without her."

"Why did you call him her daddy? He's not her father, I am," said Mr. Burrell.

"Please understand Mr. Burrell that he is her legal father, and I guess he's entitled to keep her if he wants to. He can be pretty mean, you know. I don't know what I can do. I don't want anything to hurt her but I do want her back," Rosa said.

"Don't worry, I'll get her back here in no time," promised Mr. Burrell.

Burrell pondered his options. He wanted to stay out of the limelight and didn't want to break the law any further than he had already, but now that his woman was back he would do almost anything to get his baby back, too. *"I'm a real Daddy!"* he thought with glee.

"Manfield, I need you to do me the biggest favor I've ever called on you to do," said Mr. Burrell.

"Yes Sir, I'll do whatever you want me to."

"Manfield, this could be dangerous. You got to be careful. I want you to go to Gabbettville and bring Rosa's baby back to her. You know the baby is with this man that Rosa married. I know he's a hothead. Nobody, even the whites don't mess with him. He's crazy! He's going to give you trouble if for no other reason that I fired him in favor of you. Will you go and bring my baby back to her mother?"

"Yes sir, Mr. Burl. I ain't afraid of him. I'll do it. Whatever you want."

"Manfield, I am going to let you have one of these guns to protect yourself. Don't use it if you don't have to. Do you hear me? I don't want no unnecessary killing 'round here. Do you know how to use this here gun?"

"Let me see it, Sir." Manfield takes the pistol and twirls it around his trigger finger. "Do I know this pistol, my Daddy had one just like it. We used to go out shooting just for the fun of it. I'm a sharpshooter, you know. Watch me hit that bottle way over yonder." Mansfield aimed quickly and fired, knocking the bottle five feet up in the air without shattering it. "I'm pretty good. I'll bring the baby back hoping no harm's done."

"She's all yours, Mr. Burrell said." He was satisfied that he had the right man to do the job.

"Take one of my best carriages with you and any horse you want. You know them best. You sure you don't need somebody else to go with you? Those roads are mighty rugged. They probably ain't been scraped this year. You'll find a lot of ruts." Most of the back roads at that time were not surfaced with blacktop or concrete and would have to be scraped and leveled with the big earth moving machines three to four times a year.

"No sir, I'll be just fine, Mr. Burrell. Just fine."

It was early the next morning, dew was still on the vines and the honeysuckles were still open because the sun hadn't come up yet. Manfield checked his provisions, because Gabbettville could be a long way off sometimes, he thought, and he could never be sure that he would have vittles offered to him when he arrived. He also brought along his shotgun, just in case there was trouble on the road. Bounty hunters and all kinds of stragglers and scalawags, even carpetbaggers still were lurking around because they had been dispossessed by the war. Satisfied that he had taken ample precautions, off he went to the northeast with Gabbettville on his mind.

"Whoa-a-a-a," Manfield shouted to the horses. "This here's good enough. Took me only about two hours," he figured by looking up at the sun. *"I'll turn the horses around so I won't have no trouble getting out of here when I pick up this here child,"* he said to himself.

"Hmmm-m-m, this ain't gonna be easy," he said aloud, looking around for a hitching post of some kind to hitch the horses. "This ought to be good enough", as he tied the reins to a sapling. As he walked across the yard, he alarmed the guinea hens that were scattered about to announce any stranger. The guinea hens were also kept to get rid of carrion and dangum dust as such was used by the Root Workers to cast spells and conjure the intended victims. *"These guinea hens are better watchdogs than dogs themselves,"* thought Manfield. At that moment, the front door of the farmhouse flew open with a shotgun aimed at his head.

"Miss Vi, for goodness sake, now you put that thing down! You could kill somebody. You know who I is. It's me. Manfield Harris. I work and live down on the Rose Hill Plantation. I work for Mr. Burrell Harrell."

"I don't know no Manfield Harris. Never heard of you, boy. What you doing up here on my property anyways?" Miss Viola demanded.

"I come up here to speak to Alec about a business matter. I heard he was here, but it ain't got nothing to do with you, ma'm."

"You best to get off my property, boy, before there's trouble. Come to think of it, I done heard of you. You up to no good. You better leave, right now!" Miss Vi shouted, backing up a bit but still blocking Manfield's way, still holding the shotgun at the ready.

"Like I said, Miss Vi, this ain't got nothing to do with you, so you better make it your business to get out of my way."

At this moment, a baby girl came to the door that Miss Vi had left ajar. She was a little blonde, blue-eyed toddler, not old enough to understand what was happening, but she sensed that there was trouble abrewing.

"Go back in the house, Honey, and ring the bell for your Daddy," said Miss Vi. She disappeared quickly and started to ring the bell. A tall wiry man stepped out from the side of the house.

"I know why you here, Manfield," said Alec. "You done come for my baby. The Man sent you, right? Well, I ain't going to let you have her. This is my child, and this is where she gonna stay. You're putting your life on the line, boy, and I won't spare you if you don't leave here right now!"

Alec had his shotgun hidden behind him and quickly raised it into position to fire when at the same time Mansfield whipped out his pistol, firing once at Alec and knocking the shotgun out of his hands. He took dead aim at Alec's head and told Miss Vi that he would shoot to kill Alec if she didn't drop her shotgun. She did, but threw it at Manfield. This moment of distraction allowed Alec to jump Manfield, trying to take his pistol away.

Alec was a bigger and stronger man, but Manfield was agile and fast. He managed to throw Alec to the ground while still gripping the pistol. Alec now knew that his life depended on his taking control of the pistol, so he tried to yank it from Manfield, but only succeeded in pulling Manfield on top of him. They scuffled fiercely for a moment, and then the muffled sound of the gun rang out. Both men laid there on the bare ground, motionless, for what seemed like an eternity. Then Manfield slowly emerged from atop Alec. Alec didn't move. His breathing was labored. He was bleeding profusely from the chest.

Miss Viola stood by in shock. Then she started wailing, knowing that her only brother was about to die. She ran into the house and barricaded the front door, believing that she could prevent Manfield from taking the baby. Manfield entered the house by the back door, and ordered Viola to pack the baby's things and get her ready to travel. At first she refused, but she relented when Manfield leveled the gun at her head. She somehow believed that he would really shoot.

"Miss Vi, I'm so sorry that it had to come to this," said Manfield. "Go and drag him out of the sun. Maybe he will pull through somehow. Try to stop the bleeding. But as you could see, it was an accident and in self-defense. He tried to kill me. You know that don't you? I just got the best of him. Give me that crying baby." The baby struggled for a moment. "I'm taking her back to her mama at Rose Hill. You can go and get the authorities or whatever you want to do because I ain't going nowhere, no time soon." Alec died later on that night.

A thorough review of the Troup County Superior Archives did not disclose a record that this incident ever took place; however, it was known throughout the county. Rosa was now free of this man, Alec Davidson. She decided to drop his surname as her married name, and went back to her family's name of "Winston." Her daughter would be christened as Rosa Belle Winston, born May 11, 1911. She was then just under four years old now.

Life returned to normal at the plantation. Rosa was happy to have her child back in spite of the tragedy that a life had been lost. All of the nay saying and bad mouthing of her because of her relationship with Mr. Burrell Harrell stopped and was mostly forgotten, as it is almost always the case. Babies being born out of wedlock were no big deal, and cast no lasting stigma in a black community. There was enough African culture left in the families to know that a girl had to bear a child before she could get married, in order to prove that she was not barren. This was a lenient condition, as some cultures required that the girl bear a male offspring, to prove her fitness to be married. Joy and happiness can be restored when a little child is the object of affection. The community had already forgiven Miss Rosa for her transgressions.

What the community failed to appreciate in the first place was that Mr. Burrell saw himself as truly one of them. They knew him as "Mr. Burl" at that time. But he was born and raised at "Rose Hill" in this community just like the rest of them. He was born there and raised there among all of the other children, white and colored. As children, they all played together everyday. He saw himself as being no different from any of the rest of them as they, too, saw him. He saw his courtship of Rosa as a normal happening -- just a boy and girl in love, disregarding the fact that they likely had no future, and that there could be other unintended consequences.

There was a loud rapping at the front door. "Who is it?" Miss Belle called out.

"It's me, Mister Burrell."

"We all asleep now, Mr. Burl. Can we see you in the morning?"

"Just open the door, Belle! This is an important matter. It can't wait 'til no tomorrow morning."

"Well, all right Sir, but just a minute 'til I put my shawl around me if I can find it. It's dark in here."

"Hurry up, Belle! Quit your stalling! I don't have all night!"

Belle had to find the matches so that she could light her kerosene lamp. There were no other means of getting light at the time except from the fireplace. Electricity had not yet come to the rural areas. It would be another twenty years or so before President Franklin D. Roosevelt started his Rural Electrification Project.

Rosa had been sharing her mother's bed with the baby, and she was trying to move into a back room to avoid Mr. Burrell.

"Belle, do you want me to break this damn door down?"

"If you just hold your horses, Mr. Big Boy, I'll be there, now in a minute!"

Finally, Miss Belle made it to the door and said. "I'm sorry Mr. Burl. It's not easy for the ladies to receive a gentleman caller after they have gone to bed for the night. I didn't hear no horses come up. Did you walk all the way over here? It's pitch black out there. Why, you can't see a foot ahead of you."

"I don't mean to be too pushy, Belle, but I couldn't sleep. I want you to let Rosa stay with me. I will finish building that house that I started a few years ago for Rosa. I want to live with her and the baby and raise my family right here on the plantation. Do I make any sense?"

"Not really, Mr. Burrell. But it ain't up to me no more. It's up to Rosa herself. Of course it would look bad if y'all did this but she a grown woman and now a mother. You ought to ask her. She in the back room," Miss Belle pointed in the direction of the room.

He started to go toward the back room but Miss Belle grabbed his arm. "Her sisters in there, too." Mr. Burl realized that he had shown no respect for their privacy. He flushed a bright red at his insensitivity and backed up. He hadn't even realized that the children and workers had any such thing as privacy. He was privileged and didn't truly appreciate it. That's just the way it was. He was coming into being a full-fledged member of the community.

Rosa had overheard the entire conversation and emerged with the child in her arms.

"Evening, Mr. Burrell," Rosa said. "This is your young lady. She'll soon be four years old. Say "hi" to your Daddy, Rosa Belle," said her mother. She passed the child to Mr. Burrell. He had never held a baby before in his life. Menfolks just did not do such a thing in those days.

He cradled her in his arms, and made cooing and gurgling sounds to her. She smiled at him, staring directly in his face with her cool blue eyes. He stroked her blonde hair. "Just like my Mama's," he said. "Why she's beautiful, just like her Mama. Hello, Rosa Belle. Your Daddy loves you."

"Rosa, you overheard what your Mama and I were saying. What do you say?"

"I don't care," she said. "There's no room for us here, as you can see. If that's what you want to do. But you really have to mean it, and feel truly that this is what you want to do, because there's going to be trouble with the townsfolk, you know that."

"Rosa, I love you, and nothing can or will keep you and my baby away from me. This is where I want to be, and I'm ready to die defending my right to be with the ones I love." Tears were streaming down his cheeks. He pulled Rosa and the baby close to him and held them for a long time. At last, "I have to go," he said.

"You don't have to go. It's late and you can spend the night right here. It's all right, ain't it Mama?" Rosa passed the baby to Miss Belle, who had brought another lighted lamp into the room, in anticipation that the visit was not to be short-lived. Men don't come out in the middle of the night just to pay respects.

"You can stay and have breakfast with us if you want to, Mr. Burl. There'll be aplenty," Miss Belle said as she took the baby and the other lamp with her.

The next morning, a runner came up from the Big House to find Mr. Burrell. He was screaming to the top of his lungs: "Mr. Burl! Mr. Burl! There's somebody up at the house, and they wants to see you. They done come all the way down here from LaGrange. Your Mama wants you to come home, right now!"

"I guess I had better go since I am wanted over there," Burrell said to Rosa. "I'll be back as soon as I can." He gave Rosa a peck on the cheek and off he went. Although it was early in the morning, it was already stiflingly hot. He hurried over to the house by horseback, on one of the field hands' horses. As he approached, Mr. Burl spied this stranger, pot bellied, with a big chaw of tobacco in his jaw. He was wearing a wide brim police hat, khaki clothing with suspenders and belt with scabbard and pistol, some kind of uniform, he thought. The stranger was sitting on the veranda alone. Usually someone accompanied a stranger at the house.

"Mr. Burrell Harrell, I am Sheriff Willis Farmer of Troup County", he said, flashing his badge. "How you doing? You may know or guess why I am here."

"No Sir, I don't know if I rightly do. What is it that brings you to my plantation?" Burrell smiled and looped his thumbs through his own suspenders.

"You may know that there was a killing a couple or few days ago in Gabbettville," said the Sheriff. Two nigrahs involved. One was named Mans . . . something, let me see . . . yep, I have it right here, Manfield Harris. It was said that he did the killing. The other one was named Alec Davidson. He was the one who got kilt. We, at first, thought he was a white man which is why I'm here so soon. There could be a lynching. Do you, or did you know either one of them?"

"What is this all about, Sheriff? What are you getting at? Are you accusing . . ."

"Hold your horses, boy!" said the Sheriff. "Don't get all huffy with me," he said harshly. "I need some information and I want you to answer a few questions!"

Burrell was fuming. He wanted to throw the sheriff off of the veranda or hit him or something. *"The nerve of him talking to me that way!"*

"But you going to have to tell me first what this is all about," Burrell said. "Is that too much for me to ask?" Burrell was none too happy that the Sheriff had referred to him demeaningly as "boy." Mr. Burrell was thought of as being at least of gentry, if not of aristocracy, in the area and was not about to tolerate any "big" talk from a lowly cracker of the kind that often had the law enforcement jobs. Their job was to keep the coloreds and their own kind in line. It was unthinkable even that he was sitting on the Harrells' veranda, which explained why he was unaccompanied.

"No, Sir, I'd say that's fair," the Sheriff said now understanding his place and falling in line.

"That's better, now get to the point! What do you want? I have a business to run. I have no time for this foolishness."

"I was told the gun that was used to kill that boy belonged to you. Is that right?" asked the Sheriff.

"I have no idea what you are talking about. Who told you that?"

"I picked up your farm hand late yesterday, Manfield, and he said that you gave him that gun."

"What gun? No such thing. The gun that he picked up had belonged to his daddy. I was holding it for him, the son. The son asked me for it. I gave it to him because it was rightfully his and he asked for it. That's that! Whatever he did with it was his own business. Does that answer your question? Now I do have to go to attend to my business. I don't want to see you here any more, or your men on this property again if you want to keep the peace. Am I clear on that?" Burrell walked away, fit to be tied.

"Not so fast, Mr. Harrell," persisted the Sheriff, knowing that he had been put in his place. "I got a warrant for your arrest."

"You what? Goddamit! Stay right here for a minute, I'll be right back."

Mr. Burrell hurried to the back of the house and started ringing his bell with two quick strokes. Then he tolled it once every 4 seconds for about a half a minute. He had coded signals for the tenants and the workers on the farm to respond to trouble, payday, and the like. He returned to the Sheriff walking ever so fast and said, "I want to show you something."

Tenant farmers and field hands, about 20 of them, came up on the property from all directions with their shotguns at sling arms, military style. They just stood around, not quite threatening the Sheriff, but it was a show of force. The Sheriff was no dummy.

"I am the law around here, Sheriff. Look around, as far as you can see in every direction, that land is mine. These people here live and work on this property, and they are taken care of with no interference from the likes of you on the outside. If I ever need you, I will send for you. If

28

there are any problems around here, I will take care of them myself. Best you go now."

The Sheriff realized that his badge meant nothing at all to Burrell. He backed off the verandah, checking in all directions to make sure that he was not going to be bushwhacked. He climbed up on his buggy and headed off to LaGrange. He didn't make any hay that day but promised himself that he was going to get that "high and mighty son of a bitch" one day.

LaGrange was the County seat. Several towns earlier had vied to be the county seat, but none was adequate because of their location. West Point had a good shot but it was too far removed from the rest of the county. It occupied the extreme southeast corner of Troup County and spilled over into Harris County and seemingly into Alabama as well. In addition, West Point's economy was inextricably tied to the Alabama communities of Lanett, Shawmut, Langdale, Fairfax and Riverview. LaGrange won out and a good choice it was, especially for law enforcement, because it was centrally located.

The house for Rosa was almost finished but for some small items. Mr. Burrell wanted Rosa to see it for herself to make sure she liked it. The house stood on a hill rising ever so gradually, sitting about a hundred yards off the highway and facing it. It was easily seen from the highway, and the setting was truly perfect. It could also be seen from the Harrell Family homestead, from which Burrell would always take notice of Rosa's house whenever he came to the verandah. It was more than adequate for Rosa and the baby. The rooms were big. The kitchen was especially large with an eating table so long that a whole family of ten could eat together comfortably.

"Mr. Burl," asked Rosa. "Why so much space?"

"We are going to have a mighty big family one day, just like my Daddy, Honey. He had ten. Like I said, I'll be staying with you from now on, starting tonight. It's really not safe for us anymore around here, especially since I had this run-in with the law."

Both were powerfully pleased with the house. It was now a matter of the right furniture. Many of the tenants and farmhands were standing nearby and at a respectful distance, waiting for any orders as to what they could do next for Miss Rosa, or waiting to be directed or dismissed by Mr. Burl.

Rosa was still uneasy about their staying together; as such an arrangement was totally unheard of in Georgia. She was not only afraid for herself, but for her extended family, as well as for Mr. Burl himself. But what could she do, as Mr. Burl was bull headed and really did whatever he pleased. She also was aware of the situation earlier in the day with the Sheriff, and had a feeling that he would try to get even with Mr. Burl in some way for disrespecting and belittling him in front of bystanders. But Mr. Burl didn't seem to have a care in the world. When he was a teenager, he used to hang around the adults, some were nightriders who would terrorize the colored communities, or those who would organize lynching parties, if not participate in them. He had learned how to deal with them, and seen how the powerful would handle even the less fortunate whites. It was not his nature to think that he could ever lose.

With so many people around and about and, of course, being involved in the goings-on at Rose Hill, it was next to impossible to keep the word from spreading that Burrell Harrell had taken up with a colored woman to be, in effect, his wife. These kinds of breaches of convention were not going to be taken lightly by the townspeople, and certainly not by the surrounding communities of Long Cane, O'Neal's Mills, and Salem. This was a matter of a way of life, just forming, but not too steeped in any profound tradition or deep-seated culture. West Point was the only town around with a strong sense of social establishment, as exhibited by its grand churches such as the First Baptist, First Methodist, First Presbyterian, and the United Christian Church, which was the church of the Aristocracy and a very highly stratified one at that. Neither the schools nor the clubs welcome the less fortunate whites, even though they had no choice but to accept those who came. But the gentry and the aristocracy always made sure that the whites that were the straw bosses, planters, and overseers served as a buffer between them and the colored. This system became imbedded in the ways of the South, to guarantee that the blacks would never rise to any high station in the society, as seldom would the poor whites who must, too, remember their place.

Night had fallen. All was quiet. Everything and everybody were in their right places. Supper was over. Not a creature was stirring. It was a beautiful night except there was no moon, just stars appearing as if they were holes in the inky black night sky.

"This is too quiet. Something's amiss," said Mr. Burl. "I think I had better take a look around. I don't have all of the eyes and ears I need since Manfield's been put in jail. Come to think of it, I better go and get him out tomorrow, but I'm uneasy now," he mumbled as he got up from the table. He checked his pistol to make sure that it was loaded; then he grabbed his shotgun, which he had brought in from his buggy, and walked to the entrance of the property. There he met with some of his men, both white and colored, who were posted on watch duty that night.

"Boys! I am expecting trouble tonight. You know what it's all about, or maybe I should tell you what it ain't about. It ain't about that shooting that went on in Gabbettville the other day, or anything or anybody else. It's about me and Rosa. I reckon that you know by now that we gonna keep house, and we are gonna raise a big family. It's what I want. Now if you ain't got the heart to fight to maim or kill, best y'all git off the property tonight, right now. Y'all with me?" he roared. There was a kind of camaraderie between him and his men that made them all feel that they needed each other. He was always there, bossing, overseeing every little detail. He really did not need an answer. Mr. Burl on these occasions would speak to the men in their manner of speech, in the kind of words that they used themselves. They had played together when they were little boys, and they knew that he was not only for them but one of them except he lived in the big house on the hill.

"Go and stake out your posts, and stay there until I give you the signal to leave. You know what it is, and you know what you have to do," he said.

They broke up and moved quickly and quietly around the property to their preplanned posts. Each was prepared to stay all night if necessary.

In the distance, on the road up ahead apiece, appeared six to ten headlights. They were more than likely Model T Fords. They had become popular since they were first introduced in 1908. The cars were bearing down fast, about a half-mile away. Then they started to slow down. It was still a moonless night; there was not much of a breeze.

"This is it," went through the minds of each of Mr. Burl's men.

The lights on the cars went out. It seemed that they were indeed coming to pay a visit to Mr. Harrell. Nightriders! Their footsteps could be heard marching by starlight only down the freshly scraped dirt road. There was a whole bunch of them. They came to do damage. As they approached the entrance to the plantation, they suddenly stopped, huddled for a few seconds and then spread out. The leader took a couple of steps through the entrance gate where Mr. Burrell stood in the darkness and he said: "Don't take another goddam step or I'll blow your damn head off!" The night visitors all froze in place.

"Stand right there! Call all of your men and tell them to come over here. I ain't gonna have you killed, yet, I just want to warn you. All of you throw down your guns. Now I want you to listen to me good, because I ain't in no way, shape, or form of repeating myself. Y'all understand? But first of all, tell me why you here! Why you here, boy?" poking him in the chest with his stick. "Oh, the cat's got your tongue, huh? I got you surrounded. I can kill all of you, right now. You ain't got no chance in the world of getting out of here. You ain't minding your own damn business. I'm gonna light up a cigarette and y'all watch what happens."

A dozen other cigarettes, at thirty, fifty feet away, lit up by tenant sentries at the same time. They were standing guard and surrounding the nightriders at varying distances in all directions. Then another dozen lit up. They outnumbered the visitors by more than four times. Mr. Burrell put his cigarette out. This was the signal for his men to open fire. They held their shotguns high over their heads and blasted off in unison, one volley each.

"Let's say that I don't know why you come here and I don't really care. But I think you came out here to do me and my family some harm. But I don't go for that shit. I could have all of you killed right now. I don't want to know who you are, or who put you up to do this. I'd know if I was to see your eyes, and one day I might have to kill you on the spot. I will do that. Mark my word.

"Now I am going to teach you SOB's a lesson. Take your shoes off. Throw them to the side of the road." They could barely see for it was so dark. "Now take all of your clothes off, step out of them and high tail it out of here. All I want to see are assholes and elbows. Leave your cars where they are. Get moving!" With that, Mr. Burrell fired off one shell from his own shotgun." He really meant it.

The sentries just rolled over laughing at this spectacle. When things settled down, Mr. Burl said to the crew, "Let's don't think that this is all. They might come back, maybe even tonight if only to get their clothes and shoes. We will keep their weapons because who knows when we might have to use them. So go out there and pick up them guns but throw their clothes in the middle of the highway. Take any of the shoes you want for yourselves." Shoes were indeed a precious commodity. Nobody ever had more than one pair.

"Some of y'all will have to stay right here for the rest of the night. The rest of you will have to spell them by 3:00 o'clock in the morning. I'll stay up all night."

For the first time in his life, Burrell actually felt scared. Scared that harm would come to his property, maybe members of his extended family, including his sisters who lived in the big house up the road apiece. He went back to Rosa to give her a rundown as to what happened during the night.

"Oh, Mr. Burl, I won't be able to stand all of this," she said with tears streaming down her cheeks. Then she started sobbing.

"Just cut it out, Rosa!" Mr. Burl shouted. "We said that we were going to do it and we will. What went on last night was just a taste of how things can be. We can't even think of giving in. Each time they come, and they will be back, we will have to stand our ground and even kill some of them if we have to. Now y'all come on over here." He motioned for Rosa, pulled her close and held her tightly. She felt secure like she should have never doubted him in the first place.

33

Rosa and Burrell cemented their relationship that very evening. They became almost inseparable even when they ventured into town. She would ride in the buggy or dray seated next to him. Sometimes, Rosa Belle would ride with them, seated in between. For the first time Rosa Belle, their first child, really had her Daddy at her side. He did the things that fathers do for their beautiful young ladies. He bought her pretty little dresses and always cookies and candies of her choice. He read her stories just before bedtime and even tucked her in and kissed her good night. Miss Rosa always loved these moments, as she could foresee how all of the children she and Mister Burrell would have were going to fare as they brought them into this world.

Rosa Belle had just turned five years old when the next child came. His name was George Frank. He, too, was fair of skin and blond of hair. They knew that this handsome little fellow someday would give them fits. The spacing between them was long because Rosa had had three successive miscarriages before "Sug." "Sug" was George Frank's nickname and adapted from "sugar." He was born July 16, 1916.

"I am going to name all of my boys for some male member of my family," Mr. Burrell declared. "This way we can go hunting and fishing together and never leave this vast land of ours. My old man was good to me. He left me all of this land and someday it will be our children's. And Rosa, I want the rest of them to be boys, because I need them to run and take care of this plantation." I am only thirty-one and I need plenty of boys. I am still fit to be the maker of men," he droned on.

"We will take what the dear Lord give us. I will be happy with boys and girls," said Rosa. "The Lord knows I am trying 'cause we ain't been too lucky, so far."

Chapter 3. The Depression

It was the fall of the year in 1919. It had been a bad year for farming. The spring and summer months had been exceedingly wet. The downpours were devastating. Many of their low-lying acres in the flood plain had been swamped by the overflow of the Long Cane Creek repeatedly, during planting and growing seasons, but worse during the harvest of what little was salvageable. The Chattahoochee River suffered the same fate as the Long Cane Creek, as its waters backed up in the creek onto the flood plain. There was even a cyclone in downtown West Point proper the following year, in which a great deal of damage was inflicted on the outlying communities. Rosa was frequently too ill to help with the farm work in any meaningful way, but she still took care of the children. Burrell was grateful, but how else could he be?

(The cotton, if it could talk, would retell the story that the first ever truly successful bale of cotton was created by Burrell's father, Burrell Whatley Harrell, in 1882.) The grain had been stored in the silos for the animals for the coming winter. Plenty of sorghum had been packaged for sale and ready for market, but nothing like in the prior years; however, the family was well-provided for, and there was enough for all of the farm hands and their families to have a good share and not suffer through the winter. In addition, there were shares for his mother, Miss Cordie, and his sisters who were still at home in the big house, the homestead. Burrell counted his blessings, and went back to the house to tell Rosa of the family's fortunes, though meager but sufficient to keep them going.

"Mister Burrell, I think it's about time. I have gone full term. I believe it's going to be the other little boy you wanted," Rosa said. "He's been just too frisky. I think you better call for my mother and one of my sisters to come over here. Maybe they should bring the midwife, because it ain't gonna be too long before the baby gets here."

"I'll do that, but I think I had better go over and see about my mother and my sisters, too. They are not too happy because I spend so much of my time over here. In fact, they say I spend much too much time. This little lot of mine has been too burdensome. They expect me to do everything and be everybody. Why don't they call on my other brothers or one or two of my sisters' husbands? After all they are still members of the family," Burrell lamented. He understood. He was the chosen one. There's one in every family.

He had tired of his position and responsibilities in the family. After all, he was the fourth of five boys. But he was the one that his father had put his trust in before he died. He was brave and bold. His father told him to look after his mother and his unmarried sisters, and for God's sake try to straighten out his brothers. The other boys were either sickly, or had not grown up to be solid citizens. What's more, they seemed not to care as Alfred Lee and Tom at first thought that each should have been chosen by their father rather than Burrell; yet each stood to inherit an equal share of what their father left, even though Burrell was in charge of everything now. With these thoughts on his mind, Burrell headed over to the big house to talk to his mother.

"It's about time you got over here, Burrell Floyd," Miss Cordie scolded. "You have been neglecting us."

"Yes," chorused May and Evans, who did their best to comfort their mother in her longing for their father, who had died in 1901. Miss Cordie was now 66 years old and her health was beginning to fail. She was still the proud woman, a lawyer in her own right, who had educated as many of her children who wanted to get a higher education, and especially the girls because she wanted them to marry well. She was a tiny woman, but grand enough to deliver ten children unto this world. She would demand that they come to the big house when they became adults every Sunday for a get-together. This was designed to make sure that the family remained intact.

Burrell stood there about ready to fire back, but thought better of it. He patiently waited until the grumbling died down and said, "Ladies, I am here every day. I eat breakfast with y'all every morning. I spend the night here every evening. I don't want the run of the house, although I would like to be with y'all more often. But as a family man, I have other obligations to take care of, and besides, am I not the only one in the family who is taking care of the plantation? You know we have over fifteen hundred acres of farmland planted nearly every year and nearly 5,000 head of beef cattle. Yes, I know that some of this is yours, but nobody else has hit a lick at a snake. Where are the others? Nowhere near, I'm sure."

"Oh Burrell, we don't mean to trouble you so. It just seems that you have abandoned us for that "mulatta" woman you took up with."

"You see me every day, at breakfast," he repeated. "I am a family man, and that mulatta woman is my wife and the mother of my children. What's wrong with you people? You are all educated and high and mighty, and just listen to yourselves. I am doing all that I can. I will try to do more, but this is the wrong time of the year for me to spend time not doing the farm work. Besides, I like being a father. Father! Oh my God!" he screamed. "I'm supposed to be getting Belle over for Rosa because our next baby is on the way!"

Burrell bolted out of the house, grabbed a horse, and rode bareback at breakneck speed trying to beat the stork. He didn't make it, but Miss Belle was already there with the midwife, who had already delivered a bouncing baby girl.

Burrell was embarrassed, as he broke in on the women who were doing things private to womenfolk. They handed the new baby for him to hold. He was getting used to doing this sort of thing and had come to enjoy it. He was as proud as he could be.

The new baby was Marguerite – born on September 22, 1919. She was a brunette with crystal-like blue eyes, and a beauty at that.

After that, did they start coming fast! There was Precious on January 28, 1922. Three girls and one boy. Doesn't look too good for farming. Must have more boys, prayed Burrell. His prayers were answered: John Thomas, born on April 24, 1923; Alfred Gordon, born on August 19, 1924; James Floyd, born on March 4, 1927.

"Three girls and four boys. That'll do it," Burrell thought out loud.

Chapter 4. School Days

"Mr. Burrell," Rosa said. "We must have another girl after all of the boys, or I won't have a baby to love in the house. I want at least one more child, hopefully a girl. I just remember the first one who was taken away from me for so long because we were not a proper family. I didn't get a chance to hold her and mother her the way that a little girl should be. That whole experience was bad for me, and the baby too. We may never get over it."

"It's always up to you, Honeybunch. You complained how all of children were taking such a toll on you. I want you to remain healthy so that we can bring these children up right. You know they are going to have trouble in almost every way – with the whites and the colored. In fact it has already started. I have been trying to sneak some of them in the school that the authorities just built up on the College Hill in West Point. I don't want them to continue in that no good place that y'all call a school over there in Mount New Harmony. They ain't learnt a damn thing, and won't be learning nothing either. The teachers ain't able to teach them because they don't know nothing. They didn't even finished grade school. Just where did they get their learning anyway? Right now, it's overcrowded. I won't tolerate this poor schooling no longer. Either the authorities are going to have open up this school to my children, or they will have to build a new one. I'm going back to that city school next week to see what they are going to do."

"Mister Burl! Mister Burrell, you don't seem to understand your people as good as I do," Rosa said. "They don't care about you or who you think you are. All they say is your children ain't white and they ain't, and no matter what you say or do, you ain't going to get them in that school. You may as well quit it, right now. You better come to your senses quick or we will have the Klan back on us again."

Burrell Floyd Harrell was not one easily discouraged. He would never take "no" for an answer. He was always ready to get physical if it came to that. It was a beautiful September morning. The air was so cool and fresh -- just one deep breath would invigorate you for the entire day.

Rosa had dressed Precious in her best dress with one simple ribbon in her blonde hair. John Thomas was properly dressed in a short sleeve shirt with a little bow tie. His pants were short and not too baggy, and he wore brogans for shoes. The town kids at the white school never wore brogans, as they were a dead giveaway for the kids who lived on farms or in the country. Nevertheless, these were his Sunday go-to-meetings. John Thomas was big for his age at six, and would fight in a minute if threatened in any way. He took this attitude from his Daddy. He was also blond, but his hair was rather wiry with a wave or a curl here and there. This hair form was not unusual for the whites in the area, and many blacks thought that when this trait appeared, there's been some hanky panky going on in the barnyard.

"Where are you taking us this morning, Mr. Burl?" John Thomas asked.

"I'm taking you and Precious to another school. You'll like it better there."

"I don't want to go," Precious fretted. "I like it where I go now, Mr. Burl."

"Get in the buggy by yourself, or do you want me to help you, little missy," said Mr. Burrell firmly with mild anger in his voice.

"I am not going to like it. I want to be with my friends and cousins," Precious cried out.

"Just get in and stop your whimpering."

John Thomas couldn't have cared less. He always craved new ventures. He was ready but not yet willing to go to school.

Manfield had hooked up the horses to the carriage and helped Mr. Burrell mount it. Manfield had been freed from jail at last, based on Mr. Burrell's pleadings with the judge and jury, because he was innocent of any malice, and surely would not have killed except in self-defense. Besides, he was the best employee that Burrell had, and the farm had gone down hill some since he was jailed. If they would just set him free, Burrell promised that he would keep him down on the farm forever and be totally responsible for him. The jury had accepted his plea, and

39

recommended to the judge that time served was fit punishment for second-degree manslaughter.

As Mr. Harrell headed out to the West Point Public School, as the school was then known, he rethought what Rosa had told him. Yet in his heart, he knew that he was right and that he had to go through with it. He damned himself for not having taken this action much sooner, because he had three children who had now been damaged in that country school at the church, and were going to be ruined for the rest of their lives. He felt that Rosa Belle and Sug were not of the right temperament and too far-gone to benefit from this challenge. Marguerite was the little lady who could have gone through it, but their father had the right ones in Precious and John Thomas. Precious was a bit feisty and determined to have her own way in all her eight years, and would without a doubt challenge authority. The teachers and other authorities, however, would not tolerate the slightest bit of back talk or challenge at that time. John Thomas was the man of the hour! Robust for his age and determined, he would have survived the treatment had he gone, because he didn't understand that he was "colored" or different from anybody else.

As the carriage pulled in to the school's parking lot, Mr. Burrell noticed that the other vehicles were Model "T" Fords, while his was just a horse-drawn buggy. However, Mr. Burrell was unfazed. He had not learned how to drive a car anyway. Setting his priorities straight from the beginning, he made it a point to go around to the front of this massive building rather than a side entrance, which was really more convenient. Side entrances and back doors were for the colored. The climb up two tiers of 12 steps each was tough for the kids, but worth the challenge. Perched on top of the highest hill in town, the school overlooked the City of West Point and the Chattahoochee River as it sometimes lazily flowed from upstate Georgia to its becoming the border between the State of Alabama and Georgia to the East.

The colored section of West Point was at the school's rear or east. Eighth Street to the west was tree-lined on each side of the street down to the Chattahoochee River Bridge. The setting was majestic and reminiscent of an elegant French boulevard. At the foot of the hill was a 20-foot tall white, obelisk fashioned from the very best Georgia marble commemorating the fallen Confederate soldiers from the Battle of West Point, one of the last battles of the Civil War. In fact, the war was really over at the time of the battle. It was also symbolic to remind anyone who dared ask that this was a Confederate town. Mr. Burrell resoundingly ignored such trivia, for his father had been a decorated soldier in the Confederate Army, Company B, Alabama Infantry, Confederate States of America. He remembered the tales his father told of his own fighting. He was a water boy at the age of 14 in full battle dress, but got caught up in a skirmish between the warring factions. He threw down his canteen, picked up the rifle of a fallen brother and marched into battle loaded for bear and ready to fight when a captured Confederate grabbed the breach of his rifled and said "let's go home boy, it's all over."

"What can I do for you this time, Mr. Harrell?" Dr. W. T. Harrison, Superintendent of West Point Public Schools, barked. Dr. Harrison was relatively new as the super having won the position in 1931.

"Things have not changed for my children in getting a good schooling, Professor. I come back here today to see to it that that be changed. I insist that these children be enrolled in this school, here. I know that this school is set aside for whites but look at my children. Can you tell them apart from any white child? I ask you, can you tell?"

"That is not the point! Like we told you the last time you were here, we know that they are not white," Professor Harrison said. "It's as simple as that. They will not be permitted to go here, and that's the law and I intend to uphold it. Let me just tell you what the law really says, maybe I should say policy, but it has the effect of law. Now this was established way back in 1876 when the West Point Public Schools were just being founded. It says first that "only white children, male and female, between the ages of 6 and 18; second, all children were required to spell words of three letters; third, all white children of parents living in the corporate limits, and of parents who were taxpayers but lived outside the city, and the children of the original stockholders of the West Point Female College, were entitled to free tuition." It can't be any clearer. And the next time you come here, I'll . . ."

"You'll what?" interrupted Mr. Harrell moving menacingly forward. "Don't you threaten me. You goddam son-of-a-bitch! I know my rights, and I insist that you make the right conditions for my children to get better schooling. If you don't, I'll tear you apart limb-by-limb and

41

wipe out this entire god forsaken school system. You'd better get cracking!"

The superintendent was now thoroughly intimidated by Mr. Harrell, who stood blocking the doorway. The children were standing by now all wide-eyed, and not sure of what was going on, but aware that trouble was brewing, nonetheless.

"Why don't you sit down, Mr. Harrell. And please try to be calm and patient. This whole thing is bigger than both of us. Perhaps we can discuss this further at some other time. Now nobody knows too much about this, but the City has voted funds to build a school for the nigrahs. But that won't be nearly enough, because there are so many of those little pickaninnies (peco niños, from the Portuguese) coming into the school system now from everywhere and all over. Even from Alabama. There are no schools for them anywhere but here in West Point, and LaGrange is too far for them. Their churches run those schools, and they are not very good, I'll have to agree with you. We have no idea what the enrollment will be. You may as well understand it right now; there won't be enough room for all of them in the beginning. But they will drop out like flies anyhow, and by the time they reach the upper grades, there'll be plenty of room. You get it? The boys will be trained as handymen and laborers, and the girls will be trained as nursemaids and in homemaking, because the only opportunities for them will be unskilled labor and maids for our wives and daughters. Why make them unhappy? I don't care what you say; there won't be any typewriters for the girls. Nobody will hire them as secretaries. As for the boys, their shop will be second to none. They'll be among the finest in all of Georgia.

"Now, there is this here nice little Jew fellow, Julius Rosenwald is his name. He controls The Julius Rosenwald Fund. It has been giving away loads of money in the South to build schools for the nigrahs and poor whites as well; we have applied to this Fund for some money. We think maybe twenty thousand dollars will do. You know he's the head of Sears and Roebuck Company. Bethlehem Baptist Church, that "nigrah" Church over yonder," he pointed to the church on the hill across the way, "has promised to give us the land for the School. If everything comes through, that will be a better school than this one," the Superintendent waxed on. "You see Mr. Harrell, you started us to

42

thinking the last time you were here that we needed to do something about this situation, and we are indeed coming through with a good solution."

Mr. Harrell didn't believe a word of it. "I am going to hold your feet to the fire, Harrison," he said in a manner still disrespectful of the Professor's position in the community. "This had better happen; otherwise, it's gonna to be you and me. I don't care about all of them other promises. I've got a nephew, Roy, about to be on the Board, and I'll see what he can do about this. When are you going to break ground?"

"You are getting too far ahead of me," Mr. Harrell. "A lot of other things must happen before . . ."

Interrupting again, Mr. Harrell took the little ones by the hand leading them away. He said, ignoring Dr. Harrison, "Look Precious Myra and John Thomas, you are going to have a school just like this one some day soon. Professor Harrison just told me so and it's going to be on Tenth Street. It will be ready in about two years." Dr. Harrison just stood there wondering if this man was going to try to destroy him. He had never heard of such a thing -- a white man agitating for better education facilities for the colored. Dr. Harrison failed to appreciate that Burrell Floyd Harrell was a proud and devoted father, but his concern was for his own children, not the colored in general.

"Harrison, don't you want to show me around this here place? I want to see what you really got here. You said that the new school may be better than this one. Show me what you got, man!"

"Don't mind if I do," Professor Harrison said, knowing that he wouldn't be in any trouble because his visitors "looked white" and who would know the difference anyway?

The building was grandiose -- columns carved from Georgia marble at the entrance, and floors made of Georgia granite in the lobby. Hardwood flooring from Georgia Oaks. Superb lighting for the times, coupled with large windows, allowed just the right amount of lighting exposure in the classrooms. There were laboratories abound for the science classes, all fully equipped. A spacious cafeteria set off from the

43

high school's portion of the building. The auditorium was something to behold. It was a showplace that rivaled the City Hall over town. It functioned as a performing arts center as well as the school's gymnasium.

The planners and benefactors of this school expected their children to go on to Georgia Tech in Atlanta and the University of Georgia in Athens; Brown University up North where so many of the town's aristocrats sent their children; and the University of Chicago. Many of the boys would go off to military schools the like the Citadel, VMI and of course The United States Military Academy in West Point, New York, and other military schools the likes of which abound throughout the South. A military career would add prestige, bearing and standing to a family. The townspeople had contributed considerable largesse to make this school the magnificent edifice that it was, and Professor Harrison was doing everything possible to keep as many of the gentry and aristocracy's children in the fold.

The high school curriculum to prepare these students for Ivy League-type schools consisted of orthography, natural philosophy, elocution, grammar, physical geography, Latin, Greek (for the boys), algebra, geometry, composition, rhetoric, English literature, physiology, chemistry, astronomy, trigonometry, moral philosophy, elements of criticism, reading, and penmanship. None of this was available for the school for colored, as the jobs they would hold required little or none of this.

"Very nice place you got here, Professor," Mr. Harrell said with tongue in cheek. "If the school for the colored ain't equal to this one, I'm going to give you fits, do you hear me?" I know all about that 'separate but equal' crap, it had better be at least equal! Y'all had better come through, y'hear?"

Dr. Harrison had heard about Burrell Floyd Harrell, the warrior, and did not want to tangle with him, but he knew that the powers that be in the town were more than a match for any of the plantation owners, no matter their stripe. The Harrells at best could be considered gentry but from Alabama, not Georgia.

The school was ready in less than two years – it was 1933. It would be called the "Troup County Training School for Colored." Although it was grand compared to what had been available to the colored heretofore, it was a far cry from the "white" School. It was considered "nice" and was, of course, segregated, separate and unequal. Never again would there be notions of the coloreds in town going to school with the whites. It was even out of the reach of some of the poor whites, as so few of them lived in West Point proper, or fit the criteria to include them, or even went to school.

"Training School" meant that manual arts would be paramount for the boys, and "home economics" - that is housework, cooking and cleaning for the girls. This school was intended to cement these students' lives as maids, servants, and handymen or just plain laborers. They were not to aspire to professional careers or even white-collar jobs, although they could be preachers and teachers – but to the colored only.

Troup County Training School was the showcase of the hour. All of the power brokers in the county were invited for the official dedication and ribbon cutting. The county dignitaries in their respective roles at the dedication were fulminating royally. The Superintendent, Professor Harrison, was the master of ceremonies. He introduced the Mayor of West Point and each of the county functionaries, all of whom had much to say and delivered their expectations for the students. One representative from The Julius Rosenwald Fund was invited to make a presentation. He mentioned the good deeds that the Jews across the country were doing for the less fortunate, in their role as benevolent brothers to all of mankind, whereupon he presented a sizable check to purchase an electric timing and signaling system for changing classes at the white school. This played well to the town's seven invited Jewish families, whose children attended the white school but not without occasional incident, particularly those with woolly hair.

Three colored persons were invited to participate in the ceremonies. The first was the new principal, "Professor" John Wesley (J.W.) Thompson, Sr., a rather short, dark brown skin man of some local distinction in the colored community. Next was the pastor of Bethlehem Baptist Church, the Reverend Arthur Hutchinson, a stereotypically black Baptist preacher, who couldn't make it because he lived too far away, in Atlanta, though the Chairman of the Deacon Board, Mr. Alfonso

Davidson, a diminutive, fair-skinned man who had as many children as Mr. Harrell, substituted for him. Mr. "Fonzo's" regular job in West Point was to keep the Neal - Schaeffer Drug Store tidy. And third, of course, was the janitor, Mr. Will Hart, a mulatto, fairest of skin and straightest of hair, a very useful middle-aged man who could get about town for almost any purpose without being noticed as a colored. Because of this, Mr. Will was extremely valuable to the colored community when there had to be challenges in dealings in ticklish situations with the whites. His family was as white as the Winstons, but his father was nowhere to be found.

"Now, just before we go on our tour of the building," announced Dr. Harrison. "We have our little first graders to sing a song for us."

The folding doors on the stage opened to the auditorium, and in marched onto the stage pretty little girls all dressed in white with bows in their hair, and dapper little boys with bow ties, white shirts, and black pants, to sing the song that they had rehearsed for the occasion. Miss Claudine Glover, the first grade teacher, raised her arms and motioned the children to sing:

> *Jesus loves me this I know,*

> *For the Bible tells me so,*

> *Little ones to him belong,*

> *They are weak but he is strong.*

> *Yes Jesus loves me,*

> *Yes Jesus loves me,*

> *Yes Jesus loves me,*

> *For the Bible tells me so.*

The audience applauded enthusiastically for what seemed like an eternity, as the ladies from the white community had never seen such a display of cute little "nigrah" children. The applause lasted so long that an encore was obliged.

Miss Glover was prepared and thus reassembled the children. They bowed. The audience was quiet in anticipation of the next selection. Miss Glover raised her arms, flicked her wrists, and the children burst in song again:

I washed my hands this morning,

So very clean and white,

I lift them up to Jesus,

To work for him 'til night.

Little feet be careful,

Where you take me to,

Anything for Jesus,

Only let me do.

They were so proud of themselves, and they truly appreciated the rousing applause as they grinned and shifted from one foot to the other. The guests were delighted to greet them after such a fine performance. It was as if nothing like it had even happened before in West Point. Miss Glover delighted in their flawless performances. She was a rather large woman whose proportions were quite ample. She took her bows as some concern mounted that she might not able to regain her upright posture without assistance.

Dr. Harrison thanked all of the dignitaries and guests, and the parents, too, who customarily sat in the seats behind the dignitaries and guests when they were white, and requested that they, too, join in the tour of the facility. Such was uncommon in this community as the two communities never commingled. It came off nicely.

While on the tour, one of the guests asked Dr. Harrison, "Why, Professor, those folding doors on the stage are quite ingenious, but wouldn't it have been better and cheaper though to use curtains?"

"Why, no ma'm," answered Dr. Harrison. "Those folding doors seal off the stage from the auditorium so that classes can be conducted on the stage if we need more classrooms."

"So, you don't have enough classrooms for the students then?" she persisted.

"Oh, no ma'm, that's not it at all. We were just planning ahead just in case we had an unexpected overflow of pupils," countered Professor Harrison.

Mr. Burrell Floyd Harrell, lurking in the shadows, caught Professor Harrison's eye, winked and smiled.

Mr. Harrell had come to see what had been done for his children, and with the intent of creating a public spectacle over whatever was not satisfactory to him. After having spotted Mr. Harrell in the audience, Dr. Harrison now pushed the tour at a faster pace, until one of the invited ladies raised an issue that she among others did not have sufficient time to visit the Home Economics Department. She wanted to know whether the silverware was authentic and the stemware was genuine Waterford. She wanted to make sure that any of the girls who may come to work for her later on were adequately trained to identify and handle quality utensils with care and deft. She feigned that her only interest was to make sure that others would donate the kinds of utensils, china and glassware that were needed to do the kind of work required in their houses. She was making trouble and she knew it. The Professor got the point and later made sure that quality vessels and chinaware were provided.

And then there was the manual training shop – totally empty, devoid of workbenches, tools, and tables.

"What gives here professor?" Dr. Moreman, a school board member, asked Professor Thompson. "Professor" was a title that whites could comfortably bestow upon colored professionals to avoid having to call them "Mister." Dr. Moreman was also a dentist who was a favorite of his colored patients, in that he treated them as human beings and even made house calls when they suffered unduly from tooth extractions.

"Begging your pardon, Sir," said Professor Thompson. "Professor Harrison is in a much better position to answer that question than I, Sir." Professor Thompson always spoke softly, politely, and in perfect English around the whites, and was an old pro at parrying questions put by whites to him and other coloreds that should never have been raised in the first place, particularly when an answer always seemed so obvious to the colored person. Generally, those persons were savvy, knew the "whats" and "whyfors" of when something was done, not being done or would never be done. Professor Thompson was a "truth teller" like so many blacks of his day. He recognized when the truth should be avoided in an instance such as this, for if he had answered truthfully, his days would have been numbered as principal.

"The books will be passed out tomorrow morning, Dr. Moreman, as soon as inventory has been completed over at the West Point Public School," Professor Harrison answered, groping for a plausible answer while knowingly disinforming Dr. Moreman. This really meant that the new books slated for the colored pupils would be passed out to the white students first, and the old books previously used by the white students would be redistributed to the colored students. In most instances, there were not enough books to go around so that each student could have a complete set. And in all instances most were out-of-date and in poor condition.

"I am not following you, Harrison," Dr. Moreman said. "I am talking about the shop having no tools and benches and you are talking about books. Perhaps you would want to explain later." Nearly everyone knew what was going on except Dr. Moreman, who was new to the board and not necessarily aware as to how things were done in relation to the colored community. He was from out of town.

"Again, I want to thank y'all for coming on this fine day to help us officially celebrate the dedication of this fine school," Professor Harrison said in regaining the attention of the visitors. He wanted to get this thing over with before something else may be of an uncontrollable nature could happen.

"Is the tour over? I didn't see the cafeteria. How could I have missed it?" asked Mrs. John Hagedorn in her inimitable New York accent. She knew there was no cafeteria but wanted all to see that the school board had obviously not provided equal facilities. She knew that John, her husband, the top haberdasher in town, would give her hell when they returned home as they had found a "home" here without harassment, and in the South no less, and as such allowed them to practice their faith undisturbed.

Mr. Harrell again caught Dr. Harrison's eye and smiled sheepishly.

Chapter 5. Considerations

Over the course of the last three years, two more little ones had graced the home of the Harrells. Mary Bessie, a little darling with fine blonde hair and blue eyes to match her delicately white features. She resembled the Harrell ladies in the Big House so much that Burrell took her over to meet her granny and aunties. Miss Cordie, the baby's grandmother, called for May, Evans, and Cordelia, the youngest sister, obviously named for her mother, who was visiting, to come to see the beautiful little lady. They showered her with hugs and kisses and truly fell in love with her. May even wanted to adopt her as she was now widowed and had no children of her own. It was not uncommon for "outside" children to be adopted by relatives when the bonds of matrimony had not been blessed, or some of the children were cross racial, and therefore could pass into the white race, or in instances of just plain hardship when they were white.

"Burrell, please let us keep her," begged May.

"Oh, Burrell, doesn't she look just like us?" Evans fulminated.

"Don't get yourself all worked up over anything like that. This is the first girl since Precious, almost seven years ago, so that won't happen. But I'll try to get Rosa to name her after you, May, since you are the oldest of the girls," knowingly getting himself in trouble with Rosa.

"Nothing of the kind!" exclaimed Rosa when Burrell returned to Rose Hill. "She never once came over here to help when I needed somebody. In fact, she never came over, period! I would consider naming her after your mother or maybe Miss Evans, or even Miss Ethel. I would name her Cordelia after both your mother and sister, but not Miss Mae!"

"No, no, too many "Cordelias" now. I'll just tell May that you don't like her and the way she spells her name," teased Mr. Burrell. "Just quit it. I already promised May that I would name the baby for her and that's that!"

"Don't I ever get to name any of my children? You have named all of the boys after the menfolks in your family, now you starting to name the girls. It's all right, though. You just go right ahead, but I will name the next one."

"The next one? Woman, you're 38 years old! How many more children do you want?" Burrell asked in disgust.

"And you are only 45. I'll have them till I stop, like all women, and then, that's it. You have something to do with this too, you know. I'll stop having them when you stop making them!" snapped Rosa. "I do want the last one to be a boy though. But it won't make no difference. I'm good for maybe another five, maybe six. I don't care. You want to take them away from me and give them to your sisters anyway. You would think that I'm some kind of an old cow or something," she went on and on.

The next one, who turned out to be the last one, was in fact another boy, Gaines. A fine little fellow who had the same general appearance as all of the rest of the children at birth, but he seemed a bit whiter than all the rest, including his father. His growing up seemingly without any appreciable change in appearance "earned" him the family nickname of "White Boy." Mr. Burrell didn't know what hit him with this fusillade of brickbats fired off in rapid succession by Rosa. She was always so easy going, no back talk – a perfect wife.

"Let's don't go through that again. I am going to run back over to the house and give them the good news. I'll have dinner over there tonight and I will see you bright and early tomorrow morning." He reached to hug her but she turned her back to him.

"Go right ahead! See if I care! Better yet, I ain't going to speak to you no more! I will have nothing else to do with you," screamed Rosa, mother of nine, now in a fighting rage. "You need to spend more time with your own family, Mr. Burrell!"

"Rosa, just stop that!" Mr. Burrell shouted to calm her down. It only made things worse.

"Our family is growing up and we must think about what they gonna be when they get ready to move out of here. Your place is over here with your family, Mr. Burrell," Rosa's calming down a bit. She would pronounce his name very crisply when they were not on good terms. "You're going to have to give them up on the other side of the highway one of these days so you can raise your own family right. All they do is sit out on that verandah watching them cars and wagons go by day after day. We've said that the children are going to have a rough time out there, being neither 'colored nor white.' We're going to have to talk to them about that in no uncertain terms. So far, we have kept them very close right here on the plantation. Too close! The boys ain't learning nothing about what it's gonna be like outside of the plantation. You're carrying on here like the plantation is forever. Even the ex-slaves on this farm are doing something different now and maybe better. If you want your children to be somebody, we're going to have to move away from here, maybe up North somewhere."

"Hold your horses! There ain't no way in hell I'm gonna move up to no North. I was born a Southerner and I, by the grace of God, I'm going to die a Southerner. My Daddy was a soldier in the Confederate Army, he fought gallantly, and while we didn't win, there's still no way that I'll be associating with them. They're still our enemy. I wouldn't betray his memory. We didn't lose the war that bad though, we just had to give up our slaves, but we didn't lose our way of life. Many of the older ex-slaves are still with us on this farm right here, doing what they always did. These slaves came with the property when my Daddy took it over from the Maulls back in the eighties. Of course, they were even free then, and they could leave anytime they wanted to. We pay them enough to live on, or share enough of our crops with them to live better than they have ever lived before. What's wrong with that? They're happy, right? And they love us, right? We were able to keep our land and we even bought a whole lot more. We're prosperous, I tell you, Rosa. My family may have even gained a great deal. Look at all of what we've got now. We've got almost two thousand acres planted with cotton, corn, and sugar cane, and a whole lot of cattle roaming all around out there. That's money in the bank!"

"There's no reason for the ex-slaves to stay either," added Rosa. "They don't have no land and no money. No cattle to speak of, either. They take what you give them and that's it. Their entire life centers around this plantation, taking care of the animals, slopping the hogs, feeding the cattle, shoeing the horses, plowing the fields, chopping and picking cotton. What is it they don't do? That's why we have to leave, Mr. Burrell. Our children will be just like them. If you don't go, then we'll have to leave you, and go find a better life somewhere else without you. This is still in some ways the same as slavery. Our schooling is so poor. We can't hardly read and dare not try to show we can write because our handwriting is so bad. We, together, and our children have no future. Please take us away from here, Mr. Burrell," she begged. "Please!"

"No sense in continuing this discussion, Rosa. You always get back to this old slave crap. It's over Rosa! Forget it! It's over! If you don't, y'all will be saddled for life. This is our home now, and this is where we'll stay. It was good enough for my Daddy and his family, and it will always be good enough for us. You're not going anywhere either, and neither are the children. I have made a place for them and they have been well provided for. All right, I'll stay here tonight. Hey! Are you trying to get rid of me or something?"

"Wait a minute, don't do me no favors," Rosa fussed. "It may be better for me and the children to leave without you, as you will only stand in our way or hold us back. We will no longer be the fools because . . .," Rosa trailed off after seeing Mr. Burrell turn a beet red in the face. He was getting madder by the minute.

"Enough's enough!" he shouted. For the first time, he wanted to strike her. "I get it over here and I get it over there and maybe everywhere else, dammit! I am just plain fed up with all of this bickering and feuding and fending and proving and fighting, and carrying on. All of you are going to drive me absolutely crazy!" Rosa backed off a bit.

"You must remember Rosa," Mr. Burrell said. "I'm heading two families and I'm managing the plantation all alone although I'm not the sole owner. Just think, this place would go to seed if I left it. What will happen to our inheritance? Somebody will get it that's not entitled to it. Before I let that happen, I'll stay here forever and rot if necessary rather than let this land go. This is where I was born and raised. This piece of land is like heaven to me. This Rose Hill Place! I love it with all my heart and soul!" Tears welled up in his eyes, his chest puffed up, he pounded it mightily and shouted at the top of his lungs: "It's my lifeblood!" He then let out a big burst of air and smiled.

"Yes, but have you made any provisions for your children?" Rosa started up again as relentlessly as before. "Just because you their Daddy, don't mean that they will inherit your share of the properties left by your own Daddy. And you know he didn't leave no Will neither. You know that we ain't married in the eyes of the law, so who's to say that we'll get our fair share or anything at all? Plus you don't know what final arrangements Miss Cordie done made? Did she show you the Will? You have been working your butt off to run this here farm and care for these here properties, and your mother and sisters just sit over there in the big house getting calluses on their behinds, and they still entitled to as much as you, and together even more. Do you have a Will? If so, where is it? Am I in it? Are the children in it? Who'll get the shares of the property that your four dead brothers were entitled to? And how about the Big House? You just have a room over there, and as I hear from the children's account, there's not much in it -- desk, a chair, a bed, and a table and, oh, a place at the head of the table where they eat the food that we raise over here on Rose Hill."

"Rosa, you got me thinking. I just assumed that . . ."

"Don't assume nothing, Mr. Burrell!" interrupted Rosa. "Even though Miss Cordie disowned your brother, Tom, for his gambling, trifling behavior, gallivanting and carrying on and all that, and supposedly denied him his inheritance. Did she give you his share? Who holds it? Don't you ever question your Momma's actions? She getting on up in the years now. Somehow, that disinheritance's going to come back and bite all of you Harrells in the behind. Mr. Tom's got children who stand to inherit his share if things are not in order. You need to talk to a lawyer or somebody like that. Go over to Ben Hill's to . . . Mr. Burrell, are you all right? Is there something is wrong?"

Burrell was sobbing and his head was hanging mighty low. All of these questions and issues had been haunting him for such a long time. He was hoping that they would just go away. All of his siblings and their offspring were involved. He just didn't want to think about it. There was never a large amount of money around to handle all of these problems. Whenever he got a little money, he invested it in land. The

55

more land he acquired, the richer he felt. Some of the land that he had previously acquired for settlement of gambling debts could be used to fund the needed work on the big house, but the prices were not right at the time. One dollar an acre was simply peanuts. He still was avoiding the main issue -- that of providing for his children's future. How was he going to do that? He didn't trust the legal system either when it came to the fact that his children were not considered white. Too late to worry about that.

"You keep bringing up my brother, Tom. He was disinherited for good and sufficient reasons long time ago. He wouldn't work to support his family. That burden fell on me. This went on and on until our mother decided that he had brought enough disgrace to the family, to the point that the ladies in town would hesitate to associate with them. It was the constant embarrassment that they always suffered that caused his disinheritance. I tell you, he was always getting into some kind of scrape or another with them rednecks he hung out with, shooting craps or playing poker anywhere there was a game going on. All of this was bringing down the family's good name. Then, he let himself get kilt," Burrell said, and proceeded to tell once more the tale of his brother's death.

Although no one was ever sure of the details, the story went that Tom made untoward remarks about this ol' boy's woman. He had been keeping company with her and the ol' boy knew it. This ol' boy was a policeman in Shawmut, Alabama. Nobody, but nobody, fools around with a policeman's wife. Any fool knows that, but Tom was like that. He just didn't care. He liked her, and loved to live recklessly. Cummings was this ol' boy's name. He was a mean sonovabitch. Always packed a couple of pistols. Craved being a policeman. He came home unexpectedly on this day and found them together. Tom managed to get out of the house half clothed. He jumped fences, dashed through new spring gardens racing toward the store where he had left his buggy. Cummings was so furious with his wife that he failed to notice Tom's escape. Cummings toyed with the idea of killing her on the spot. Realizing that such wouldn't do him any good, he decided to pursue Tom. There were not too many places for Tom to go or hide in Shawmut. It was nothing more than a hamlet with a general store, post office, and a cotton mill. He made the mistake of going to buy him some smokes to steady his nerves. Cummings, in hot pursuit, flung the swinging doors of the store wide open with such force that he almost tore them from their hinges. He stood there, baring his pistols, just staring at Tom with fire in his eyes and hands at the ready, waiting, and daring Tom to move. Tom was defenseless. There was no getting past Cummings.

"Get out of town! You sonavabitch!" Cummings shouted now having one gun drawn. "I don't ever want to see you in this neck of the woods again, do you hear me?"

Tom moved cautiously as he slid along the wall to get past Cummings. Cummings motioned with his pistol signaling Tom to make it snappy. "Don't try no funny moves or I will blast you to kingdom come," Cummings barked. Cummings was a cop. A mean cop. There were certain things that he could not do regardless of his feelings. But he was waiting for any excuse to bag Tom, even with the slightest provocation.

Tom managed to get to the door and slipped outside. A crowd had gathered to witness the ruckus. Tom ran to his buggy, mounted the cab and yanked on the reins for his horse to move out. The buggy had to be turned around; wasting precious time, for it was headed in the wrong direction to get back to Georgia. As the buggy turned, Tom wanted to wipe Cummings out, he was so embarrassed for being caught red-handed, so he reached under the seat and grabbed his own pistol. At the moment the buggy straightened out, Tom fired two quick shots at Cummings while the buggy was picking up speed. He knew that he could outrace anybody, so he took the chance. One bullet nicked Cummings in the arm, and the other grazed off his forehead. Tom was a good shot, but not good enough on this day. Cummings, now having the upper hand and thoroughly incensed, took careful aim at the cab of the buggy while steadying his hand, still not knowing if he could fell his prey. He gently squeezed the trigger. He knew how to fire this weapon. He trained on it in the Army during World War I. He was a marksman. Three rounds popped out, one hitting Tom in the back thereby lodging in his kidney.

Tom slumped over letting out a piercing scream. Two bystanders already mounted on their horses caught up with the buggy and brought it to a halt. Tom's horse had panicked, as he was not used to gunfire. All he had ever done was to pull Tom's buggy on his rural mail route from one mail box to the next, sometimes waiting for Tom to make his daily appointed rounds in rain, sleet or snow while showering the ladies with his masculine charm when their companions were derelict.

Cummings dropped his head and then his gun. He had just shot a fleeing man, even though it could be said that it was in self-defense. He just stood there. He slowly stooped and picked up the gun, walked over to the police station, and handed it in.

"Lock me up, Sonny, I've done wrong. I don't deserve to be no policeman. Take my guns. Here's my badge. Open up that holding cell and I'll walk in it," Cummings said to Sonny, the deputy on duty.

Tom died the next day, Sunday, March 28, 1920.

"It's hard to lose a family member no matter what. It hurt us all," Mr. Burrell said. "We really never got over it. It's things like that that stick in your craw and make you wish that you never lived," Mr. Burrell said as tears again welled in his eyes. He loved his brother so.

"We all took it so hard even though he had it coming. He still was a good enough fellow in our eyesight. A husband, a father, a brother, a son, an uncle, nephew, cousin and friend. We loved him! He was buried the next day over in Pinewood Cemetery in West Point. The family really turned out real big. In fact, everybody was there. All of us Harrells were there, the Floyds, the Combs, the Wallaces, the Stricklands, the McClendons; you name them, and many more relatives and an army of friends and neighbors. He had a lot of colored friends, many of them his gambling buddies, too, and they were there as well. Tom would have given anything to see the fuss that all of us made over him. But he left two sons, Roy and Willard, fatherless. He was only 41. Only 41!

"Roy was seventeen, the same age I was when my Daddy died," Mr. Burrell said. "I just hope that Roy won't have to come up like me, with all of this God forsaken responsibility for a bunch of people who think that they deserve to live like royalty and yet show absolutely no appreciation. After me, Roy is the oldest male Harrell after my generation."

The following appeared in the *West Point News*:

In Memoriam

Thomas Gordon Harrell, of West Point,

deceased March 28, 1920, was shot in

the back at Shawmut, Ala., near the burial

Ground of Samuel Harrell, pioneer of

Virginia. On that fatal Saturday was cut

Off a keen, discerning intellect, a heart

That beat but with kindness. Idealistic,

Yet judicial, he advocated practical

Humanity ever championing the lowly

And oppressed. The colored population

adored him.

Pre-eminently peaceable, amiable and

Witty, he won many true friends. Suffering

Bravely, making pathetic attempts at joking,

He met death in a beautiful spirit. When he

Began our Lord's Prayer, there was not a dry

Eye in the room.

Brother, farewell.

The family's account of the shooting was not markedly different from that given above, except it included the detail that there had been a continuing argument and an altercation between Tom and Cummings. The newspapers indicated that there were too many variations as to the likely reason for the shooting, but never declared any specifics. Men don't willy-nilly shoot one other, and the rumor of a romantic entanglement was indeed credible.

The following Monday, Cummings was arraigned in the Chambers County Circuit Court in Lafayette, Alabama, the County Seat. He was charged with manslaughter and bound over to the Grand Jury, then released on $2,000.00 bail. The trial would be held when the circuit court convened in September.

"Now I don't mean to hurt your feelings or nothing like that, Mr. Burl, but why are you going all over this again. You are just trying to dodge the issues. We are talking about our children and their future. Believe it or not, things are not always going to be the same. You can hold some people down only so long. Sometimes it seems to me that you ain't got the sense you were born with. If you do, why don't you realize all of this?"

"I don't even know what you are talking about, woman," Burrell blurted out. "Just what in the hell are you driving at? What do you know or suspect that's going on?"

"That's just it. I don't know what's going on and these are your responsibilities. Your Daddy expected you to see after your Mother, your sisters, and all the affairs of the plantation. I'm just saying that you had better get involved, because our boys are getting older and growing up and ready to take some of the load off your back. You're going to have to put some of your responsibilities in their hands, and not be afraid of what your family or your gambling and drinking buddies or other white folks might think about it or do. It's time you truly accepted them as your real family.

"Don't look so surprised. I know you a big time gambler. Some nights, you say you're going over to your Mother's when you go out gambling with your buddies, you know who I'm talking about, and I know their names, too. And I even know where you go. You go over to Belle

60

Billingsley's. Everybody knows she run a bawdy house. It's called a house of convenience. That's funny. But she don't allow no colored men there. I hope you feel that you don't have to do what the other white men do. Everything you need and want is right here waiting for you at any time. The children pick up on all of this stuff from the workers and keep me in the know. I'm just saying, Mr. Burrell, it's about time for you to see to it that these here children of yours are provided for. Without you, we are nothing. You said it yourself so many times. I hear tell that your family is embarrassed about your relations with us. Right now your children are ashamed of who they are, too, and they are teased by the nigger children in town. It don't matter too much to me because I know I am a good woman and I ain't looking for nobody's approval. What's more, I've got right with God and I've been right with God for a long time. I just want you to do right by our children and put on paper what you are going to give them. Is that too much for a mother to ask for her children from their father?"

"Rosa, this makes me think that you don't trust me."

"For God's sakes, man, it ain't no matter of trust now, Mr. Burrell! If them lowdown, dirty crackers get a hold of your property, your children won't see the light of day. It's got to be on paper, and filed in the county offices and soon as you can! You know that! Don't put this off. My heart hurts me so!"

"Well, if it's going to make you happy, but I'll need to have a talk with all concerned, and that means talking about Tom's share, too."

"Tom's dead. He ain't got no share. He been disinherited. It ain't about trying to make who happy, it's just that you have to do something pretty quick for your family before it's too late. That's all."

"Yes, but he was my brother. Well, everybody knows what I want to do with my land. My boys are gonna to get all of the land on the south side of Highway 18. That's always been known as 'Rose Hill Place.' The girls are gonna get the Hogg property, that's the parcel on the other side of my property north of the highway. I 'acquired,' he chuckled, that from Ol' Al Hogg to settle a debt. There is also some Hogg property east of the Hamilton highway that's mine. That's going to the girls, too. Everybody knows that and that's the way it's gonna be."

61

"Mr. Burrell, things ain't like they used to be. The honor system is done for, gone with the wind. That's all talk."

"Yeah, yeah, yeah, May's been after me to do something for the children too, but I don't see that's such a big problem."

"If Miss May give you her property, you won't have no problems, because she's got no heirs, but you be aware that if she give it to Mr. Tom's children, there's gonna be a heap of trouble, and it will come from the first male relative who asks to help you solve your problems," warned Rosa. "And you know who that's gonna be."

"You sound just like Mama and May, always quoting from Shakespeare as to underhanded plots and motives. Them's real educated dollies over there, they are as clever as the devil, and they are always imagining terrible things about to happen. I'm aware of the value of land, and I will take care of it. I know what I'm doing. Look at all of this property I've accumulated." Rosa was no Shakespearean scholar and was not likely to have heard of him.

"Mr. Burrell?"

"Yes, Rosa?"

"Is it too late for you to consider sending one of our boys on to lawyer school, so he can look after things of yours in the future? If you thinking about using Mr. Roy, Mr. Tom's boy, to take care of things, you know he don't care for his cousins -- our children. Don't let him have a thing, because he will take it all. He's already upset that he don't stand to inherit much of anything, because his Daddy was cut out. You know that Mr. Burl. You know that! Don'tcha?"

"Yeah, Rosa. A guy's got to be fearful even of his relatives. Do you think that Alfred is the right one, or is it John Thomas? Alfred is bright and a straight shooter, and will stand for right, wouldn't you say? Now John Thomas is a straight shooter, too, but bull-headed. John Thomas knows about running the farm, and I'll always need him here. Alfred's been helping me with my books and knows my business. The only thing I'm really fearful about him is will they do business with him, or any of our children for that matter?"

"Well, there's Precious!" she murmured.

"What do you mean, 'There's Precious?' he shot back slightly angered.

"She smart and feisty and can run circles around all of them. You ought to think about her."

"Rosa, sometimes I think you got loose rocks in your head. There's no way they would even talk to a woman lawyer, let alone one who's mixed with colored. Have you ever heard of one?"

"There's always a first time, Mr. Burl, and you don't have to get nasty about it," Rosa fumed. "Women are smarter than men anyhow, and you know it."

Rosa and Burrell went on about the business of parenting and schooling the children as best they could given the ways of the South. But both were overwhelmed with the enormity and dependency, not only of the overall family, but most of the workers on the farm looked to them, too, to provide support or get work for their families. This was an outcome of slavery, as the workers had never done anything but depend on the "master" for their welfare. There was never a truly large cache of funds available to them, either, because Burrell had no choice but to support his mother and sisters in the manner that they had been accustomed. They didn't know where the money came from in the first place; in fact, they seemed not to appreciate that it took money to get things done, to buy food, and other necessities. Things just happened, they thought, particularly with the niceties. They just took things for granted. Rosa had high hopes that the children would move on beyond the farm, and establish themselves in a big city up North or somewhere, to support their aims until they could get on their feet. The trouble was that they had no relatives in the North, or in the big cities of the South. The South still had not truly recovered from the ravages of the Civil War, nor had the country from World War I either for that matter. The horrid economic times of the late twenties and early thirties had nearly wiped everybody out. Those who owned land fared so much better because they only tilled the soil, raised whatever they ate, bartered for what they needed, and were able to support others who had less resources to depend on. But the taxes didn't let up. There were always the taxes. And if you wanted to vote, you had better ante up with your poll taxes as well. The vote was power. It meant that you could have a say in your community; it meant that you could participate in your own government. Without the vote, you were nothing.

Burrell was more concerned as to how he was going to keep those boys down on the farm to help him manage the plantation. He made sure that they understood how to run a farm, how the buildings and houses had to be maintained; that Rose Hill was a community, and not just some ordinary plantation; and that in spite of itself, it was going to continue to exist almost as it was back when his father bought it in the eighteen eighties. The previous owners of the plantation had been good to the overseers, drivers, ex-slaves, and their descendants, all of whose jobs it was to bring forth riches so that their masters could live in luxury and prosper. They were cared for in nearly every way, so there was no need for self-reliance. Burrell repeated the stories that his daddy told him about his having bought this plantation in the eighties, that when it was being run as if it were still slavery time. He was now considered the Master, and all the overseers and planters reported to him just as they had to his Daddy. This was a way of life. His Daddy had tried to change the workings of the plantation, and had encouraged many who were no longer needed to leave; yet they had stayed on because life on the outside was really an unknown to them. They simply did not believe that they could cope.

Burrell Floyd had been born on this farm two years after his Daddy took it over again. He never left it. His view of a family was as his Daddy's. Everybody had a role to play, including the women and children. Nobody was to be idle, except the women in the big house, yet even they were encouraged to lend support to slave women and to the indentured servants' females, to see to it that they were healthy and that their children were cared for and properly nourished. After all these families were part of the assets of the plantation. Burrell had been a good student, and had taken all of this in, as he intended to run his family the same way, with only a slight adjustment or two. But life was changing radically beyond the farm, and the inhabitants on it were being left behind -- they became "country folks" -- people who didn't really know the real time of day, and were therefore out of touch with the new times.

The depression set in. The nation was clamoring for change in Washington. Herbert Hoover was president. He did phenomenal things to try to stave off the devastation that was sure to follow, but all of this was for naught. It was too little, too late. Franklin Delano Roosevelt became the man of the day. He instituted all kinds of change and reform. New agencies were created to deal with an economic crisis of gargantuan proportions. There was work for nearly everybody. The Works Progress Administration (WPA), the Public Works Administration (PWA), the Civilian Conservation Corps (CCC), the National Relief Agency (NRA), the Rural Electrification Agency (REA), and many other agencies were established to bring the country out of the depression, and establish relatively modern conveniences for the country folks. Many of the colored country folks barely survived these times. When there were no more jobs to be had with the WPA, PWA, CCC, and other federal government agencies, a small stipend of fifty cents a week was provided. This was the beginning of welfare, as it was known to many people and for many years. These "small" but inadequate stipends still exist in places today.

Many of the whites resented the blacks getting jobs with the WPA. They called this Roosevelt's emancipation of the farmers and farmhands. There were not enough workers around to do the hard labor required on the farms, and many of them went out of business. The poor whites benefited as well as the blacks, and maybe better, because their kind ran the Agencies. Those who did not have means of their own felt ashamed to have to depend on the government; even the children derided the workers by scrawling graffiti under W.P.A. as "We Poke Along."

Burrell borrowed money through the banks, through the Farm Land Bank Corporation, the corporation set up to insure the loans, of course guaranteeing payment by the Federal Government. He was able to repair so many of the of the sheds and barns on the farms, prop up the houses, and buy for the first time a couple of tractors, which could be used to plow in a day several times more than what the horses and mules could ever do. He bought balers for his cotton. He set up a cotton gin on the Long Cane Creek, using his water resources to generate all of the power he needed for a big time operation. He was now able to plant all of the fields that would yield bumper crops. Because most everybody was still on the farm, he was able to sell all of the cotton, cane, and corn that he could produce. Good times had come again. Full electric power had come to the farm! There was enough money on hand now that every obligation could be met. Wages were even being paid in cash to the sharecroppers and field hands.

The United States Agriculture Department had organized the farms and the farmers so that Government money could be parceled out to all of the farmers. The County Agents were the powerbrokers, the kingfish that handled the largesse, at many times bypassing the state officials to get things done in a hurry. Practically none of the funds went to the small farmers and very little, if any, to the colored farmers. Suits were being lodged against the Government charging it with discrimination against these farmers. Some of these suits are still being pursued and are pending today still without satisfactory resolution.

Chapter 6. Establishing a Family Legacy

The Winston-Harrell family was now complete. They knew their place and kept it. They were reasonably satisfied with their lives at this point in time. They knew who they were but not necessarily who and what they were going to be as there were going to be so many unknowns and the racial climate was still volatile. They reinforced their ties to the colored community not only in the rural but also in town particularly since Rosa Belle had married and moved into the city of West Point. Rosa and Burrell maintained their relationship and were unperturbed. Others knew the value of an education and pursued it through high school although having been damaged by early failures in the educational system. The account below gives some indication of the challenges they faced.

Rosa Belle

Rosa Belle, the oldest, was in her early twenties and married. Rosa Belle did not really care for her father, as she blamed him for allowing her to be taken away at such an early age. She was his own child, and entitled to be loved and regarded as a valuable human being. She felt as she grew up that he had neglected her, notwithstanding the social mores and norms in effect in West Point or Troup County or all of Georgia and Alabama at the time, even the nation. Her upbringing was estranged, even though her mother and Mr. Burrell started housekeeping in earnest when she was only five years old. In her view, he was just an interloper in her mother's life. Her schooling was pitifully inadequate when he, her father, could have sent her off to school somewhere else. She remained on the farm, mainly because the outside was so much worse. She could only leave if there were a serious man in her life. They were hard to find.

She married Walter Parker, whose father's property bordered Mr. Burrell's. She met Walt through her mother's visits to Mrs. Parker, one of her few friends nearby outside of her own maternal family. The Parkers were considered fairly prosperous through farming whose output was more than sufficient for their own subsistence. Walt and Rosa Belle courted for a while, until Mr. Burrell got wind of their relationship and forbade her ever to see him again.

"I am a grown woman!" Rosa Belle screamed at her father. "You can't tell me what I can do anymore! You have kept us under your thumb and have not allowed us to grow up. You treat us as if we are your slaves, not your children. Not me, I am leaving."

"You will always do what I say. It is not safe out there for you two." Mr. Burrell said in trying to be calm. He was not used to anyone defying him, let alone a daughter shouting with all of the disrespect that she could muster. "You are a white woman, and he will get both of you killed." Rosa Belle was so white that it was impossible to distinguish her from any white woman. She was still blonde and blue eyed, and her body make up was more of a white person's than a colored. The colored women's bodies were shaped by the hard labor they endured -- the clothes washing, field work, cotton chopping and picking, and pulling and lifting heavy bags of cotton. "Do you have any idea what you are getting into? Those savages will string up both of you, and riddle your bodies with bullets. He knows what I'm talking about," pointing to Walter. "Just ask him yourself. Better yet, I forbid you ever to see him again. And boy, listen to me good, I don't ever want to see you on my property again, you understand? I have to protect you from yourself! Rosa Belle, you can't ever leave the farm again. Ever!"

"All right," Rosa Belle said, knowing very well that the best thing for her to do at this time was to leave, but she could not do so at the moment. She would steal away at the first opportunity. Miss Rosa, her dear mother, was quiet. Her heart was breaking. She also knew better than to get involved, as Rosa Belle would always have her way in the long run.

Her brothers and sisters were watching and taking all of this in, realizing for the first time that their lives may indeed be captive and in this dilemma forever. Miss Rosa hugged Rosa Belle as her sisters were in a manner of speech "tugging at their mother's dress tail." The boys ran out of the back door and went off to play. They were accustomed to these outbursts brought about by the women, or at least they thought so.

George Frank

George Frank (Sug) was a maturing teenager, and having no particular interest, had quit school altogether as he was, if anything, a professional truant. And when working on the farm, he dedicated too much of his time drag racing his father's tractor around the fields. He was a farm boy, but believed in having a good time. He was friendly with the farmhands, shot craps with them, could drink any of them under the table, as well as commiserate with the males of the white sharecroppers. He was well liked among the farmhands, but Miss Rosa considered him a "good for nothing" wretch. He was still a good contributor to the well being of the family and the farm, but was just wayward. Mr. Burrell, too, found him useful but incorrigible, and decided it was best just to leave him alone. When a young fellow such as Sug turns out the way he was, his demeanor is not entirely due to his own bearing. He was devoted to his Dad, and always loyal and obedient. He was his Daddy's favorite. He was anxious to stay on the farm for the rest of his life as much and as long as his Daddy wanted him to. There are many influences that direct a young man's development; many of them are beyond his ability to control. The many young ladies considered Sug a "dandy" as did women around the community; he considered it his duty to deflower or oblige as many of them as he could, although he did maintain a steady girl friend – a not too distant cousin. Wherever he planted himself during the day, there was always a good meal being prepared for him, and a bed to relax in. He remained on the farm for his entire life; never getting married, and established a small bootleg whisky business for himself that would have been highly profitable had he not dipped so often in the product. It was easy to maintain the business, because this vast farm could conceal any number of illegal whiskey stills. Sug's as well as the other bootlegger's outfits were never raided by the "revenooers", because Mr. Burrell would not allow any of them on his properties. Sug, turning the entrepreneur, eventually abandoned his own activities in favor of taking a cut on the others' operations, as they were squatters on his Dad's property.

Marguerite and Precious

Marguerite and Precious from day one were striking beauties. During and after their school days, their range was from home to school and back again. Mr. Burrell actually forbade them to court or have boyfriends. He only wanted them to stay near and dear to him. He was dead set against their dating black men and turned away all of the local whites who appeared to have an interest. Mr. Burrell openly declared that he did not want his girls marrying any blacks because he wanted no black males to own any of his property. Only "blood" males, heirs, could inherit Harrell property, and his property could only be passed to males with Harrell blood, and his Will would actually show that. He decided further that none of his girls would be given property, and if they did marry and acquire any of the property, it would revert to a Harrell male. He did not consider his children as colored or black, per se. Insofar as he was concerned, they were all white, yet he was unable to resolve that view truly for himself. He didn't consider or even entertain the old rule created in early slavery in Virginia that when a child was born to the union of a white and a black, the race of the child would be that of the mother. The opposite was never envisioned. At the same time, he didn't really treat his children as other fathers would treat their white children. He never invited them to the big house when other members of the extended family gathered for their Sunday get-togethers. These happened without fail except in the wintertime. The Harrell offspring from all around Georgia and Alabama would gather at the homestead. They didn't have to bring anything but themselves. Grandma Cordie and Uncle Burrell furnished the fixings. Enough farmhands were corralled to do the cooking and serving, and all had a good time. The whole family was there except for Uncle Burrell's children, who were never expected to be there, or ever acknowledged by the rest of the family as really existing. Some one of them were always hanging around, hoping that one day they could go up to play with all of those other children from over town. But Uncle Burrell was never anxious to have his family associate with the other side of the family either, and deliberately kept them apart. Precious and Marguerite would go over on occasion to comb, brush, and braid their aunties' hair as little girls would often do and sometimes help around the house. Burrell was not too crazy about this activity as he wanted his sisters and his mother to stay out of his affairs.

At Miss Cordie's Sunday gatherings, the young grandsons would play games that involved scuffling and horseplay, while the granddaughters would hang around their mothers to listen to the poetry being read by their aunties or Miss Cordie herself. The menfolks just hung around smoking cigars or telling stories until the ladies were ready to go home. They would talk of their business connections, successes, and conquests in economic matters of the day. Burrell was always anxious to get them moving, as he would not have seen his family on this day.

Precious and Marguerite were apt students, and both of them dreamed that one day each would be free to leave the plantation and do whatever each wanted. They each graduated from Tenth Street High School, formerly Troup County Training School for Colored, in 1941 and 1943. They led rather uncomplicated lives without ever availing themselves of a complete college education, which they could have easily had, but over Mr. Burrell's dead body. Precious did go to Paine College in Augusta for a couple of terms, but she dropped out, as parental or family support was not forthcoming. Finally, each moved away, got married, had their families, and remained out of the clutches of Mr. Burrell, not returning even for his funeral many years later.

John Thomas

And then there was John Thomas. "Son" was his nickname. Nicknaming was customary in the South. He was the second male born in the family. As it turned out, he would be the strong male in the family. His Dad saw in him the makings of a manager -- a boss. John Thomas was going to be like himself, not the oldest or the first son but scion of the family. Mr. Burrell decided to grow John Thomas into what he himself always wanted to be. Mr. Burrell was going to be able to leave his world in the hands of John Thomas. This was mighty pleasing to him. John Thomas was a go-getter. He even played hard and for keeps in anything he did. He, like the girls, was determined to get an education, but he would rather not leave the farm, yet. He dreamed of becoming the controller of all of his father's properties, providing for his own sisters and brothers, as well as his Aunts who lived up the road in the big house. He knew eventually that there would be problems with white heirs in the family, but he thought he could handle them. Just like the rest of his sisters and brothers, John Thomas quickly became aware

71

as he moved into his teens that his world was going to be proscribed, being neither black nor white but having to conduct himself as if he were a black. Like Sug, John Thomas had a full head of tousled blond hair. He had to come to terms as to what he had to be, as opposed to what he wanted to be. He would have had no problem passing for white, but upon reflection, decided that he didn't want to be white. He ticked off the advantages of being white, but against those, he knew that he would have to give up his family, and once he crossed over, he could never truly come home again. In fact, if he ever did return, it would have to be secretly and always under the cover of darkness.

What set John Thomas apart from his siblings was that he was into sports. These activities required him to scrimmage, to stay after school for basketball practice, and therefore to make friends with the other boys in the game. His socialization was complete when the cheerleaders teased or picked at him and found him to be a cool cat, for some day he would be out of school and hopefully would take a wife.

He enjoyed playing sports in high school, basketball in particular. He was a big guy and a star. Over six feet, and would someday become a two hundred pounder, a very big guy for basketball in the 1940's. He played the game with such gusto and riveting enthusiasm that during one tournament, "Bangs," as he was called by his teammates, banged the basketball in the opposing team's basket. His embarrassment caused him to go on such a scoring tear that he scored 10 successive baskets before the other team could recover from his gratuity. He was a good, mild, and rather gentle person – a real gentleman. He knew that he was going to succeed in any venture he undertook, but he recognized that this "race" thing handicapped him. Troubled that he didn't want to leave his family after high school, he knew there was nothing for him to do in West Point but teach, or perhaps he could possibly get a white-collar job at one of the West Point Manufacturing Company's local plants. But no colored had ever been employed in white-collar work at any one of the six West Point Manufacturing Company plants up to that time. He came to understand that sports had to be his way out. His heart was set on it, and in trying to pursue this approach of getting away, he sought a basketball scholarship at Clark College in Atlanta. He decided that if it were granted, he would accept it regardless of the outcome on the farm. He didn't even realize that this would be his opportunity to escape the farm, for he had never really felt that he was bound to it, as did his sisters.

He waited for the letter he thought would never come. Finally, it arrived. He jumped for joy. He ran all of the way from his home house over to the Big House where Mr. Burrell was about to mount the buggy, shouting, "It's here, Mr. Burrell, it's here!"

"What in the world are you yelling about, Son? What is it?" Mr. Burrell asked.

"It's my scholarship! My basketball scholarship to Clark College, all expenses paid. I'll be going in the fall. Maybe even before then just to visit the College and be given an orientation."

His father was taken aback. "Son, you never said anything to me before now about going off to college. I didn't know you were interested in leaving our farm. It's basketball, is it? So that's why you got all of them hoops hanging on the houses and trees, and anywhere else you could stick one."

Mister Burrell was talking in the manner of the field hands and sharecroppers, as he was raised among them and spent so much of his childhood as one of them. He also talked to his children in this way, for his "real" family was more of the same. But his manner of speech to his mother and others on the white side of his family was more refined. Miss Cordie insisted that family members at all times speak correct and perfect English, and those who slipped were scolded mercilessly. When John Thomas was talking to Mr. Burrell in private, he, too, was given to correct English in a manner of trying to impress his father so that he would become aware of his education. He was always anxious to please his father.

"I thought you knew that I wanted to go to college, Mr. Burrell," John Thomas said. "To manage this farm right, I'm going to need more than a high school education. I intend to do big time farming. But I promise that I'll be back as soon as I finish."

"But Son, don't you think that you should've talked to me before you got into something wild like this. You don't need no college education

73

to run a plantation like this one. You know darn well I need you right here on this farm to help me run this place. Someday this will be yours. I would not have been able to do it without you so far, and insofar as I know, I can't do without you now. There ain't nobody else that I can really trust. Your brothers ain't up to it yet, if they will ever be. Not to say that they ain't good workers, but they just don't have the calling. And I am not about to let Roy have a free hand in running the farm. He'll eventually take everything for himself.

And just think, you won't fit in up there with them city nigrahs; these are different kinds of nigrahs. Most of them won't know nothing about farms and the kind of life and workers we have right here. You know all about community, working and running things that'll make you a man. You don't want to be with'em no how, do you? They won't know any practical things like how to run a farm from a business standpoint. They won't go into business. They are like these ladies that I have here on my hands. They will read and discuss Shakespeare, recite poetry, write little ditties, and things like that. What kind of living can you make with that sort of stuff except to be one of them, huh?"

Mr. Burrell was not aware that mulattoes and other fair-skinned Negroes were privileged in their communities, especially in the halls of higher education in the black colleges and universities. He may not have even been aware that there was any such thing as a black college or university. In fact, a great many of the top posts and professorships in the so-called colleges for blacks were held by mostly fair-skinned coloreds, and a large percentage of the student body would also be fair-skinned; furthermore, they would generally be better educated and more accomplished than their darker-skinned brethren. This is not to say that there were not a large number of darker blacks in the colleges, or that they were not treated fairly, but the appearance was that the darker blacks were less favored. Generally when a real black man was at the helm, he oftentimes took a very fair-skinned wife, for social reasons, it was presumed. This was the outgrowth of the system that blacks found themselves in, and in many instances mimicked the Jim Crow system that was established by whites. It was wrong, but that was the way it was.

"Bay can help you, Sir," pleaded John Thomas. "Bay" was Alfred's nickname. "He'll be coming out of school next year, and he can do all

74

of the things that I do and maybe better. He's not planning to go off to college or anywhere else. What's more, I'll be back, just like I said. You just wait and see."

"Once you leave here, Son, I just know I'll never see you again. Haven't I been a good Daddy to you? I took care of all of you kids, didn't I? You can't leave me now stranded like this when I need you most."

John Thomas had never seen his father in this light before and wondered what was the matter. What was the real problem?

"What's the real problem, Mr. Burrell? You can tell me. Surely you won't try to keep me from getting an education and just as I said, I'll be back. I just came over to tell you that I'm going off to college, not to ask you could I. I also thought that you would provide some help if I ever needed it."

"What is this? You're double-talking me! At first you said that you had all expenses paid. Now you are trying to tell me that you might need some help. You are running away, ain't you? Well, you ain't 21 yet, mister."

"Honest to God, Daddy, why in the world are you making such a big deal out of this? If you truly need me to stay, I'll stay. For your information, I am 22. I will never leave you and Maw. You know that. I love this place as much as you do. This is my home. I'll always come back."

"Did you hear yourself then? You called me "Daddy." That makes my heart feel so good. It makes me feel like a real Daddy for the first time. Do y'all feel like I'm a good Daddy to you? I always wanted to be closer to all of y'all. I wanted you to be as free as white children but I didn't want to risk you getting hurt or harmed by the folks around here. I did the best I could." Mr. Burrell lowered his head in his hands. He shivered ever so imperceptibly, raised up, tears in his eyes and asked John Thomas to take his hand.

"I just can't spare you now, Son. I need you. You can't go!"

John Thomas was flabbergasted. It was like somebody had knocked the wind out of him.

"I wish you hadn't said it like that, Mister Burrell," he said, being careful not to slip and say "Daddy" again. He wasn't sure how he would feel towards his father from hereon after this session. "I will stay only because I know that you do need me no matter what, although I know that we would all be better off in the long run if I went to college."

Mr. Burrell was as much dejected as John Thomas. There were many things on his mind. He had no friends to confide in anymore, as he now had become suspicious of all white relatives and friends around him, and he hadn't grown as close to his children as he should have. He never had a role model of his own, no Dad or any other of the white men around. On occasion, he slept in the Big House where his sisters resided. But he kept to himself while there, oftentimes, just talking to himself and getting no solutions to the problems that beset him. There were many opportunities but he was unable to break with the ways of the South -- the precepts of the Confederacy that he still harbored. It was the segregation, the ostracism, and other social constraints that the system imposed on him, as well as his family. He had not yet admitted to himself that he considered himself to be superior to his own children, principally because of their admixture with "black" people. This in his own mind took away nothing concerning his love for and his relationship with their mother or them. It was the way it was. It was the way he was raised, even though he never really felt that he had made a mistake by entering a common law arrangement of an interracial nature. He didn't know how not to have his own way. With John Thomas' having confronted him, and in defiance at that, he now felt that he must start unloading and sharing some of his burdens with this son and heir apparent if it were not for the ever-present Roy, his true successor as the "head" of the Harrell Family.

Earlier, John Thomas had also received his "greetings" from the Draft Board and had been getting ready to report when Mr. Burrell found out that he was planning on going into the service. At the time, John Thomas was a junior in high school. But no one could get a deferment from WWII at that time unless they were sick, illiterate, or had considerable family obligations.

"What's the meaning of this?" demanded Mr. Burrell. "Don't you know that you have to put me on notice where you are going and when and all of that?"

"But the Draft Board sent me a notice, Mr. Burrell," John Thomas said. "We have no choice. We have to go to fight for our country."

"Like hell you do!" Mr. Burrell fumed. "In fact, I'm headed over to that Draft Board right now and give them a piece of my mind. They got no right coming out here and messing with my family and interfering with my workers like this. I am going to put a stop to all of this shit once and for all time!"

"Where's Manfield?"

Mansfield was always lurking around where the action was. He was still a wily and crafty old character at the tender age of 62. He knew what was going on, but never alerted Mr. Burrell, because he liked the boys and knew that Mr. Burrell would pitch a fit. But whenever Mr. Burrell got into a ranting and raving mode such as this, he knew to hitch up the horses and prepare for a little traveling action.

"I want you to drive, Manfield. We're going overtown. I got some business to take care of."

The last time Manfield had made this trip, Highway 18 was a dirt road. The wheels on the carriage were made for dirt surfaces. He expected Mr. Burrell to demand a fast pace, so he pointed out that if they were going to go into town more often, perhaps while there, maybe he could buy some balloon tires and maybe a new undercarriage. Mr. Burrell ignored Manfield altogether, although he was fully aware of his new needs, but his money was getting funny again.

"I'm aware of my needs, Manfield. Whenever I need your help, I'll ask you!"

"I'm so sorry, Sir," mumbled Manfield and then says to himself, *"I wonder what got stuck in his craw?"*

Manfield observed that the Tenth Street School campus looked mighty good since that new principal, 'Fessor Traylor, took over. "Did you hear tell of him Mr. Burrell? I hear your boys talking 'bout him all the time. 'Course, I didn't understand all of what they was saying. They said that Mr. Amater Zeale Traylor was a progressive man. He changed that school, fixed up the building, painted everything, all with student help. He furnished the shop with them benches and tools that was promised in the 1930's. Ain't that campus beautiful, Mr. Burrell?"

Mr. Burrell remained silent.

Primarily the boys in the upper grades did this work during their shop periods until it was finished. Five male students, juniors at the time, protested Professor Traylor's project. The class included John Thomas Winston. H. C. Copeland, Jr. (H.C.) and Allison Davidson both of whom were very fair-skinned, in fact, the latter, a mulatto, led the protest. H. C. was John Thomas' first cousin on his mother's side. John Thomas' mother, Rosa, and H.C.'s mother, Janie, shared the same grandfather, who was white. H.C.'s father, Mr. Hill Copeland, Sr. was also a mulatto thus making H.C. technically a mulatto as well. These "near-white" boys refused to do manual labor as neither felt that this should be required of them. They were there to get an education not do yard work. John Thomas didn't have these kinds of problems, as he was a farmer. He in turn, informed his Dad as to what was going on and Mr. Burrell told him flatly that he could not participate.

Mr. Traylor was a disciplinarian and would not tolerate protests of any kind. He was ready to expel all of them. H.C., Allison, and Priestley Martin quit school and transferred to Lanier High School in Lanett, Alabama from which they graduated. Another of the protesters dropped out leaving John Thomas as the sole boy in the class. The project was completed in style and the community was buoyed by the appearance and the success of it. It was kind of a monument as to what can be done when a community pulls together.

Mr. Traylor had another project in mind. He was going to create a football team and use a square block of nearby vacant land, which in effect separated the white and colored sections of the town, for the football field. This proved infeasible because the male enrollment had been decimated by the draft for WWII. The defection of the three boys to Lanier High pretty much quashed any further attempts.

That vacant land was sold to J.G. Roberts, a white entrepreneur, who was one of Roy Harrell's fiercest competitors for providing housing to the poor blacks. They were fleeing the outlying farms into West Point from rural Georgia and Alabama as far south as Opelika some 22 miles away. J.G. Roberts threw up hi-density substandard 'shotgun" houses modeled on Roy Harrell's successes to accommodate the influx. He painted the houses a very dark green, trimmed in white. These "attractive" additions were the first houses to be seen when entering the colored community from the white. A picture of this cluster is included in Travels through Troup County, A guide to its Architecture and History, a publication of The Troup County Historical Society, 1996. These houses should not necessarily have been considered representative of those in that community.

The grass at the High School was always neatly trimmed and new shrubbery had been planted and pruned. Lawns, if any, were not customarily well taken care of in the colored section of town, and one could bet that there were no public dollars to take care of a lawn at the colored school. The school was considered an asset to the community for social functions ranging from Boy Scout meetings to the summer vacation Bible School. Bible School was a favorite activity of all of the children. Mrs. Virginia Cook, wife of Edmund Cook, head of the Batson-Cook Company, sponsored it, and ably assisted by Mrs. Mary Jimmie Thomas. Mrs. Cook was a great supporter of the black family and benefactor of the colored community in general. She was also a key factor in funding the education of so many of the young ladies who went on to college after high school graduation. Everybody loved "Miss Virginia" not only for these many deeds, but also for her nobility personified. The colored families' incomes were most always allocated to things that were considered necessities for the family, such as food and housing.

"Mr. Burrell, you don't take Miss Rosa overtown wit' you no more, do you? Is there something wrong, Mr. Burrell?" Manfield nagged on.

Manfield recalled when Mr. Burrell would take Miss Rosa to shop on a regular basis for small grocery items in local markets. The local markets used to be owned by the colored folks, but for some reason, they all went out of business. Word had it that they extended credit, and the creditors did not or could not pay. Manfield delighted in getting the wagon ready because he didn't get to do very much any more for "Miss Rosa", as he characteristically called her. Mr. Burrell would say to him to hitch up his two finest horses to the wagon, but not the carriage. The carriage was used for special occasions, and this was just shopping at T. P. Haralson's store on Tenth Street. This store and others like it supplanted the stores owned by the colored merchants. The new stores carried a wealth of goods that never appeared on the shelves of the colored-owned stores including refrigerated goods as well as fresh meat. It was just across from Tenth Street High School. This is where the students dashed off to buy goodies during recess or at lunchtime. Mr. T. P. had everything you would want to buy in that store, including fresh meat. *"I know, 'cause I was sent there many times to buy stuff for the ladies in the big house"*, thought Manfield. *"I don't know why they don't send me no more."*

The Haralsons lived in the back of the store, which was in the colored section of town. Mansfield thought "it was strange that this here white man lived in the colored section with his family. Of course they was real nice people. He didn't have or give nobody no trouble. His business was strictly cash and carry, and he never gi'd nobody no credit. His children played with the colored children, but they went to the white school up there on the College Hill. His boy, James, was smart. He built racing cars for the Soap Box Derby, and made all kinds of things like monster kites and teepees with the colored kids. He was a favorite of all the colored boys. When this here boy went off to college, he went up there in Atlanta to Georgia Tech and left all of his friends behind."

"Manfield, did you hear me? Are you back there daydreaming or something?"

"Oh, no Sir," Manfield lied. "I was just remembering when you took Miss Rosa to the store and I would be hitching up the horses."

"Manfield, I only ask you to come along to drive me, not to keep me company," Mr. Burrell said coldly. Mister Burrell knew not to scold Manfield too much as he, Manfield, was now the only "old friend" he had left.

"Begging your pardon, Sir. I'll just keep it to myself. I was going to tell you something that you ought to know, but since you don't want to hear it, I won't tell you then."

"OK, what is it?"

"Oh, if'n you don't want to hear it, maybe I shan't tell you. You don't treat me nice no more. Is it something I said or done?"

"Why don't you tell me on the way back. This way, I can keep my mind on what I'm going overtown for. Is that all right with you, Mr. Manfield?"

"Be it far from me to meddle. Suits me fine, Sir. Suits me fine."

Manfield went back to his reminiscing. Mr. Burrell would drive the wagon down Tenth Street at a fast pace, not wanting to slow down the motorized traffic trailing him. Miss Rosa would hold on for dear life. He would cut across the oncoming traffic, bringing the wagon to an abrupt halt right in front of T. P.'s store. If it wasn't for the shed overhang, it would have blocked the entrance. Mr. Burrell would hop down and help Miss Rosa alight and they would go into the store together to shop. He always brought the big wagon, and they would buy stuff not only for themselves but also for his sisters and his Aunt Josephine who lived in the big house with them. Aunt Josie was his mother's sister and one of the last members in her generation of the Combs family alive. Miss Rosa didn't mind, because she enjoyed shopping, why, she would shop for anybody, even for Mr. Burrell's sisters. Manfield didn't think they cared much for Miss Rosa because she always occupied so much of their brother's time.

No matter when Mr. Burrell arrived, be it at lunchtime, break or after school, the neighborhood school children got the word out real fast that he was at the store because the first thing he would do was to buy candies, fruits and nuts and pass them out, especially to the little ones. He delighted in this as much as did the children.

Meanwhile, back on the wagon, traveled through the white section of town. All of the lawns were beautifully manicured, houses seemingly were freshly painted. Beautiful trees surrounded the properties. He decided to travel on eighth Street. This way he would see the that great High School and the Confederate Memorial. This charged him up a bit. He was on Highway US 29 and made his turn to go straight into town. He was going to see the Huguley House. Relatives of his owned it. It was a gleaming white two-story mansion, kind of narrow but with white 25-foot columns surrounding the east and south sides. Eighth Street was wide. It could have accommodated four lanes. It really was a boulevard. They now crossed the Chattahoochee River Bridge just before entering town. The river was high and muddy from the red hills of Georgia, flowing very rapidly, and still quite a bit swollen due to the recent rains upstate. A relic from the old pontoon bridge that spanned the river just after the 1919 floods poked out of the water. In times of drought, a lot of the old bridge's structure could be seen. It was never removed, because the river served no useful commercial purpose, and therefore it was never considered to be worth the expense of removing it. It was said that the river was navigable up to Columbus. But the river's natural function was to drain the mountains and the upper reaches of Georgia with its myriad of streams.

As they entered town, one of the town's councilmen spotted Burrell on his way. He made a hasty telephone call ahead to Mayor Barrow that Burrell Harrell was headed in his direction. Many of the whites were leery whenever Burrell made unexpected appearances in town, mostly because when he did, he had Rosa with him. But they also knew that when he left her home, he was out for blood.

The carriage pulled up to City Hall, a white painted two-story brick, boxy building, which contained all of the offices and functional activities of the city, including the courtroom and the jail. Parking accommodations were still maintained for the horse and buggy crowd. Manfield tied the reins to the hitching post while Mr. Burrell stormed into the town's administrative offices, demanding: "Where in the hell is that Draft Board woman? None of that 'Oh, Mister Harrell this, and oh Mr. Harrell that, we're so glad to see you shit;' where is she?"

"Please have a seat, Mr. Harrell, she'll be right with you," the receptionist said very calmly. They had been forewarned.

The Mayor strolled in. "Burrell Harrell, dad blast it! Now, ain't you a sight for sore eyes. Where in the hell you been, Boy? You missed a few poker games several Thursdays in a row now. Something wrong?"

"You damn right," said Burrell. "You folks here in town been messing with my boys. You want to call them to the draft. They are farm hands, and you know better than to call them. How the troops going to get what they need if you take the farmers away? I want to have these folks once and for all to stop this here harassing me and them, y'all gonna drive me crazy. Just let me see the papers you have on them, Johnny."

"Just hold your horses, Burrell, she'll be out here in a minute. Just lighten up. Watch your language, we have ladies in the office. You getting on up in the years, you know. You must cut out some of this ranting and raving. You gonna have a stroke, pop a blood vessel or something. You know that this draft board stuff is not my business. This is State and Federal Government stuff; not even in the jurisdiction of the State."

"Well, if it ain't Mr. Burrell Harrell! King of the road! How long has it been since I laid eyes on you? You big ol' lug. Five, ten years," said Miss Claudia, the head of the Draft Board, as she entered the room. "I sent you a letter a year or so ago asking you to be a member of the Draft Board, because we didn't have any real knowledgeable farmers on it, and I could only think of you. You didn't even answer me, you scoundrel!" chided Miss Claudia, at the same time flashing her eyes in a flirting manner.

Burrell melted in his tracks.

"I know what you here for. That was a mistake on our part to send them notices to your boys. We have deferred them all as well as your workers. I just declare! I sincerely apologize. We should have told you about it. I guess we just never got around to it. Don't you want to take me out to dinner tonight? Come on now; don't give me that shy look. Well, maybe some other time, then, huh? I know you are extremely busy all of the time. You are going to come back to see me, you hear, you sweet ol' thing?"

"Well, I don't know what to say, Miss Claudie," Burrell smiled.

"Oh, that's all right, Burrell, you go on and finish up your business with the Mayor and I'll talk to you later. "Bye." Miss Claudia gently sneaked out of the room, thereby avoiding a confrontation over a problem that really no longer existed.

The Mayor escorted Burrell back to his carriage asking, "Burrell, don't you think it's about time you bought yourself a Ford or Chevrolet truck or two? In fact, you may need several with all of the business you're doing. John Davidson or Huguley-Scott got the right ones for you. They've got plenty of 'em on their car lots. It must be costing you an arm and a leg to take care of all of them horses and mules and wagons and things over there.

"Burrell?" continued the Mayor. "I want you to level with me. Are things going all right for you out there? You seem so troubled. What's wrong? Why are you fretting so? Is it about your family? The boys want to leave, don't they? You can't keep them down on the farm forever, you know. I hear that the Interstate is coming through your properties out there. You should be able to get a nice piece of change for all the land they need. You gonna need yourself a good lawyer to handle all of that. Don't you have a nephew who lives around here somewhere who's in the law business? You will need a relative who is a friend, somebody you can trust. "

"You talking about Bubber Johnson, ain't you?" Burrell asked. "Bubber is my youngest sister's son. He's just like his mother. He'll take good care of business."

"There's talk in town about what's going to happen, and we think that Bubber is your best bet. Want me to get in touch with him for you?"

"Naw, let me think it over. I'll get back to you." Burrell was never anxious for anybody to get too involved into his business, even family.

On the way back home, all was quiet except for the clatter made by the horses' hooves when striking the asphalt road surface. The horses were driven at a nice clip to speed up the journey – a little more than two miles from overtown to the farm. Manfield didn't dare start up a conversation, as he was unsure of Mr. Burrell's mood. Manfield was always one to size up a situation before getting involved. He decided to wait for Mr. Burrell to break the ice.

"What was it that you gonna to tell me on the way overtown, Manfield?" asked Mr. Burrell.

"Oh, h'it twas nothing, Sir. H'it'll keep. I done plumb forgot whatever h'it twas anyways. I'm getting a little feeble 'bout the head, and I keep forgetting stuff," Manfield whined.

"Manfield, you and me, we been together for a long time," Mr. Burrell said. "I want us to stay close, you hear? I credit you for so many of the good things that have happened around here to me and my family, you know that? What I'm trying to say is that I value your comments and advice, even when I don't ask for them. I guess I have to say, too, that I'm sorry for cutting you so short when we were on our way overtown. Now, what in the hell did you want to tell me?" he demanded.

"You have to understand, Mr. Burrell, Sir, that I ain't so sure of what I'm 'bout to tell you, but I think you ought to know as much as I do. You see, I was over there at Zachry's Store and I was minding my own business just chawing on some sugar cane, when I overheard these here two white men talking. They was talking about Mr. Roy. They said that he had been up to LaGrange looking over the deeds and the Harrell family papers and things. And whatever that meant, I thought that you ought to know about it. He may be up to something. You know he always upset and after somebody 'bout something."

"OK, Manfield, this is always good information, but don't you tell nobody else what you just told me. Roy has never rested since that his Daddy was disinherited from the family. We are going to have real trouble with him sooner or later. You can put up them horses and carriage now, and I will see you later, and much obliged."

Alfred Gordon

Alfred, nicknamed Bay, was the sixth child and third son. He was the quiet one, and steady, friendly, but he had no friends and was a loner. He made no waves, was quite unassuming, but was always there to help. Alfred was the "whitest" of the children in the sense of mannerisms, looks, and straightness of hair. He was the intellectual who pondered profound notions, but nothing that would benefit the farm. He was there to do the bookkeeping and was smart as a whip. He kept to his books, himself, remained in school, and tended to world affairs. World War II was still raging while he was in the tenth grade, and he had already mapped out the strategy as to how the war was to be won.

The first period of each school day involved discussions of current events. Mrs. Margaret Traylor, the principal's wife, who had a master's degree in English Literature from Atlanta University, led the discussions. This daily exercise was an enrichment program initiated by the Traylors. The first of its kind at the school. She taught the students the English language as it had never been taught to them before and exposed them to English and American literature. The Traylors were Godsend. All of this was right up Alfred's alley. He knew all of the important generals in the Allies' camp, and some of the enemy's too. He especially liked the manner in which Marshal Konstatin Rokossovski maneuvered the Soviet Forces to cut off the Nazi retreat on the Eastern (Don) front as the Battle of Stalingrad was coming to a close. The war was going so badly for the Germans. He quoted verbatim the General's appeal to the Nazis to surrender. Alfred recited it as follows:

"The situation of your troops is desperate. They are suffering from hunger, sickness and cold. The cruel Russian winter has scarcely yet begun. Hard frosts, cold winds, and blizzards still lie ahead. Your soldiers are unprovided with winter clothing and are living in appalling sanitary conditions . . . Your situation is hopeless, and any further resistance senseless. To avoid further unnecessary bloodshed, we propose that you accept the following terms of surrender: . . ."

His fellow classmates sat spellbound as this story unfolded, waiting for the time to ask questions.

"They were honorable and reasonable terms, but the German Commander had to appeal first to Der Fuehrer, Adolf Hitler, himself," Alfred said.

"Marshal Rokossovski gave the Germans twenty-four hours to reply. It was an impossible demand, and it was unlikely that this could be met.

"Surrender" in the German Army was unheard of, and at the time forbidden by Hitler".

Alfred, in effect, held court every day, because no one else had a personal radio or maybe sufficient interest to listen, and no one else consulted the morning newspaper, _The Atlanta Constitution_, on the progress of the war before the school day began. Alfred had been up since daybreak tending to his chores on the farm, in addition to have eaten a full country breakfast of sausage, ham, bacon, eggs, grits, and biscuits with all the fresh milk he could down.

Alfred graduated from Tenth Street High School in May 1945, just after the surrender of the Germans in World War II. He was already twenty-one years old, quite late for graduating from High School, but he had started late at the country "school," for what it was worth, but planting and harvesting the crops had a higher priority than education.

Alfred's stature grew in the eyes of his white cousins by the way that he handled their Uncle Burrell, and insofar as Roy was concerned, Alfred would be a much better person to deal with than either Rosa Belle or John Thomas. Alfred never showed any high ambition, and would be content to stay on the farm to provide for his mother and siblings if that were necessary, and to help Mr. Burrell whenever he could. He didn't even have a girlfriend, if for no other reason than that the prospects were slim to find the "right" girl when he was not even searching for her. Mr. Burrell had plans for him though.

Alfred would go into the service after Mr. Burrell loosened his grip. All of the boys were eligible for the draft except for Gaines who was too young. Alfred had wanted to go into the Army prior to his getting out of high school, but Mr. Burrell would have none of it. He delayed his entry into the Army primarily due to Mr. Burrell's opposition to the drafting of farmers. On this issue, Alfred knew better than to challenge him, as John Thomas had already lost that battle.

After the war, Alfred did join the Army, and rose to the rank of Master Sergeant in the Quartermaster Corps. He chose this area because he could be a supply specialist and as such he could work by himself and be secluded as much as he liked. Alfred didn't fit in the segregated Army, because he was in effect white. He looked "too white" for the blacks although he was accepted by them, but he didn't want to betray his heritage just to be white. It was not that he didn't get along with either the whites or the blacks; he was just a plain loner – and a real lonely man. He could talk "black' or "white" when the situation dictated it. He could "act white" or black, too, but he didn't want to be like the whites, and felt it was best to just be himself and by himself no matter his looks. He did the jobs he was assigned, and when he had had his fill of the Army, and his enlistment was up, he returned home to West Point and Rose Hill. There he built a new home for himself and eventually for his mother, and that's where they stayed until his death at the age of forty-five. Mr. Burrell took his death very hard. If he had a favorite at the time, it was Alfred. He had named him for his great grandfather *Alfred* Lee and Uncle Thomas *Gordon*.

Chapter 7. Good Times

Mr. Burrell continued to realize, not for the first time, that all of their lives were going to be a mess if he, within his power, didn't straighten things out. What's a man to do? First he mused that he and Rosa were going to have a long heart-to-heart talk, something that they had postponed far too long. This now was a long-running crisis. Some of the children were indeed old enough and big enough to leave home, but they had not really been prepared for the cruel, cruel world outside.

"Why must there always be a crisis, Burrell?" he asked himself. "Aren't there any very good times? Any easy solutions?"

"It shouldn't be hard to think of good times, Rosa. Let's give it a try. I'm going to start it off. The chaps are good size now. We all live for the weekend. Just seeing the weekend itself is a good time. When Saturday rolls around, we spend the whole morning getting things ready for the next week, taking care of all of the chores and fixing things, otherwise the place would fall apart."

"Yes, Mr. Burl. It's like that in the house too. Things that don't seem to amount to a hill of beans do have to be taken seriously. Just little things around the house. And then it's time to go overtown for the next week's provisions. It looks so funny when we leave, you and me seated in the front of the wagon with two or three of our chaps sitting up front or in the wagon bed with us. They have so much fun when they play in the wagon bed like that. They know they are gonna have to sit still on the way back 'cause there'll be so much stuff, no room, that they will have to sit on the bags of hog shorts, and barley, and feed and stuff like that for the cattle. We are so fortunate, Mr. Burrell, to grow almost all we need, so we don't have to be bothered with going to the store so often. Yes sir, these are the good times.

"Mr. Burrell, those hog shorts were not for the hogs as you remember, they were for making home brew. You didn't want the field hands to be making their own liquor and home brew. That was something that I had to do and then parse it out to the women so that their menfolks would stay half sober during the week. You know, don't you, that these men also made their own whisky. They bought a lot of stuff the same that you were buying, so that they could make their own whisky, and they sold it too. I know that you knew that our boys oftentimes went out at night to work with them when they were making whisky. You knew that, didn't you?"

"Yeah, the older boys would go off to the 'Rooty Hole' for a Saturday swim, and sometimes through the week when the weather sometimes got too hot to work. Oh, they would have such a good time," Burrell mused. He ignored her talk about making whisky. This was not the women's business, and they should not be poking their noses into it. The first thing you know she would be accusing him of going out nights making whisky. "Yeah, Honeybunch, but the Rooty Hole is a mighty dangerous place. That's near, you know, where the Long Cane and the Flat Shoals Creeks meet. That water is so swift that when it turns that bend, it keeps on carving out a deeper hole and washes out a lot of soil from around the roots and trunks of the trees that hang over the bank of the creek. That exposes a whole lot of the roots. It was dangerous because some of the boys could get their legs or feet tangled up in the roots and if not quickly freed, they could drown easily. Don't you remember that Saturday when we come back to the farm and they couldn't find that little boy who always came in from town to play on Saturdays?"

"Yes, I do," Rosa said. "That was Taddyroll. He lived in town. A mischievous little wretch. No bigger than a gnat's eyelash but swift as a cat. Was always getting into trouble. He was eleven years old, but about the size of a seven-year old. He went swimming with our boys, and some other boys from town and around the other farms out here. Mr. Burl, I'm told that they swim naked there, and swing out from the trees to drop off in the creek. They would throw their clothes on the bushes or right on the bare banks. Sometimes the girls would sneak around to spy on them and steal or hide their clothes. This one day, a big storm done come up all of a sudden. They all got out of the water like a blue streak so they wouldn't get struck by lightning. When that storm was over, everybody was accounted for but Taddyroll. His clothes were still hanging on the bush. They searched and dragged the bottom of the creek, and in between the roots for fear that Taddyroll's legs had got caught on one of them. Remember Mr. Burl, the boys come and got you to go down to help them search. You got several of the men from the farm to go with you, and y'all dragged that place well after dark, but no Taddyroll. Y'all come back nearly exhausted. Word got around in town that Taddyroll had drowned at the Rooty Hole. Gloom set over the whole town because Taddyroll was missing and he was so well liked. The next morning, you took them same men back to the Rooty Hole with your axes and saws and cut away all of them roots so that this swimming hole would be a whole lot safer to swim in. That was so nice of you to do that. That's why so many people really like you because you did so many good things like that for them." Rosa touched Burrell's arm affectionately. He smiled.

"It wouldn't have been so damn bad had we not seen this little fellow, still no bigger than a gnat, smiling from cheek to cheek standing right there on the banks. 'What you so happy about boy,' I called out to him?"

"Nothing," he said.

"What' your name anyway?" I asked.

"They call me 'Taddyroll!' Sir."

"Taddyroll!"

"Yes, Sir. Who might you be?"

"I am Mr. Burrell Harrell."

"I know 'bout you. You Mae Bessie's Daddy, and Son's, and Bay's, and Little Bay's Daddy, right?'

"Right! Taddyroll, I'm going to have to take you back into town and parade you around so people can see that you're not dead."

"Me dead? I didn't know that I was supposed to be dead. But can I come back with you, Mr. Bud Hal?"

"You bet you can, Taddyroll, but first, you'd better tell me what happened that made you run away like you did from the Rooty Hole yesterday, Little Fellow,"

"Well, you see it was like this. I heard that loud clap of thunder right after the lightning struck, so I was getting out of the water when this wide mouth water moccasin come right at me. I jumped up on the wrong bank of the creek and this snake chased me and I run as fast as I could. The first thing I know, I was at home. And that was all there was to it."

"OK, Taddyroll. Now we can go back to the farm because we are having a big feast out there today. Everybody else will be glad to see that you're OK. Come on in and say 'hey' to Miss Rosa."

Nearly all of the farm families would come out for the big feast that was put on once a month by Mr. Burrell. Miss Rosa was in charge. Food was spread everywhere and all of the kinds that the farmers and their families liked. The big event was the open pit barbecuing. Two burley men would straddle each pit to turn giant hogs over and over as they cooked, while another one or two basted it with swabs soaked in the best home made barbecue sauce in all of Georgia. This took a few hours. The hogs were prepared the morning before. Big pots of Brunswick stew were served before the hogs were sliced for the big feast. The delicacies were the pig feet, pigtails, and the pig ears roasted right there over open charcoal flames. The little ones were clamoring always for more and forever in the way. Ears of corn were being roasted in their husks or shucks, and were called "roasting ears," and when they were ready to eat there was nothing better. It sounded as if the roaster was calling, "Come git your "roeshenells." The kids always came a running because they were so good – all basted with fresh butter.

The women took care of the internal organs, the liver, the heart, maw, brains, and especially the hog guts, both the large and small intestines, that were called "chitterlings" or just plain "chitlins." These were the crème de la crème of the delicacies.

The most interesting part of the preparation of the chitterlings was the cleaning. They were separated by either tearing or cutting away the membranes that bound them together. Once the separation was finished, the intestine was strung out and a hose was inserted in one end, while the kids supported by hand a section that was maybe 20 feet long. The force of the water pushed the hog's waste along the way with a little help from an experienced woman, but being very careful not to remove all of the morsels of waste for that was where the flavor came from. They were then washed and sent to the right pot for final cooking.

The fish fry was just as big a hit as the barbecue. Many of the boys and some women on the neighboring farms would go fishing in the Long Cane Creek early that Saturday morning. The Long Cane was chock full of fish. Everything they caught was brought to the party. It provided one of the staples for the farm families. It was like manna from heaven. They were fried in lard, "the king of fat" that made everything taste so good.

"But Rosa, this is not what I meant. I meant actual fun times. Times when we'd go over to Zachry's and park the dray nearly all day, we'd go in and get us a big strawberry soda, a belly washer, and guzzle it down as fast as we could to see who could down it the fastest. Then we would buy a big bag of parched goobers, and eat and drink to our heart's content. But the big contest of the day was between the men, to see who could drink a whole ice cold 'Co-Cola' in one gulp. It was hard to do. No matter, tears would flow, eyes would pop, your ears would ring, and when you finished, you could hardly stand or breathe. Your heart thumped so hard like it was going to jump out of your chest. Man, that was something! Wipes you out just thinking about it. Whew!"

Burrell was now fifty-six years old and a bit worn for his age. He had worked in the sun all of his life. His skin was leathery and heavily tanned, as was that of many white men, because of their having worked long hours in the blistering sun. The Georgia sun was always unforgiving. He looked quizzically at John Thomas as they crossed the yard towards the big house.

"Son, I'm beginning to think that somebody is trying to steal my property away from me. "They" had me to make out a Will in 1941 and it was not quite the way I wanted it to be. Of course, I went ahead and signed it because I'm going to be here when they are all gone. There's nothing in the Will that spells out what Rosa and you children are to get when I pass on. I want you to see it. I want Gordon to look over it, too. But come on in the house. I got a desk in my room where I keep my things. We can sit down in there and go over it." Neither John Thomas nor any of his brothers or sisters had ever been in their father's room before. It was Spartan and sparse – a bed, a dresser with a washbasin and a pitcher of water, and a table with a high-backed chair. There was only one window with the drapes barely open, just to let in enough outside light to keep from bumping into things.

"Let me turn the lamp on at my desk. I just picked this up on sale last week at Skinner's Furniture Store overtown. Son, the Skinners and the Harrells have been friends and neighbors for a long time; why they own property next to ours. But you know that, don't you? If you ever get into trouble and I am not around, one of the Skinners will help you. I just want you to know that. How you like this setup? Watch it! Don't trip over that electric cord. There are no wall outlets in here. I had this whole house revamped back in '22 and none of us thought to put wall plugs in. I guess we didn't really know about them. We were so excited about having electricity throughout the house for the first time that we just plumb forgot about things like that. When you build your house, make sure that you have enough wall outlets; they are as important as having enough closets. We had another chance just after Roosevelt got in, when a whole lot of electricity projects and many other improvements came along. Then I was a bit stingy and didn't think we needed 'luxury' stuff like that. I was just plain backwards – a country bumpkin."

"Mr. Burrell!" John Thomas called out. There was no response. Mr. Burrell just kept on talking in a low mumbling voice. "Mr. Burrell!" John Thomas shouted. "You are stalling."

"Son, I guess you're right," Mr. Burrell said looking somewhat startled. "I really forgot why I brought you in here. I'm getting a bit senile and slow now. Just be patient with me."

John Thomas looked his father in the eye and steadied him as he staggered forward. He placed his massive hands on each of his father's shoulders and held him close. Mr. Burrell wrapped both arms around John Thomas and hugged him as tightly as he could and almost broke down. He had come to bond with this son for the first time. At a time when men didn't show physical affection for one another. He even shed a few tears thinking of how long he had deliberately withheld affection from his children. This was a tender moment and it had been building up for a long time. John Thomas accepted this as a gesture of his caring, but was not ready yet to believe that this was true fatherly love.

"Now, what was it? Oh yes, it was the Will. But let me tell you this first. "The Feds are bringing that Interstate highway through here, right through our property, Son. And they want to reroute the Long Cane Creek that supplies the waterpower for my cotton gin and gristmill. I am going to need you boys more than ever. I don't know who I can trust, and I don't really know how to handle this transaction all by myself, and I am afraid that I didn't prepare you boys for this kind of thing either. I am so sorry. But it's not too late."

"I think you ought to tell Bay about this," John Thomas said. "Maybe there's something we can figure out together."

Chapter 8. Extending Family Involvement

"What a day this has been," Burrell thought to himself, as he returned from the Draft Board. "Something's always coming up. I'd better look in on Gaines to see what he's up to. I don't see him much any more. Haven't ever had much time for him. I'll just check up on him tomorrow. I'll just go in a take a little snooze." He clambered up the back steps to enter his room and bumped into John Thomas.

"Son, you still in here! Goodness gracious! You scared hell out of me, Boy!" Mr. Burrell exclaimed. "I thought for sure that you would be back at Rose Hill by now. I guess you want to keep on talking about what I need you to know. I suspect that Roy is trying to take legal action in reclaiming his Daddy's share of the family's properties and what not. I have always suspected Roy's intentions in being so helpful to me particularly when we drew up the Will. My eyesight is getting so much worse but I never read that Will completely that was put together back in 1941. I want you to read it. Have Gordon to read it, too, and let me know what you think, and get ready to help me out." Mr. Burrell handed the Will over to John Thomas.

"Son, I want you to have dinner with us tonight here in the big house. I know you are going to be a little uncomfortable here with my sisters 'cause you ain't never had too many dealings with them. But they your aunties and they know all about the whole family. Their dealings have been mostly with your sisters 'cause women handle these things so much better than us menfolk for some reason. Come on through the house and meet them. They are out on the veranda where we usually see them. They have been sitting there it seems forever just watching the cars go by not lifting a finger or hitting a lick at a snake. From the way they dress, they couldn't do any work anyway. Their dresses would hang to the ground and they always wear bonnets. Just like they did in the twenties. I tell you what they looked like then. You remember seeing that painting called, "Whistler's Mother" – that's the way they look. Weren't too many cars on the road then. I know you have seen all of them at some one time or another, but it's best that you meet them now. They are up in the years, you know. Come on into the parlor."

Burrell went through the hallway to the front door and asked his sisters to come into the parlor. They deferred each to the older one before proceeding to their places at the table.

"If Mama was alive, she'd be sitting right here," he pointed to her chair. The parlor had high ceilings and tall windows befitting a house of the Greek Revival Architectural period. There was a wide hallway opening up to as many as four rooms as well as the dining room with a big kitchen. The drapery was made of heavy tapestry in hues of green, gray, gold, and purple that were received in payment from some bartering deals that Burrell made in exchange for cotton products with some European merchants. Golden tassels and tiebacks draped each panel perfectly. Hanging on the long wall in the parlor was a grand antique Brussels tapestry depicting John the Baptist presiding over a baptismal ceremony in the Jordan River. The floors were of Georgia red oak hewn from these grand trees on their own property. The ladies sat very properly in their customary places when receiving company. Burrell went around the room with his introductions.

"This is John Thomas, y'all. I call him Son. He's my second oldest boy." Burrell would always speak flawless English when among the ladies except when he wanted to rile them up.

"Son, This is where my lovely mother sat. Cordelia Alpha was her name. She just loved her name. She was really named Alpha Cordelia, but somewhere along the way, it got reversed. As you must already know, everybody called her 'Miss Cordie' -- a brilliant woman, petite, and quite pretty – a true southern belle. Her picture is hanging right over yonder. She knew all about all of y'all, Son. I guess you are wondering why wouldn't she? She was all about education. She even moved down to Auburn so she could be close to the girls when they went to the Institute down there. It was called "API" then, which stood for Alabama Polytechnic Institute. She was from Cusseta like nearly all of the rest of the family that settled in West Georgia. That's the homestead, you know.

97

"When Mama moved to Auburn, she took the four youngest children with her. That was Ethel, Evans, Sam, and Cordelia. She left me and Robert here to see after things. Mostly me. 'Mr. Robert' as we called him was never all there – he was "slow." Auburn was quite the community for everything that was going on even for some in Troup County, Georgia. Of course, Georgia Tech was our school only because we all were born in Georgia, but our roots are in Alabama. We were so conflicted when they played football against each other, I don't know what to say. Well, we just didn't know who to root for. Auburn is a pretty town. The Institute is the driving force down there. It's a college town and full of life. You have to go down there sometime to look around.

"Here's your Aunt May. She is the oldest of all of the children and has always been a "mother" to all of us. She has always been the main driving force in the family. When anybody needed anything, anywhere, she was there - Birmingham, Saint Louis, Boston, New York, you name it. She kept her bags packed and was ready to travel anywhere at anytime. She was very much like our mother."

May was taken aback by Burrell's referral to her as "Aunt May." In all of her days, she never had to consider herself as an "Aunt" or relative to any "colored" person. She was a Confederette. All sensed her awkward reaction. John Thomas and his father ignored her; nevertheless, her sensitivity had registered. The family's supposed acknowledgment rather than acceptance of Burrell's family was tacit and merely window dressing, and to the public, it was non-existent. Burrell's family was simply "invisible" to them as were most all colored at the time.

"This is Aunt Evans. She is powerfully educated. She's got a degree in Architecture, areas that women don't get into. She's also smart and I'm told that she is rich. As you get to know her, she can tell you more. She's been to places like New York. Got a degree from Columbia University and like your Aunt May and your Aunt Ethel, she done taught school everywhere.

"And this is Aunt Verne," Burrell continued. "My other sisters, Ethel and Cordelia are with their families living somewhere over there in Alabama or down in Florida. Who knows?

98

"Ladies, I have invited John Thomas to have dinner with us tonight because we have to talk about some important family matters of the future. Who knows, he may be our saving grace. I want him to review the Will that was put together in 1941 just after Mama died. I don't know about y'all but I was never really satisfied with it. There was pressure to get it done quickly but I don't recall where it come from. My dear ladies, I need each of y'all to tell Son and me what your true wishes are for the disposal of your properties and belongings regardless of what it says in the will. I will then try to fix it just the way we all want it to be without outside meddling, family or otherwise.

The cook, Carrie, opened the French doors to the dining room and announced dinner. Carrie was a bit on the heavy side and getting on up in the years, but she loved the ladies and wanted to do as much as she could to help them out from time to time. She was also able to eat better there than at home even though she furnished many of the vegetables. She also did most of the cleaning and gardening, for these ladies never, never engaged in such lowly chores.

"Ladies and Gentlemen, getting down in here!" she boomed.

They proceeded to the dining room. The table seated 12 adults comfortably. It was of sturdy mahogany material, just right for the10 children of Mother Cordelia Alpha and Father Burrell Whatley Harrell.

"John Thomas, I want you to sit in my place, here," Mr. Burrell pointed to his spot, "this evening and I will sit in Poppa's place. Nobody's sat there since Poppa passed on back in aught one. I will sit in his spot as I am the man of the house, head of the family, I think." He looks around sheepishly for reaction. He was totally ignored. "We will keep Mama's place vacant this evening." They were all seated. "Now, ain't this just like family?"

"Burrell, your English is less than perfect," Verne scolded again.

"I knew that would get a rise out of you, Mama, I mean, Verne," Burrell teased her.

"Burrell, no slang please! You sound just as your field hands do," countered Verne.

"That's a whole lots better than smelling like 'em, Verne," Burrell guffawed. "May, you be first."

"There is no substitute for the use of good English at all times. Oh, why don't I just give up on you? There is absolutely no hope for you, Burrell Floyd."

May turned to John Thomas. "John Thomas, I am so delighted to meet you, boy, after all these years. I just declare, Burrell always kept you boys so close and away from this house for some reason. He thought we didn't know about y'all. Of course we did, I have seen all of y'all from a distance, not knowing which one was who, but I didn't realize that you were so white, and so big, and so tall. We Harrells are not tall folks, you know. Why, I do tell, you look just like any white boy. I am a widow now, you see. I moved back here after my husband died and have been here with my sisters ever since. You should come over more often and talk with us. We would just love that, wouldn't we?" Evans and Verne nodded their heads in agreement.

"I'll do the best I can ma'am," John Thomas said. "Thank y'all for welcoming me this evening." John Thomas turned to his Aunt Evans and smiled.

"Son, you ought to remember me. I am the one who went down to Florida, came back and tried unsuccessfully to get your mother to let me take your sister, Mary Bessie, and brother, Foy, back with me to live down there and get them a good education. They were so cute. You just couldn't resist loving them. I felt that all of you children were too white to be raised up here as colored. All of y'all must have suffered so. Mary Bessie and Foy would suffer so terribly here, but your mother would have no part of it. In fact, Mary Bessie, who was not more than 8 years old at the time, said very forcefully that she did not want to leave her mother nor did she want to leave her friends in school. It's too bad that children cannot make good decisions for themselves. Now, Foy was raring to go. He was about 6. He was looking for adventure. Furthermore, I saw a great future for y'all although I understood your mother's reasons particularly having had so much difficulty with getting her oldest child back. That was such a sad story. I am sure that it's hard for any mother to part with any of her children under any circumstance.

100

"Sometimes, I recall our discussion; it was not a discussion, it was more like a lecture on my part. I really couldn't understand very well what the emotional situation was. I was never married, never had a child and was never very close to anyone who did. I think I was being selfish, but really, I truly thought I was doing good. As I have gotten older, I came to realize how brazen I was for going to her like that. It boiled down to that I didn't respect her. And it was not about race. Then again, maybe it was. I look at that as my upbringing. I practically barged into her house. She didn't even know I was coming let alone why I was coming to see her. We had never talked before and I don't think that we had ever met each other. Come to think of it, we did but at the time she was working in our household a helper to her mother. What I had in mind for the children was so good for them really nobody could reasonably object. Just think what they could be today. Free from all of the troubles you people suffered from. When I went to New York to study at Columbia, I got the chance to see and feel another world where everybody seemed to be free to do almost anything they pleased and associated with them, too. I knew that your brother and sister would never have that kind of living here in Georgia as colored people. Florida was a different story although not too much different from here, but Mary Bessie and Foy would have learned to be white and do the things that white folks do. Go to places where white folks go and not even think about it. Your mother didn't understand that. Rosa almost had me understanding at one time that no matter how many children a person had, they are all dear to them. She told me that if she would let them go, they would never come home again. They would not even know their brothers and sisters. They would have no real family and no matter how much attention they got because it would not be real love. They would be messed up.

"I failed, John Thomas. I failed them. I did try. I think the whole thing blew up when Mary Bessie started to cry and told her mother that she did not want to go. That she wanted to stay at home with her, her mother, and family, and cousins, and playmates. And as I think of it now, she was wise for a little tyke but kind of impudent.

"I'm back home for good now. We are here to look after your Daddy," she giggled. "You probably wonder why in the world do I have a boy's name. Well, it is like this, it comes from my grandfather on my

101

mother's side. He was named James *Evans* Combs. Our sister Cordelia has a son named Evans, too. As you get to know the family, you'll see that most all of us have names reflecting someone's family name from the past."

John Thomas nodded in thanks for her comments. He said, "please Aunt Evans, don't feel that way. Everybody understood what you were trying to do. I think what you were trying to do as good too. We are OK as to who we are." Evans was pleased that he called her "Aunt." He then turned to Aunt Verne.

"John Thomas," she said. "This has been a long time coming. Didn't any of you children ever want to come over here and visit us? We all wanted to go over to see y'all but somehow and for some reason, that never took place. But we are here now and biding our time. I am a widow, you know, and I am sickly and can't do much for myself, but thanks to my dear sister May, she's an angel. My husband died in a car crash some time ago. He was a military man. Lieutenant Colonel Cole was his name. Our best years are way behind us. All we talk about now is the past and the dead past is gone forever. We do a little Shakespeare now and then. His plays – we even play the roles.

"Romeo, Romeo, where forth art thou?" chirped Miss Verne. They all laughed, as did John Thomas.

He was familiar with this line but chose not to let on as he found this camaraderie amusingly strange but welcome. He also wanted to play down his education as many of the colored hid their knowledge of events or goings-on from the whites so as not to rile up their sensitivities. They would usually think that the colored were uppity, or trying to measure arms with them, and further appearing to disrespect them.

Miss Verne continued, "And we took turns at reading his sonnets, everything he wrote. Isn't it wonderful that we can engage in the finer things of life like this? Just in case you don't know it, John Thomas, we are all very well educated. Some of our family members are even college professors and leading members of society, as well as captains of industry, and social mavens no less. We never found too many of the ladies around here as suitable company in the West Point area or to marry our brothers off, not that they were not nice people or the brothers even marriageable, but that seemed to be just the way it was. We came from Alabama and somehow these Georgia folks seemed to think that they were a bit better than we. We did not understand why for some reason as they were not nearly as well educated; but we did, however, think that we were better than they. Note my use of the English, John Thomas. We think, too, rather privately though, of course, that we were a bit ostracized because of Burrell's family situation, if you know what I mean."

"Now you wait just a damn minute, Verne!" Burrell fumed in anger at the comment. "Like hell it was! I don't remember a single time that me and my family were not fully supported by all of y'all. Come on out and say it! Or maybe you're telling me something now for the first time and I was being used all along. It had nothing at all to do with me. But I know it was because of all the scrapes that Tom got into. Besides, he was only a mailman and got hisself kilt coming out of a crap game or something like that or for some other reason that nobody will tell. And am I to understand that that was not true either? So why don't you level with Son, he needs to know the truth, too."

May interrupted forcefully, "Verne, how often do I have to tell you that there are some things that you don't talk about. You just opened up another can of worms."

"Well, let us not fret about it," Verne said. "We really need to get over it. We welcomed all of y'all, besides Burrell was the man of this house here and the boss of our family. He really has taken good care of us, too. But enough about us. Tell us something about yourself, John Thomas," Miss Verne asked as John Thomas if he was previously instructed to call her rather than "Aunt Verne."

John Thomas looked over at Mr. Burrell seeking guidance as to how he should respond to this new challenge.

Burrell interrupted by saying that the food was getting cold and why not all dig in and talk could continue at the table or after dinner.

"Very well," Verne said, then turning to address the cook, "Carrie, why don't you tell us what you got cooked up for us this evening."

"It's the usual, Miss Verne. If I had knowed though that y'all had a guest for dinner, I would've fixed up something real fancy. But we do have broiled chicken, I got a mess of greens from my garden along with some okra and tomatoes, and I done fixed some potato salad. I went to y'all's storehouse and got some sweet potatoes for candied yams and I have banana pudding for dessert, and all the iced tea y'all can drink. And oh yes, some of the best cornbread this side of heaven. Do y'all want me to serve y'all or do y'all want to take care of yourselves?"

"Just serve the bread, Carrie, and that will be all," Miss Verne said cutting Carrie short, after all, she was becoming all too familiar for a servant. "That will be all and thank you so much. And oh by the way, bring Mister John Thomas a larger glass for his tea. He is a big young man as you can see."

"Yes ma'm, Miss Verne," Carrie said. "Please pardon me though Miss Verne but ain't this here, Son, Cousin Rosa's boy?" The question was raised by Carrie to deflect her having to call John Thomas "mister." In Verne's eyes, John Thomas was "white" and the servant must call him "mister" notwithstanding his being otherwise.

"Oh, I thought you knew all along. John Thomas, do you know Carrie?"

"Oh, yes ma'am, I do. She's my mother's cousin."

"Well I'll be," Verne said with utter surprise. "Nobody ever told me that.

Carrie you never told me and why not?"

"Well, Miss Verne, first of all, you didn't ask, next, nobody never asked me and I learned long time ago, never to give out no information to white folks if you was not asked."

"Let's get on with the service, I'm starving," said Burrell. "You get Verne started talking and we'll be here to all night."

Momentary silence fell over the dining room except for the clinking of the silverware and dishes striking each other while all helped themselves. There were two big electric fans going full blast as this was

August and it stayed hot late into the evening. The helpings were ample. There was always plenty of food as the field hands and the sharecroppers willingly shared their vegetables and fruits from their gardens with the ladies in the big house. Carrie also had a garden of her own at home and she always contributed the canned condiments such as tomatoes, pickled cucumbers, pepper sauce, chowchow, okra, and beets. The meal for the cornbread had been ground right there in Burrell's own gristmill. The ladies had become a bit feeble and were not able to eat as much as they used to but gave fair credit to the cook for a well-prepared meal.

Throughout the dinner, John Thomas dazzled and peppered them with stories of the plantation and all about the relatives especially his Uncle Bob who was his maternal grandmother's brother. He went on to tell them that his grandmother, Belle, was born on the Rutledge plantation in that big mansion that sits off the road a piece to the north on Highway 18. The story goes that she was born in the kitchen as her mother, Lillie, was fixing dinner.

"She was born right after slavery time, you know and she and Uncle Bob were said to be the children of the master of the plantation. Their father or one of the family members was said to be one of the signers of the Declaration of Independence. They were from South Carolina," blabbered John Thomas. He felt very comfortable with them now. He was talking his southern can off. After all they were, in his mind, merely family now.

Mister Burrell wanted John Thomas to curb his stories but somehow was unable to get his attention. Finally, Mr. Burrell interrupted, "Son, you are going to have to come back again when we have less pressing business to take care of. Remember, we want to hear these fine ladies tell us how their shares of the plantation are to be divided up and who gives what to whoever."

"It is 'whomever,' Burrell. Not 'whoever'" said Miss Verne.

"Oh for God's sake, Verne, nobody talks like that around here but y'all. So will you just can it, please? Now can I get back to whatever I was talking about? Christ Almighty!"

"Never use the name of the Lord thy God in vain," his sisters chorused.

"In addition, Son," Burrell's finally ignoring comments, "I need you to read the Will to me before you go this evening. My eyesight's getting to be so bad. Can we bottle this dinner up and get on with it?" There was always the lingering doubt as to whether Burrell could really read effectively even though his signature was so skillfully crafted. But because his demeanor was so overbearing, no one dared challenge or impugn his literacy skills.

Burrell's real aim at this point was to avoid any further talk about the social life or race mixing on the plantation because it was leading to situations that dealt with the co-mingling of white men and colored women during slavery and, of course, afterwards. Little did he suspect that his sisters were already thoroughly savvy and very much aware of the goings-on and happenings on the farm and beyond for that matter. They felt that it was best never to broach the subject about such behavior and that they really had reconciled it as a way of life and in this way, the peace was kept in the family. So many of the women seemingly reconciled that it was better to be spared the "drudgery" of loveless sex than to have to engage in it.

"Did you enjoy the dinner, everybody?" Burrell asked.

"Yes, we did. It was a delight. Thanks to Carrie; she is the best cook in the world."

"I am going to tell everybody what Mama wanted us to do with the properties back in 1941 when we first wrote the Will", said Burrell. "Poppa, may God rest his soul, never had a Will so Mama "inherited" everything from near the West Point City limits line clear back for three miles or more along the north side of Highway 18 with some Skinner family property sprinkled in between. I have a map here if y'all want to look at it. Pass it around. On the south side, the land goes for about two miles from Skinner property on that side. I really never heard how this got so messed up. But anyway, Rose Hill is on the south side. Poppa bought that from the Erwins back in '82 just two years before I was born. That's the richest land out here in the country. It came with the ex-slaves on it and their descendants. He had just come back to West

Point from Cusseta to start farming in a really big way. He wanted to raise a lot of cotton and cattle. He did all right for himself.

There are seven of us left now. Mama wants that divided up in seven equal shares to do whatever we want to do with it. A lot of the land out here I bought myself or got through dealings with others around here by whatever means." He would never mention how or why he acquired many of the properties, but it was generally well known that it was through the settlement of gambling debts owed to him, although gambling was considered a God-awful sin. "So, much of that land is not included in those shares, but we will share the common property and share alike. How'd you like that, John Thomas? I sounded just like one of them bigwig city lawyers, huh? My Grandpa, Alfred Lee Harrell, bought the home house even before 1882 and gave it to Poppa. He bought it from the Maulls and all of the property surrounding it. That's why you hear it sometimes called the Maull House. It was a treasure. That's where I was born -- this very house where we are right now. This here 1910 map here of Troup County you are looking at right now shows the owners of all of the property around here, near and far. All of our properties are shown in my name as you can see with a couple of "et als." That's the way Mama wanted it at the time. She made me pledge to do right by all of y'all. I think I have done just that. And in doing so, I have nearly worked my damn fool self to death. I'm beginning to get a bit peeved and a little feeble now so I think that it's high time to set things straight. I want Son to hear all of this. Now he and his brothers and sisters and his Mama are not included in the Will at all. It was not an oversight nor a mistake but I didn't know how to handle this because of the times. That was not my intention but I was advised that those were just details and could be easily ironed out later. I think I wanted Roy to take care of it. Well, now is later.

"So May, why don't you start things off," said Burrell.

"Just remember that Mama said, "Rose Hill is yours, Burrell," no questions about it. This was not included in the seven shares. Just make sure that those children of your'n are taken care of. Don't make a mess of their lives, too."

"And I do remember saying, 'just what do you mean by that Mama?'" Burrell recalled.

107

"Any ways, I am the oldest of the children and have played the role of Mama sometimes and even Florence Nightingale to all of them including Burrell," drawled May in a quavering, high-pitched voice still showing a bit of upset over Burrell's challenging their mother back when. "I won't comment on whether what we are doing is right or not, all I want to do is to get Tom's family included. That's what I want to do with my share. Now why do I want to do this? As some of you know, Tom was cast out of the family and cut out of the will because of his rowdiness and disgraceful conduct. He brought shame on the family, so he had no share, and his estate, if any, has no share. I think it was wrong to cut him out, and because of his transgressions, his family has suffered unduly. His family ought not to be made to suffer. But that was the way things were done at the time. So I am giving my entire share to Roy, Tom's oldest child so he can do with it however he pleases."

"John Thomas, it was not so much that Tom was disinherited," Mr. Burrell said, "as it was that Mama had spent a small fortune on getting his killer prosecuted which in her own way should have been sufficient for an inheritance. She failed to realize that she was the beneficiary of her actions, not Tom as he was dead. Really, It was not fair. That has bothered all of us and this is high time we to get that squared away."

"Verne, your time," Burrell barked.

"What is there to say? We are all just about gone. We don't have all that much time to be here on this Earth. All most of us have to our name is land, land, land. That's all we talk about anyhow. Land is cheap. What is its value, maybe a little more than a dollar an acre? How many acres are we talking about? Two thousand, . . . five thousand acres?

What was it the last time somebody counted? Anybody know? Who's going to buy it? Farming isn't prosperous anymore. We have come to the end of an era. We have lots and lots of land but no money to speak of. We are cash poor but land rich. If Burrell didn't grow and sell all that cotton, sorghum, corn and stuff, there would be no cash at all. We all have Burrell to thank for this and all of those workers out there who toil on a daily basis just for us. They are not slaves anymore but for the good it's doing them, they may as well be. I have a little money put away myself. I have a Will of my own and it includes a portion of my

108

share going to Cordelia and some to Roy. Maybe he will heal one of these days because he bore the brunt of our family's decision. It's too bad that Tom can't know this. He was our flesh and blood, our poor brother, may God rest his soul. It's so heart wrenching whenever I recall that 'In Memoriam" piece in the newspaper. May, didn't you write it? I memorized it. I want to recite it again. It's kind of funny, too. Please tolerate me.

"Oh-h-h no-o-o-o, not again!" Evans exclaimed.

"Let her do it for goodness sake!" Burrell chided Evans.

In Memoriam

Thomas Gordon Harrell, of West Point,

Deceased March 28, 1920, was shot in

the back at Shawmut, Ala., near the burial

ground of Samuel Harrell, pioneer of

Virginia.

On that fatal Saturday was cut

off a keen, discerning intellect, a heart

that beat but with kindness. Idealistic,

yet judicial, he advocated practical

humanity ever championing the lowly

and oppressed. The colored population adored him

pre-eminently peaceable, amiable and

witty, he won many true friends. Suffering

bravely, making pathetic attempts at joking,

he met death in a beautiful spirit. When he

began our Lord's Prayer, there was not a dry

eye in the room.

Brother, farewell.

Most of this passage reflected Tom's deathbed lament in his last minutes at the hospital. It was he who recited the Lord's Prayer and others in his hospital room joined in his recitation of the Lord's Prayer to pray for his soul. May, his sister, composed the Memoriam.

"My health is beginning to fail," continued Verne as she no longer paid any attention to Burrell, "and I am just not up to this kind of thing anymore. I was feeling so good while we were talking about other things and listening to John Thomas' tall tales. He speaks so nicely, not like the other nigrahs."

Burrell interrupted, "Verne, don't you ever call John Thomas no 'nigrah!' He's my son, and you just remember that. He's not a 'nigrah.'"

The term "nigrah" was not intended necessarily to be insulting or demeaning, but white southern speech patterns in general were so corrupted that little time was taken to enunciate words clearly. Furthermore, they didn't know what term to call the blacks that was acceptable to them, or perhaps they really didn't care, all they knew was that they were different from "them." They just knew that they had to be named or called something different without demeaning them because "race" was such a big factor in the daily lives of nearly everybody. There were so many of them, too. The colored population was as big or bigger than the white in many areas.

"But I am not finished, Burrell. There's much more that John Thomas should know. I should have started at the beginning.

"OK," Verne said, not fully understanding why Burrell was so riled up as she didn't see anything wrong with what she said. "I am so much better off that I have met him and would like to become acquainted with the rest of his brothers and sisters some time soon. I am going to give my entire share to John Thomas for his sisters but through Burrell so that things can be worked out through the system without any trouble.

"Even though it's early, I am ready to turn in. I am just plain tuckered out. I won't be having dessert with y'all tonight. I will stay here just a bit longer because I want to see John Thomas off."

"Evans," Burrell said rather softly as she was demure and the classiest of the sisters. All of this blood letting was beginning to get next to him. "Your time."

"I was only 12 years old when my Daddy died. He left 10 children to be raised by Mama. We didn't have a whole lot of money, but we did put it to good use through sacrifice and support for one another. I went off to Wesleyan College in Macon and later transferred to Auburn where I received a bachelor's in Architecture in 1911. I was the first female to receive such a degree from Auburn or maybe anywhere else, who knows? That wasn't the point though – I had the talent. Now, women were not in those kinds of fields in those days and I suffered as I could only get jobs as a draftsman. I was angered at this blatant discrimination. I believe that was the beginning of my efforts to work for women's rights. Among other things, I truly became a suffragette! Well, don't let me take up any more of the time, I'll tell you more John Thomas when . . . .

"That's enough for now, Evvie," interrupted Burrell. "We . . . .

"Burrell, there is so much more that John Thomas needs to know. We won't get the opportunity to meet all of his brothers and sisters and he can tell them what he has just heard from us," Evans said. "Just let me tell him a little bit more and then we can be on with it."

"Aw right, go ahead."

"Auburn was and is "our" school; our brother, Sam went there, and became an electrical engineer. After I couldn't get into the field of

Architecture, I went back to school to Teachers' College at Columbia University and obtained my Masters Degree back in 1928. Cousin Bubber went from Auburn on to the University of Alabama to become a lawyer and Roy's older son went to Auburn as well as his wife, Julie. But good ol' Colville went to Georgia Tech.

"You see, Son, these dollies can go on and on."

John Thomas sat there quite puzzled. Most of this he had never heard mentioned before even though there were many questions in his mind as to Roy's involvement in the family's affairs. After all, Roy was nothing more than a first cousin to him and a stranger, if that. Roy did carry himself as if he were the equal of his Uncle Burrell. Roy really had inserted himself in the role that his own father may have played had he been on the scene, except Roy was beginning to displace his Uncle Burrell as the head of the family. He was "too often" on the scene to tend to his aunties' needs as well as his Uncle Burrell's. Tom would have never been successful in this role; however, he had two sisters older than he. John Thomas also realized that he would not have been able to handle the system as Roy would have exercised it no matter how "white" he appeared. The townsfolk would have never allowed that to happen knowing of his background and furthermore he had no desire to challenge them or more than that, he feared them. Mr. Burrell knew that, too.

There was momentary silence in the room except for the sound of the grandfather clock. Almost at once, everybody at the table noticed that the clock had the incorrect time.

"Whose job is it to set the clock, May?" Burrell asked.

"Nobody's really, we tell Carrie to wind it sometimes. But what difference does it make? We are not going anywhere, we don't do anything, and we are never expecting anybody anymore. It's just an old relic. Time is not important to us anymore," May sighed with resignation. "You could say that we are waiting for the Lord."

"Oh, don't say that," said John Thomas. "I will be over here all of the time to see about you."

Dinner was finished. Carrie was called in to remove the dishes from the table and while doing so, she asked brusquely, "Dessert anybody?" Carrie was never classy. The quiet continued. John Thomas had his stomach set on some of that banana pudding but he realized just before Mr. Burrell spoke that it was not going to be tonight.

"Why don't we all pass, Carrie. It seems that we have taken too much time for dinner anyway and there is still a whole lot of work to be done tonight. You have outdone yourself, Girl. When you get done in the kitchen, I'll make Manfield take you home in my best carriage. We'll see you early tomorrow morning," Mr. Burrell said.

Carrie caught John Thomas' eye as he had previously ignored her and beckoned for him to come over. "Son!" she whispered, "They ain't never gonna let you git that land, if you don't find a good lawyer who will take this up for you, 'cause Mr. Roy, gonna git it. Watch my word!" Carrie tried to eavesdrop on nearly everything that was going on in the big house so she could to pass the word to Rosa to protect herself, if need be. Rosa was fearful that when Mr. Burrell passed on, they would all be evicted from Rose Hill.

John Thomas followed Mr. Burrell to his room. Legal papers, the deeds and the Will, had been spread all across his table. The lighting was dim. There was only one chair in this massive room. "Son, why don't you sit down in this one but get one of them dining room chairs 'cause we gotta work some long hours here tonight to get this thing ready by tomorrow morning. Hurry back, you hear?"

Carrie waylaid John Thomas again but he brushed her off quickly as he felt he couldn't keep Mr. Burrell waiting for long as he considered Carrie as nothing but trouble. "But be careful, Son," she warned. "Be careful."

Chapter 9. Bringing up the Rear

The last three children in the Winston family were the beneficiaries of the experiences of the older ones who had adjusted to their being and living. These younger boys were going to become farmers as well because there was enough land for everybody to plan out his future. The youngest daughter would not be so much better off than her sisters for she was not to own land but hopefully get married and raise a family; her only duty on the farm was to carry water to the field during harvest time.

James Floyd

In the meantime, back on the farm, James Floyd Winston was born on March 4, 1926, and died on September 1, 1968, a year after Alfred. He went as far as the third grade in school and abruptly quit. He was a fun guy, who ran around with his buddies who were elementary school dropouts just like him. James was good in the real life role of "Johnny Appleseed" to the budding young lasses of the surrounding farms. Although he was a good-looking guy and the girls found him irresistible, he looked "too white" for some of the them. They didn't want to have his babies. He, like his brothers, was a blond, blue-eyed, young man, but unlike them he hung around with the classic-looking "black" kids. They were mostly unmixed, solidly black with full lips, kinky hair, and prominent eyes. They wore the black mustache, a sign that they were to be considered virile men and ready to become fathers. James was one of the boys, and had no use for any of his father's tenant whites around the farm as running buddies. He was always involved in some scrape or other from which Mr. Burrell had to rescue him. He was just a big kid, had no purpose in life and saw no reason why people should complicate their lives being serious about such things as going to school, working, or accumulating things. He was, however, the most entrepreneurial of the boys in that he made the best whiskey in the county, which earned him the distinction as being a leading "Whiskey 'Nigger'" in the business. The demand was great, and he would always oblige as well as imbibe. Imbibing led him to an early grave. He was just 42.

114

Mary Bessie

Mary Bessie was the last of the four girls. She was the "Belle of the Ball" so to speak, a pretty thing but strong and healthy looking, a prom queen, the beauty. She was smart and apt and the businesswoman par excellence. She truly was a "white girl" in manner and looks, and she was loved by all of the colored folks. In spite of her white appearance, she fit into all of the plays at school, the many projects which girls usually get themselves assigned to and the like. But she wasted no time in leaving school everyday and getting back to the farm on time. Not that she had any duties, but she had a curfew. Mr. Burrell saw to it that his girls wasted no time with black males and he wanted none of them to marry "black" under any circumstance. Mary Bessie's brothers acted as her protectors or chaperons no matter the occasion. John Thomas was her main protector, but a watchful eye was cast by any of the other brothers around.

Mary's popularity won her the Miss Tenth Street High Pageant Award not only for her prized looks but also for her drive to succeed in any endeavor. She raised absolutely the most money, which was key to winning the title. The girls who didn't succeed in winning thought that her raising "big dollars" was due to Mr. Burrell's "millions." They believed that he gave her everything she wanted. In truth, she did her winning with truly hard work in baking and selling pies and cakes with her team members, and raffles. She won handily. The King of the pageant, Ernest Johnson, crowned her "Miss Tenth Street High." There was the feeling among the aspiring girls that Mary Bessie would win the title every year no matter how hard they worked. But the truth of the matter was that Marry Bessie won only once, and competed for the title only once. Mary Bessie's aggressiveness was so overwhelming that none dared attempt to compete with her and they withered at the thought that any other of them had a chance at all. There never was the slightest inkling to her that her victory was due to her whiteness or looks. Even if it were true, no one would dare raise the issue or acknowledge it. Because "colored" folks came in all colors, one could not consistently discriminate, as there were many in every family who may not have even had the same father. No self-respecting colored woman or girl dared find themselves alone after nightfall for fear that they would become prey and abducted for some roaming white man's pleasure for the evening.

The boys at school all secretly pined for Mary, but the most aggressive was Jim Earnest Fannings. She had no particular interest in him at first or anyone else for that matter. She considered him and them more of a nuisance than anything else. But his persistence paid off. He won his lovely prize soon after his being dubbed the "rejected one." Jim had the persona of the Black African male glistening in the sun at high noon. He was thoroughly aware of Mr. Burrell's distaste for black males particularly as prospective suitors for his daughters and worse Jim's pursuit of Mary. Jim somehow never found the occasion to meet Mr. Burrell and never even remotely considered asking him for Mary's hand in marriage. This was a "white" family and there was no room for a "black" person especially of Jim's hue. Jim knew that one day Mr. Burrell would be proud of having him as a son-in-law, but he was not yet ready to acknowledge that; however, once married, he would spirit her away before Mr. Burrell could learn of their union. Jim was a smart "cat." After the wedding, he didn't hang around for the celebration and all of the congratulatory offerings and gifts; he high-tailed it out of town with his bride the very next morning. This was an extremely dangerous journey for them both. The year was 1947. The ways of the Old South were still intact. Segregation was still king and legal. The perennial lynchings were extant. They caught the "Special," the early morning train, the next morning. It was one of the last steam engines still in service with at least 10 passenger cars plus a dining car as well as an observation car. Both of these were off limits to Jim and therefore also to Mary unless she chose to pass.

There was something sentimental about the Special. It was the "alarm clock" of the day. Its whistle blew so loudly each workday morning that it almost woke up the dead. This was the wake up call for the entire Valley – some 25,000 people. Time to get up and go to work. The Special departed West Point at 6:05 AM, on time, every day. Notwithstanding that, the Lanett Mill whistle blew at the same precise time every morning except for Sunday. The Mill whistle was official, after all where else did everybody work?

Mary and Jim were worried because blacks were as much concerned about race mixing as whites; it was strictly forbidden by the white power

116

structure in addition to its being abjectly unlawful. There had been known instances where blacks were lynched just for looking at a white woman, let alone being her companion. Although it was not unusual for a black man to accompany a very fair-skinned "black" woman, it was still just plain hazardous. The railroad car "reserved" for colored was the first passenger car on the train. The worst feature of this car was its discomfiture because it was next to the tender. Whenever the train moved, the shock created by the coupling and decoupling were more intensely felt next to the engine's coal car, the tender. The railroad tracks at that time were not precisely laid; there was no such thing as ribbon rails; they would be available at a much later time. The noise of the wheels, the clickety-clacking, against the rails was quite disturbing and every rider suffered from that. As the train moved forward, it would snatch, and jerk the passengers senselessly. The passengers in the first car felt the greatest discomfort. There was absolutely no advantage in Jim Crow for the Colored.

"Tickets! Tickets!" called out the conductor. He was ready to collect or punch tickets of those getting on in West Point. A Porter always accompanied the Conductor for some reason. This was Jim and Mary's honeymoon voyage. They would see the USA and spend the evening the best way they could.

The Porter was the first to spot the couple. He inched ahead of the Conductor to check out the situation, although, the Conductor usually preceded the Porter. The Porter was always black, the Conductor white.

"Where y'all going this morning?" smiled the Porter. He took a long look at Mary Bessie. "Y'all together, Ma'm?" he asked.

Jim knew the reason for the questioning, but feigned not understanding the need for its being asked: "Is there a problem, Sir?"

"Not yet," the Porter answered. "But there could be if y'all know what I mean."

Jim nodded knowingly, pointed to Mary Bessie with his right index finger and then pointed to the back of his left hand with the same finger. The Porter understood.

"I see," the Porter said. "What might be the occasion, may I ask?"

"Of course," they said at the same time. "We're newlyweds!"

"Well, congratulations to the both of you! This is mighty fine!"

Of course the other passengers nearby were listening in and burst into applause with that pronouncement.

The Conductor turned at the sound of the commotion and asked, "What's going on here, Rufus?"

"Nothing much, Sir. We all were just congratulating the newlywed couple."

"By golly," the Conductor said. "Let me get in on this."

As the Conductor approached, he was horrified to see this pretty little white thing sitting with this Negro, black as the back. "Wait just a minute, I ain't gonna have none of this on my train," he bellowed. "I am putting y'all off this train at the next stop and I'm gonna turn both of you over to the authorities in LaGrange. Y'all know what the law is!"

The Porter tried feverishly to smooth things over and calm the Conductor but he would have none of it.

Mary, not being willing to tolerate any more of this foolishness, stood up and said forcefully to the conductor in her best "colored" speaking accent, "See heah, suh, I'm colored. My Daddy's white and my Maw's colored, so I'm colored. 'Course she very fair herself that's why I look the way I do. But you don't have to put us off. My Daddy's nephew, who is white, gonna board this here train in LaGrange anyways and he'll tell you that everything's all right. Is dat all right wit' you, Sir?"

"Well, I don't know what to say. Why I surely did mess things up, didn't I? I was gonna come and wish y'all congratulations," the Conductor said rather warily. "But I _was_ minding my own business! Well, if'n it's all the same to y'all, congratulations anyways."

They nodded and looked away.

The train steamed into the LaGrange station. It was now running late. It had stayed too long in the West Point station for some unknown reason. More passengers than usual perhaps needed to come aboard and all of the visitors had to dismount. The train took off nearly as fast as it entered the station without a single visitor boarding. Visitors were allowed to come aboard as well wishers to say their goodbyes to the departing passengers; however, this day there was no time for such. Mary was upset that her cousin was unable to see them off. Jim thought that she had made up the story about her father's nephew coming aboard, which he felt was very clever. Her cousin indeed was there and Mary spotted him on the platform just as the train pulled out. She managed to get his attention and waved frantically to him as the train sped out of sight.

Jim began to wonder, would it always be this way? Too much damn excitement! They would have to change trains in Atlanta. There he had reserved a compartment and for the first time in their hours-old marriage, they would be alone together. He felt that the compartment was best as they would not be meeting other passengers and their privacy would be assured. They were headed to Detroit, the motor city, where they would take up housekeeping and be relatively free from intrusions.

When they arrived in Detroit, they found work in the automotive industry at first. Later Mary saw an opportunity to take over a restaurant, owned by Lebanese, catering to a mostly white clientele, and turned it into a Sports bar and Restaurant. It was located on Seven Mile Road where there were legions of auto dealerships.

Mary and Jim modernized the place and heralded the Detroit Sports teams, The Tigers, The Red Wings, and The Lions. This became a haunt for stars like Alex Karras, Bob Lanier, and many others. A black may never have been able to acquire a place like this bar and restaurant and of this caliber in the location that it was in. These kinds of enterprises were reserved for white ownerships only. One wonders how the Lebanese got in except they were the foreign merchants to the world at that time and at a glance appeared white. Nobody, but nobody, knew that Mary Bessie was not white. Nobody asked and nobody told. Only Jim Earnest knew. He stayed out of sight and out of the limelight, and managed mostly in the kitchen or worked in the back office keeping the books. Even though the Detroit enclave from West Point knew that they were there, they never came over to the restaurant for anything. They realized the situation and were not about to expose this relationship. There was a cardinal rule in the colored community throughout the nation that members of the fold never "outed" a "passing" brother or sister no matter the situation.

Mary, at first, had trouble with this arrangement, as she felt that she not only was denying her husband but also betraying her race. This was the first time that she had knowingly or openly paraded as a "white" woman, even though she didn't declare this herself. She never consciously or deliberately passed for white even for business reasons; and it was not at her insistence, but the presumption of the person believing she was white or didn't think anything about it. This is the way it should have been if America was to be "raceless." This in her sight was forgivable as she and her family accepted being colored for the longest and embraced the so-called "black culture." Jim had it the roughest, although he played his role to the hilt in this masquerade. He was the "darkie" in the kitchen as long as it was necessary to establish the business and see to it that it prospered.

They changed the menu, added "Soul Food" to the selections, such as chops, fried chicken, chicken and dumplings, greens, both turnip and collard greens, introduced chitterlings, hog knuckles, pig ears and pig's feet, which were now considered delicacies of sorts. These were the leavings of the butcher shops and pens, and were at one time the mainstay diet of "poor people," black as well as white, yet were foreign to a northern or non-southern clientele. This change in the menu also brought in many southern whites that had moved to the Detroit area for defense work during World War II. They came from "Down Home" so to speak and their tastes were indistinguishable from the blacks. Mary and Jim also brought in the relatively new European and Asian dishes to appeal to immigrant tastes, so many of whom were affected by the GIs having gone to Europe and the Far East. In its heyday, this was the place to be seen; it was bustling; it was magic! Many of the GIs had married Europeans, especially Germans, and found this place extraordinary because of the heavy pork selections on the menu, and because somehow they perceived that they and their wives were welcome. Maybe it was the vibes that Mary gave off, silently signaling that she was one of them, a kind of a "war bride?"

Jim and Mary decided to start a family. Although the business could not spare her, she decided to go back home any way to deliver her first child. This was prompted by the many concerns she would have in the hospital, and believing that she would not be received well because of her color or better yet the color of the eventual baby. Back home in Georgia, if she chose a mid-wife, it would be not only traditional but also out of necessity as babies were delivered at home. If she could now choose the hospital, she would still be in familiar surroundings and with family, especially her mother and sisters, and friends. In addition, the hospital staff to include the doctors, all of whom were white, would know her background. Beverly, her first born, came in December of '48, born in West Point, Georgia. She was as white as new-driven snow. Suspicion in the colored community set in almost immediately as to whether Jim Ernest Fannings was the true father of this child. This was reasonable, as when both parents are of mixed race, perceptible black admixture can usually be discerned but on the other hand you can't tell what you are going to get. The situation here was that Mary's appearance was that of no black admixture at all and Jim's appearance having no white admixture whatsoever. In the black community, Jim's skin color would be described as "black as the back" meaning the soot-covered back of a wood- or coal-burning fireplace. It was therefore obvious that Jim must have had white ancestry in his family, even if not apparent, and there was no question as to who was the baby's father -- certainly not in Mary and Jim's minds.

Race has always been a burning issue in America ever since its founding; however, there has never been the resolve to come to terms with it. And whenever any situation is allowed to fester, it only gets worse. It has become popular in the scientific community, except for perhaps the medical field, to declare that there is only one race; and that one is the "human" race as each apparent distinct group is interfertile, meaning that offspring can be reproduced or interbred from such a mating. This declaration has been established as fact as a result of the successful "Genome" Project.

After a relatively short period of getting that home-sweet-home motherly love and family care, Mary was headed back to Detroit, with

121

Jim accompanying her as he had come down to witness the baby's christening at her home church, Emanuel Chapel CME (Christian {formerly Colored} Methodist Episcopal). Travel in the South by blacks "through the country" was always met with a loathsome fear as to their safety in the event of a car breakdown or if they were stopped or challenged by southern policeman for whatever reason. Most of the law enforcement establishment at the time was white, hence the apprehension. In this instance, this couple appeared as a white woman with her white child and black male companion, his being at the wheel.

"Jim, why don't you go on back by yourself," Mary's Mother, Miss Rosa said. "Let Mae Bessie return by train just the way she come down here. I see nothing but trouble if something went wrong on the highway. Every traffic light where you would have to stop could set up a problem, and there won't be nowhere along the road to stay for the night. There ain't no restaurants where you can stop to eat, no motels where you can sleep, nothing!"

"Please don't worry yourself, Miss Rosa," Jim said. "I'll be careful. You've fixed us some fried chicken and other goodies. The baby's got milk and enough bottles to last her until we get north. It's wintertime and nothing will spoil. And if anything does go wrong, I'll have Mary stay out of sight depending on what the problem is. You know she's very nervous about being taken for white and the terrible things that could happen to me. We've been through this once before, you know."

On the way out, they drove past Tenth Street High School, their alma mater, over to Highway US 29 North. It was 2:00 o'clock in the morning. Such an early start would get them past farm vehicles and Atlanta and many other areas, where there could be traffic problems and possibly unpleasant encounters with the police. They planned the trip this way so as to leave at night, as most other colored travelers did at that time to avoid encounters with the law, as well as the local whites that were most often hostile to any black. The timing was to arrive at their destination before nightfall the next day.

Flashing red lights were closing in fast from the rear. Jim realized that he was moving at a pretty fast clip. He slowed down as the police car approached and came to a stop at the side of the highway. Mary was asleep. Jim shook Mary forcefully to awaken her. "Mary, Mary! We

122

got trouble. The cops are after us. Just make like you're asleep, cover your face a little bit and turn your head toward the window and don't make a sound. Let me handle everything even if it seems to be going bad. Just don't make a sound."

"Michigan car tag, huh? Let me see your driver's license and registration, boy! Is this your car or is it stolen?" the cop rattled off.

"Good morning, Sir," Jim, sweating profusely, said as pleasantly as he could muster under the circumstances thinking of the worst that could happen.

"Your driver's license looks OK, boy, but this here registration is for another car. You got another car?"

"Let me see that one, Sir. Oh, yes Sir, that's the one for my wife's car. I keep mine here in my wallet. Oh, here it is."

"Looks like you're OK, boy. What you doing in this part of the country at this time of night any ways? Looks like I'm gonna have to run you in for speeding though," the patrolman said.

Jim apologized outright and said that he was trying to get his wife and baby back home as quickly as he could. They had both been in the hospital in Georgia, but he didn't mean to break any Tennessee laws. The baby's still sick and we need to get her to the doctor as soon as we can.

"In that case, I'm gonna let you go this time. Be careful if you plan to get home in one piece. Y'all have a nice day, you hear?"

Jim didn't really know what to say. Such cordiality he never expected.

Mary whispered, "Just say, 'Thank you, Officer.'"

Five years later, Mary pulled this caper one more time but with Jim Junior. This young gentleman's skin color was a light brown or tan, absolutely nothing like Beverly's, but it raised no eyebrows, as this was the way he was supposed to look. Jim and Mary's family was set. Their years together prospered. Jim's career in the Federal Government was quite successful as an accountant, as well as his having joined the Michigan National Guard, rising to the rank of Master Sergeant.

Little by little, however, the crowds thinned as the auto dealers on Seven Mile Road moved to other locations around the City or farther out following the money as more and more southerners both white and black moved in. Mary had "lost" her lease before things started spiraling downward at a rapid rate. Many thought that her identity as an "African American" had been revealed, even though she made no overt effort to conceal or deny it.

They lived a good life, made a few bucks, but decided to give it up. There was the lure of West Point. There was something magic about the area that beckoned for the prodigal son and daughter to return home in 1985.

Gaines Tyrone

All of Burrell's boys were named for the Harrell males except Gaines, the last child, who dropped his middle name of "Combs," the maiden name of his paternal grandmother, Miss Cordie. Gaines changed his middle name on his own to the more popular "black" name of "Tyrone." The guys called him "'Rone" after Tyrone Power who was the popular, swashbuckling Hollywood debonair dandy of the day and of course because of his good looks.

The rest of the family was so involved in their own battles and interest that few paid any attention to Gaines, or Foy, as he was known. He had dropped out of school after completing the tenth grade. The reason was that the West Point Public Schools board had decided that its schools should be on the nationally popular 6-3-3 grade method, rather than terminating its high school education at the eleventh grade. No consideration was given to allowing those who were planning to graduate in 1949 to finish up at that time. It was abrupt. This edict applied to all students regardless of race. The graduating classes of both schools would have been the largest in either of their histories. (As a result of this change, the white school's football team won the State Championship due to the repeating experienced senior players.) A large number of the black kids dropped out altogether. Gaines now found that it was all just a waste of time. There was nothing new there. The books were out of date and as far as he was concerned, he was not learning a damn thing from those teachers. Many of them were marginal and did not challenge him either at home or school. He blamed the teachers for not fully realizing that his troubles were cast upon him many decades ago resulting from the failure of the Government to uphold its bargain to make the schools "separate but equal." He was smart kid just like Alfred, and was content to be all by himself. He didn't particularly care for the young ladies who were interested in him, or for anyone else for that matter. He hadn't connected with Mr. Burrell in such a long time; he just didn't bond as did the other boys. Mr. Burrell was now 61, too old to "play" with a 17-year old boy even though he was his son. Foy was the "Prince" -- the Baby Boy. His sisters fawned over him all of the time and really looked out for him. He was Miss Rosa's darling.

Mama Rosa and his sisters were waiting for him to come by for his evening meal. They waited and waited. Finally, he showed up.

"Foy, where in the world have you been?" his mother admonished.

"Oh, I dropped by to see Mr. Burrell."

"What for?" they exclaimed.

"I just thought that it would be nice to tell him that I volunteered for the Army."

"You what? Why didn't you come over to tell us first? Why did you go to him?"

"He is my father and boys must keep their fathers clued in as to what's happening in their lives. Also, he raised holy hell when Son got his draft notice, so, I thought I had better clue him in before he had another conniption fit. But I don't think he really cares now, but he did give me $50.00. Maybe that's why I really went by, I needed the money and he was always so generous. He knows that there is nothing around here for me, so I'm in the Army now!" he sang in the tune of the World War I song: "You're in the Army Now." He continued,

"You're in the Army now,

"You're not behind the plow,

"You'll never get rich,

"You son of a - - - (oops!)

Everybody laughed for a moment but "Maw."

Miss Rosa started wailing inconsolably, "My baby!" she moaned. The sisters joined in. There was no one around to comfort them. Sug and Alfred came over and had a few drinks with him and bade him goodbye just like they did in the movies, only they seldom went to the movies and when they did, they sat among the whites.

Gaines reported the next day to Fort Jackson, South Carolina for induction, orientation and processing. The Korean War was raging. The Army was taking casualties but that didn't matter, some soldiers will fall. If it were God's will, you'd come back home with a sound body after the war was over.

Gaines reported afterwards for basic training at Fort Benning, Georgia – much too close to home, just 40 miles up the Chattahoochee River. He wanted to get away from there. He soon found that there were a whole bunch of activities to occupy him without longing to go home and receiving the comforts provided by his mother. His orders showed him to be classified as a "B." The letter "B" was the Army's personnel racial classification code for "Negroid," the letter "A" denoted "Caucasoid," as one would expect. Gaines so indicated on the questionnaire that he was a "B" when he filled it out at the Induction Station, Fort Jackson, South Carolina. When he presented his orders, the clerk, a corporal, without checking them steered him to the Company that at the time was reserved for A-types. As no one had explained the situation to Gaines, he truly did not understand what was happening. He woke up when he noticed that all of the troops in the Company were white -- not a single colored soldier to be seen. While he expected to see an integrated Army as segregation was by now supposedly old hat in the Army, he certainly didn't expect this. He came to realize that he had been assigned to a previously designated all-white Company. This was even more confounding; as he understood that President Truman's Executive Order 9981, dated July 26, 1948, had desegregated the Armed Forces and this

126

was 1951. What was the problem? Strangely enough, three years later, the Army had not gotten around to complying fully with the Executive Order. Gaines, in turn, requested that he be assigned to an all-colored unit.

"What in the hell are you talking about, soldier?' demanded the Corporal.

"I believe there's been a mix-up here," Gaines said rather innocently. "It seems that I have been assigned to an all-white unit but I'd rather be assigned to an all-colored unit if this is the way it's gonna be."

"Come again? Ain't this some shit! Now just why in the hell do you want to do a stupid ass thing like that, soldier?" the clerk demanded. "Are you crazy or something? Why would a white boy want to be assigned to a unit with them? Huh? Just tell me and you'd better make some sense."

Before Gaines could respond to declare his race, the First Sergeant walked up behind the clerk, tapped him on the shoulder and said, "Looks like we goofed on this here recruit, we didn't read his orders right. It says here that he is classified as a "B." You know what that means, don't you?"

"Sure I do," the clerk said. "You mean he don't belong in this unit. You got to be kidding. Look at him, do you think that . . . . ?" The clerk was a "Yankee" and this was a new experience for him.

"Yep, and in that case, I'd better tell the "Old Man," the First Sergeant said. "This is our first case like this and we'll be gigged for not complying with Presidential Order.

This was not an oversight, as the full Army just had not gotten around to it – some three years later. No rush. This was a minor or a non-issue at all. The President was told that it would take time to get this done and that there would be dire consequences if this thing were rushed. The unit-level was not responsible for implementing these kinds of directives. Headquarters, Army, Washington 25, DC, had the full responsibility but had not yet bellied up to the bar in many areas

127

especially down South. This was a failure on the part of the higher echelons of the Army to execute faithfully, willful or not.

The Presidential Order was the first of the national efforts to de-institutionalize segregation (or racism) in the Services. It was said that the Army was the first of the Services to comply fully; however, the Air Force did not have much of a problem as it had just been formed a year before under the National Defense Act of 1947 before the Order was issued. Whatever problems it had were left over from the Army Air Corps. Once it was recognized that the Government was serious, restructuring went well and without a hitch – but it did take a relatively long time to filter down.

Once the Order was given, integration was swift. Integration had a positive effect on Army personnel especially at the enlisted level. For the first time in the history of the Army, personnel were thrown in from all over the country regardless of racial classification, especially blacks being thrown in with whites. Probably the group that benefited most were the young southern white soldiers. What became immediately apparent was that the Civil War was still being "fought" all over again between northern whites and the southern whites. The northern whites instigated most of the aggressive acts of razzing, name-calling, and taunting, the response was spirited and sometimes nasty, but the situation rarely got out of hand. Fort Benning was "Rebel" territory, and the cadre-in-charge were mostly southern non-commissioned officers who were mature enough to prevent any serious altercations, again this was the Army and there was no tolerance for disobedience. The most surprising aspect that grew out of the integration of the Army was that the southern black and white soldiers seemingly became fast friends – socialized together, were drinking buddies and went into town together where it was tolerated; this is the early 1950's, even before national declaration for the desegregation of the schools. Gaines had friends in both camps and seemed to have integrated himself very well with the whites, but suffered socially when it came to sharing the company of white lasses, as he was a self-proclaimed black regardless of his phenotype, and he had been thoroughly indoctrinated at home by his older brothers.

Gaines rose through the enlisted ranks achieving Master Sergeant within his 15 years of service. He was very bright, being known as a mathematical genius of sorts since high school. His talents were appreciated in the Army and he was offered several topflight assignments plus a chance to become an officer, all of which he declined. He realized now particularly after his first racial incident of coming into the Army that he should have always insisted on being categorized as a black. He was always so frustrated in trying to correct those who identified him racially as white. He decided just to let things be, come what may. In other words, he allowed himself to pass without so declaring whiteness. Whatever they thought he was, that's who he was. He realized the pitfalls in passing, therefore, and he was feeling guilty of deserting or betraying his "social" race. But in his own mind, he was just being practical.

Now he had no more buddies from either side and that prevented him from having female company. Lone wolves don't fare well. His difficulty with the black girls was that they did not want to have a "white" boyfriend, and Gaines was "too white" although they knew that he was black. Having a white man as a "lover" was considered disgraceful. The white girls didn't know any better because to them he was white, but that created a dilemma for him. "I've got to get out of this man's Army," he realized. "I just can't take it anymore." With no buddies to pal around with anymore or anybody to confide in, he practically became a basket case. He was going stir crazy, and knew it. What's a guy to do? He was hemmed in not knowing how to deal with this dilemma. He found comfort in imbibing. He pulled a couple more stints or hiding out in the Army and felt that he had had enough. He was so close to having his twenty years in for retirement, he went back home without the benefit of retirement and settled back on the farm and lived an unremarkable life at the behest of his sister, Mary Bessie and her husband, Jim, for over five years. They managed him as best they could. He was messed up and was this way when he came out of the Army. He had no visible means of income or support, but managed somehow to scrape together enough change to keep the booze flowing. This "change" was said to be coming to him because his Dad, Mr. Burrell, instructed Gaines' his first cousin Roy, who in turn instructed his sons, Roy, Jr. and Colville, that if anything ever happened to him, "Foy must always be kept in money." It more than likely went for booze.

Mary didn't know where the money was coming from, so she asked her sister, Precious, to drag it out of him at the first opportunity. She did, took the money from him and marched off to her cousin Colville's, rapped on his front door, and when he answered it, she threw the money in his face, screaming, "We don't want your dirty money!!"

Gaines fell to the bottle while still in the Army due to his nightmarish experiences as an infantryman in Korea. He and his platoon were engaged in hill fighting and were trapped in a hole near the summit of the hill they were trying to secure. He, as the platoon leader, was the last one to leave as he had hoisted others out; how many survived enemy fire, he never knew. He tried to dissuade them from trying to escape because the enemy surrounded them, but it was their decision. He knew somehow that they would eventually be rescued. He covered those who decided to go. He waited it out -- the last one walking so to speak. He didn't dare leave, himself, because there was no one left to cover him. There he remained for seemingly an eternity, alone, surviving off rations dropped in by helicopter. He was regarded as a hero and was honored later for this act of gallantry. This was the hellhole from which he never thought he would recover. He really didn't.

The draft of southern black and white males during the Korean War bode well for the nation and could have been a harbinger of things to come because they were becoming friends. This is where the race problem laid -- a contest between the males – the blacks and the whites competing for sexual access to each other's females, at least in the minds of some – the prize in the contest. The whites had the upper hand and had to keep it that way lest they themselves would be "colored." The prize eventually in all wars was the female. It was all about sexual privilege and perhaps everywhere. A culture was created around this contest, not just in the South but nationally. Laws were promulgated to enforce the separation of the races and a judicial system so biased that "justice" was wrought in the harshest way. The Volunteer Army eventually supplanted the draft and today, many of the old race problems are back.

Chapter 10. The Entrepreneur

While not one of Burrell's boys, Roy Wallace Harrell was the eldest in Burrell's children's generation, and was to play a major and deciding role in the distribution of Burrell's estate. He was born in 1903. His lot, like the rest of the Harrells, was from a "creeping" aristocracy but not sufficiently exalted, so to speak, or recognized by those who were indeed the genuine article. But the family was prominent. Roy had a rather normal childhood, but was always the kid who would dominate. He was a fighter. Even his friends were scared of him. He was a fierce competitor. Crafty and bold, he seems to have always gotten what he wanted even if he had to take it. He left nothing to chance. He also was a hustler. He had the craving to own things, land, and money, even as a boy, to be important but only to one girl, that's the girl that he married. Now she was indeed of the genuine article from McMinnville, Tennessee.

Roy started out to own land so he could build his "empire." He bought dilapidated houses at first and fixed them up with his own hands and sold them for a pretty nice piece of change. This method was not a fast enough track to real wealth for him. He recognized too that more and more "nigrahs" were coming from the farms and rural areas to live in town – from the old slave plantations, and had to have some place to live. The sharecropping system was failing. The sharecroppers were being roundly cheated out of their earnings. There was an unease with which they could not cope in the new system. They had no recourse because the system did not support them. So, Roy bought land in the colored sections in town around West Point and the Valley and stuck up shanty after shanty of such density that outbreaks of sickness and unrest, to include weekly killings, were feared as a constant threat to the social order because of the bad living conditions fostered in such close quarters. The truth be that there was never a social order. He somehow convinced the town fathers to hire more policemen, all white except for the first time, two blacks were added to the force, Willie Canady and Ralph Palmer, to patrol certain areas to keep down the killings, mostly over women and robberies. (Willie and Ralph's sole function was to keep the black's behavior under control.) Each had come from the prominent black families in town and according to the thinking of the town fathers, they could be more effective in reducing crime. Such could not have been further from the truth. The blacks saw this for what it was; Ralph and Willie were made nothing more than Uncle Toms or lackeys for the whites. If they had encounters with white lawbreakers, they could hold, but not arrest the perpetrators until white policemen arrived. This experiment was short lived.

Roy had no trouble finding tenants for these shacks as they came from "Good Bucket" and other redlined areas in West Point, but his troubles were mostly about collecting the rent. There were too few jobs, little or no money for rent – just for food and maybe clothing -- sometimes begged, sometimes borrowed, too often stolen. The jobs they found would pay them only in clothes or broken down furniture instead of cash that they rightfully expected and certainly needed. The renters couldn't make the whites pay for the services rendered. Some of them were paid with broken down bathtubs and toilet stools. These were leftovers when running water was installed in the remote white sections and they were upgraded from cesspools and sanitary conditions like that. These poor souls couldn't use them because they didn't yet have either running water or cesspools. The Jim Crow system was unfriendly to them and they really couldn't do anything about it. They acquiesced because what else could they do? Before, these poor souls were never conditioned to providing for themselves as they were not much more than chattel, still almost slaves, something Roy did not fully appreciate because he was born in town, and perhaps never a slavedriver. But he did a commendable thing by installing modern bathroom fixtures in their bathrooms.

He came acalling every Sunday morning to collect the rent. He banged on doors and announced himself by shouting, "ROY HARRELL!" If he didn't get the rent money then and there, it was rumored that he beat up on the renters, heads of the household, male or female, whoever was supposed to be responsible. It was only hearsay as no proof existed of this demeanor. Some said he always had a shotgun with him as a little inducement to pay up. No one ever saw a shotgun, this was legend as harsh measures were always used to make the colored pay up. This fit. Eventually, he had no trouble collecting. The belief that he would engage in these practices worked with the renters. He firmly believed that if they owed him, anybody, he should've been paid. He didn't fear the law. The law wasn't for the white folks; it was for the blacks, no two ways about it. The rent charged was from three to five dollars per week. There were never enough jobs for all of these "squatters." Those who did work got their income from the cotton mills or more likely from the poor whites who also worked in the cotton mills and were in just a little bit better shape. Almost everybody, one way or the other worked in the cotton mills, the cotton industry, or for The Lanett Bleachery and Dye Works which really was still the cotton industry. Roy, by now, had at least a hundred houses in West Point and the Chattahoochee Valley from Lanett as far south as Cusseta and west to Lafayette, the Chambers County Seat in East Alabama. From this, he earned what became a rather nice living for the times. Collection became so easy that he was able to use his nine-year old son, Colville, to do much of the collecting; he was a real businesslike little fellow. Roy Junior, too, helped on occasion, but he was an egghead and when he did play, he preferred to play with the colored kids. They seemed to have more fun at play. Colville's call for the rent in his little squeaky voice never put the fear of God in any of the renters but they knew if "Mr. Roy" ever got wind of their giving little Colville a hard time, they thought he would pummel the hell out of them. Colville was a spunky and industrious fellow who would grow up to be somebody, as he would always deliver. Everybody knew that he was going places some day.

Chapter 11. The Second Will

Burrell and John Thomas worked late into the evening reviewing and making changes to his copy of the official Will.   Both men were tuckered out by now but kept on going for another hour or so.   John Thomas read aloud from a copy of the first official Will, and then a passage or two from the codicil that Mr. Burrell had marked up to revise the original Will. The original Will, itself, was kept by Roy because he was the executor. The impetus to change the official Will came about from Mr. Burrell's coming to understand that his "colored" family may not be dealt fairly when he was gone. This was a change of heart for him although he had been suspicious since learning of Roy's visit to the Hall of Records at the Court House in LaGrange, as Manfield had alerted him. What was his business there?   John Thomas, in silence, wrote down Mr. Burrell's every utterance as to who was going to get what. Mr. Burrell knew that this codicil had to survive. He always had misgivings about Roy's faithfulness because of late he had become too eager to help no matter the situation. He would take this one to that new lawyer named Simon Wuerfel in LaGrange so as to be out of the sight of family. Burrell had to put faith in this new lawyer's hands because he wanted to establish his practice as well as his integrity.

John Thomas and his Dad continued to tick off his wishes one by one: that the Rose Hill plantation itself be left to his boys, this was solely his own and no other family member's. This property extended from the east bank of the Long Cane Creek up past the Old Hogg property bordering Hamilton Highway, Georgia Route 103 (see Troup County map). He also wanted it stated that his boys would take care of their mother, Rosa, if anything should happen to him, and that the Hogg property, itself, be set aside for his four girls, his own daughters, Rosa Belle, Marguerite, Precious, and Mary Bessie. He noted that it was not the going thing to leave property to females, as the land was generally held in trust for them so that no males from other unrelated families could ever get their hands on property not passed directly down from a Harrell to them.

Mr. Burrell could have done all of this, himself, without the force of a Will, by simply conveying the property by means of a warranty deed at any time directly to his children. But somehow he felt inwardly that this action would betray the family trust. There was always the stipulation that only those with Harrell blood could inherit Harrell property – heir property. Perhaps he thought of his children as not being Harrells. This suggested that in cases where the father was white, the offspring, even though illegitimate, were considered to belong only to the mother – and therefore the offspring were declared as nonwhite. Legitimacy has nothing to do with biology. Otherwise the children would possess the rights and privileges of the father, and access to his property and other means of wealth. The socio-cultural legal system, in place, denied the usual transfer of such wealth and rights to the nonwhite offspring.

Dr. Joseph L. Graves in his book <u>The Race Myth,</u> puts it more succinctly:

> *"The state of white male sexual privilege created contradictions that the ruling elite had to contend with, for heterosexual activity creates offspring. These offspring were half European and half other. How would they be dealt with? What would happen if by virtue of their ancestry, they attempted to claim the rights of their fathers? How would the wives and offspring their legitimate marriages deal with their half kin? The solution was simply to classify them as nonwhite and thereby deny them the rights of their fathers."*

It had been a long day. They finally finished up and called it a night.

"We gonna meet in this new lawyer's office tomorrow morning in LaGrange, Son. I'd better invite Roy because he needs to be there. You can drive me up there in your truck. See you tomorrow morning, early," Mr. Burrell said in bidding John Thomas good night.

The next day, Burrell walked into the law office of Simon Wuerfel without knocking and said, "Simon! You a newcomer around here. I picked you 'cause I'm sure you don't know your way around the South. I want to hire you to do a change to my Will."

"Yes Sir!" Rising to his feet, Simon said, "Good morning, Mr. Harrell."

"Right nice office you got here, boy. You doing any business? Here's a copy of the original Will that I told you about. It was drawed up in 1941. It don't read quite like I thought it should. If you note it, my nephew, Roy, along with my sister May are the only beneficiaries. He is also the executor. And that part about leaving the property to Roy 'and his children,' I don't know nothing about that. He must've added that himself. He's got the original papers, but I don't think I appointed him to that position. He took it. Now, I did sign all of them papers that he and the others shoved in front of me. Somehow, I believed that they could be trusted. I thought that they had carried out my wishes. Who knows, maybe they did. It was my goddam stupidity and carelessness not to read it, but so be it. I must be getting old and maybe, I hit the bottle too much.

"Simon, I want you to be part and parcel of this here one. Roy is a tough customer – bull-headed. You got to ride herd over him. While he ain't no lawyer, but he's got a good understanding of the law. Remember, he is nobody's fool and he been around the horn a few times. His position in my family will command some respect from you. He's gonna pull out every stopper because he's top dog in the next generation of my family. He knows every real estate trick in the book. He learned that from that Wallace-Strickland clan of his, his Mama's folks, up there in Meriwether County. They say that they are all for self and nobody else. I hear tell also they 'own' the police, the sheriff, the courts, both city and county, everybody. It seems that everybody works for them. It's a power thing with Roy. You know the story from that murder up there in Coweta County. You read that book? It was Roy's Uncle John Wallace who did the killing. There was this here newspaper woman, editor, or something like that, Margaret Anne Barnes or somebody like that, who wrote all about it. She wrote this here book. She's from somewhere around here. I heard tell that it was a best seller. It's called <u>Murder in Coweta County</u>. Well, Roy's mother, Lura, was John Wallace's sister, his Mama was a Strickland, and them Wallace and Strickland folks took the law into their own hands; would kill you at the blink of an eye and show no mercy. But all of that meanness and lust for power came strictly from the Strickland side, not from the Harrell side of the family, you understand. We, the Harrells, are a kind and peaceable lot." Mr. Harrell waited for an "Amen!" Simon didn't understand.

136

"Roy's grandmother, Miss Myrt, was a Strickland. Man, she had that mean streak just like them there men, but she was the power. She taught her children and grandchildren everything, even how to be mean, if you know what I mean. Ha, that's funny, my rhyming. Well, you'll hear the story, time and again. The State of Georgia electrocuted Ol' John Wallace and that nearly tore up Miss Myrt and Roy's mother. They never got over it. Them folks somehow went so far as to try to avenge John's execution. They even went after the State people. Roy's just like 'em – mean as a snake. Learned his ways at his grandmother's knee. That's him all right! 'Course now, his mother was a real nice woman and caring, too. She taught school in West Point for 36 years. She was my brother Tom's wife, you know? He was Roy's father.

"Son, and Simon, y'all have to be careful with Roy. He'll take you out. He's out to avenge the treatment that our family dished out to his Daddy, my brother, Tom. Tom was our dear brother and with two sisters ahead of him, and being the second oldest boy, too, he didn't stand much of a chance to be nothing but a "toddler" holding onto Mama's skirt tail. He had the run of the whole place. He was spoiled rotten. He grew up carefree and devil may care. After a while, Mama couldn't do nothing with him. We really were surprised that he ever got married. Of course us Harrell boys didn't seem to fancy marriage at any rate. But only Sam and Tom got married. And Sam got tricked. I should also say that I really got married, too, sort of, but it's only common law but it's recognized in this here state except for me and Rosa, ours is illegal. I don't have no piece of paper to show for it. Most of the people who got married back then don't have no paper to show neither. I didn't even make no public announcement, but it was there for everybody to see. Tom turned out to be no good. He was a gambler, a good one, a poker player, and a crapshooter, sort of like me. I never thought of myself like that before. But he was better at gambling than me. His problem was that he loved it. He shot craps with the po' white trash, lowliest folks alive! And with the nigrahs, too. I got nothing good to say about them, neither. Always adrinking and agambling and acussing, killing and fighting. He was just a no account rural letter carrier and always getting into scrapes. Had a family to take care of. Through his winnings from shooting crap and that mere pittance of a salary he got from the Post Office, he was able to make ends meet. He didn't understand that you couldn't run around with lowlife folks and high hat them either, especially in public. They will kill your ass. He couldn't even bring them home with him. Mama and my sisters would no longer suffer the constant embarrassment coming out of his tomfoolery. So they voted him out of the Will. Nothing was left to him. Not one red copper. He became dejected and was worse than before.

"Word come in that he had been kilt. Seems like he had won the pot and decided to quit because he had won most of the money anyway, got up and walked away but still taunting the biggest loser. He boasted that he had screwed this guy's wife. That sonovabitch pulled out his .44 and blew Tom to kingdom come. In the back. We, the family, was all broken up. Now this was one version. There have been many and we really don't know what to believe, but they had the trial in Lafayette, Alabama, and his killer was convicted.

Everybody hates to lose a loved one no matter how. Further embarrassment fell over the family and nothing was done to reinstate Tom's inheritance meaning that nothing would be left to his widow and family. Our family could act small like this at times. I thought I had cleared matters up by allowing Roy to be the executor but he wanted it all if for no reason other than he had been denied and deprived because of how his father was treated. No question that Roy and his family suffered. Roy will get it all if y'all ain't careful. Do you hear me? But he was driven to do this, driven."

"Now where's Roy? He should've been here by now."

"No sense in getting started yet. Let's wait until he gets here before we start. Let's have a Co-Cola."

"Couldn't be here on time, folks," Roy said as he burst into the office. Roy never apologizes. "One of my houses burned down last night, goddammit! It was half gone by the time that sorry bunch of excuses for firemen got there to put it out," he said in utter disgust. "The trouble is they need telephones over there in the colored section to call in cases of emergency but them Laniers and their Interstate Telephone Company won't put enough phones in for the nigrahs for some reason. Don't they realize they could put in a thousand phones in and make a whole lot of money? It's just plain stupid. Them bastards just love to talk. What y'all cooking up here, Uncle Burrell?"

"Roy, we gonna redo the Will. That first one we did had nothing in it for my children. I am gonna tear it up. I don't know what I was thinking of. Where is it at? I want it to say so right in the Will itself, you understand me?"

"Of course I do, Uncle Burrell. I got the Will right here. I told you before that I would take care of everybody at the right time."

"I remember now but nevertheless, I want it spelled out. Is that OK with you?"

"Why, yes Sir. We should get on with it right now because I got some other business to take care of because of the fire."

"Simon, go over it with Roy. Roy, you still going to be the executor, but I want, Son, John Thomas to you, to be in on this from now on. Understand?"

"Not a problem at all, Uncle Burrell," Roy said. "By the way, what's been eating you lately?"

"Me? What do you mean by 'What's been eating you lately?' I should be asking you that question. Should something be eating me? I just have a sneaking feeling that you won't carryout my wishes," Uncle Burrell was never one to mince words. He was livid.

"Just a minute! Haven't I always been faithful to you, Uncle Burrell? I'm doing your duties right now by taking good care of those 'dollies' as you call them. Haven't I even taken care of you when you couldn't do for yourself? Who's putting this foolishness and all of these crazy ideas in your head? I have always been loyal to you," Roy puffed feigning that he was truly hurt. "Who's been putting me down?"

"But why didn't you take care of things the way I asked you to the first time? What went wrong? Tell me," Uncle Burrell demanded.

"Taking care of what - the farm or the Will?

"You know I'm talking about, the Will! That's what I'm talking about! You just trying to confuse me." Uncle Burrell ranted.

"I reckoned you trusted me so I didn't have to go to all of the trouble of dotting every 'i' and crossing every '*t*.' Anyhow, I was going to work directly with your boys to make sure that they were satisfied when the time came." Roy could never bring himself to call them his cousins or by name as they really weren't raised to think of his Uncle Burrell's children as kinfolks because in his mind they were simply "nigrahs' and no matter how white they looked, they were still just plain nigrahs. "I am really hurt, Uncle Burrell. I didn't know that you felt this way about me. I still don't understand then because you signed, not initialed, every one of them sheets in the Will. Look at your copy."

"Roy, I'm saying we are gonna do it different this time so we won't have the kind of squabbles or misunderstandings that we having right now. I also want Simon to draw up a codicil, that's what they call it when you are making changes to the existing Will, and I want a signed copy in John Thomas' hands. He's going to be looking out for his brothers and sisters' interests," Uncle Burrell declared. "I am still the head of this family and don't you forget it. Somehow though, I get the feeling that you're disrespecting me." Uncle Burrell's temper seldom flared of late but he felt that things were going on behind his back and there was nobody to shore up his interests. He was aware that he was not the man he used to be. He was not seeing after the crops like he used to. When harvest time came, he was not out there running the show. In fact, he was gone for long periods of time from the Big House. The sisters were always uneasy as to his whereabouts – afraid that something had happened to him. Somebody else was supposed to be taking care of the business. But who? He had been hoping that it was Roy, but then again Roy had his own businesses and full-time job to attend to. He believed that John Thomas was still doing his chores even though he never really had entrusted John Thomas with the overall responsibility for the farming business, but who had really been minding the store? Was the cotton being picked on time and was it being baled so that it could get to market on time? How about the grain? Was it still being harvested and stored in the bins and silos for feeding the cattle for the next season? Just who was in charge? Why had it all gotten this way? Didn't May always make the payroll? What's the matter? Didn't his overseers know what to do? If not, whose fault was it? He held his thoughts for a moment. Maybe it was his. Certainly it was his responsibility. He knew that he had stayed away from the fields far too long but that was no excuse for the others not to do their work. He was still paying them. These were the days when he went on his drinking binges and without the headman around, and with nobody seemingly in charge, nearly every facet of the business was sloughed off. Couldn't a guy take a day off for a change? Or have a little fun? But these were not merely days, but sometimes weeks at a time. But where was he? Those in the know didn't have to guess – he was over at his Rosa's, at home where he wanted to be. John Thomas took care of his area but dared not interfere with what was solely Mr. Burrell's domain, that is, who was supposed to take care of this? The weight of Mr. Burrell's world was coming down on him, as he had not prepared his successor.

"Not so fast, Uncle Burrell," Roy said. "If you don't trust me, why don't you just put your John Thomas in charge, right now?" Roy demanded, standing up quickly. "Why did you call for me to come up here anyways? I get so damn tired of the family accusing me and questioning me about all I'm not doing for them. What is the real problem? What is it? You can't carry out your duties as you promised Grandpa you would, can you? I don't need you to tell me everything to do. Any damn fool can see that you can no longer provide for your sisters, either, and that woman you have kept all of these years. I know it's tough. Me and Bubber have been helping out to the extent we needed to and it's a strain. We got families of our own. I know. I lost my Dad at 17 just like you did. I have been the man of the house for my mother and my brother and sister but still providing what I can for my Aunties and you. And this is all the thanks that I get. Who pays your bills? You? From what? That land? No, Mr. High and Mighty Burrell Floyd Harrell, His Highness. It's been me and Bubber and mostly me." Roy was fighting mad but feigning his hurt. Too much was at stake for him just to walk away and he was fully aware of it.

"You've been waiting a long time to say your piece, haven't you boy? You rascal you!" Uncle Burrell shot back. "Just simmer down yourself and get on with the business of why we are here. Now you just sit down, don't get all huffy with me, and let's finish this up, right now!" Uncle Burrell was firm and felt good that he seemed to have been taking charge again. Roy backed off a mite. Simon was quiet as any good lawyer would be under the circumstances, but he had to be more than that – a peacemaker, confidant, and stood to see how Mr. Burrell

141

Harrell's properties were going to be disposed of. He was letting things play themselves out.

"Roy, just calm down," said Uncle Burrell. "No need for you to get all riled up. You know why you've been chosen. You the eldest living male of the next generation. Bubber's next. Then, it's John Thomas. This involves all of the family's properties, not just mine, and rights. John Thomas can't represent them and y'all know why. This system like it is would not allow John Thomas to run the show nor would the rest of our family. Neither would those who are identified as colored be accepted by the courts, the legal profession, or the business folks. I don't like it but that's the way it is." John Thomas knew this as well, so he made no effort to push it. "Now can we get on with it?" Uncle Burrell demanded. Roy held his tongue. "I say, can we?" Uncle Burrell uttered once again directing his ire at Roy.

"All right, let's go on," Roy said in deference to his Uncle and now asserting his apparent ascendancy to the head of the family. "But I ain't gonna be no hero. You made this mess Uncle Burrell and you ain't going to stick me with it."

"Simon, read it to him just like we worked it out." Uncle Burrell went on.

Simon started reading Mr. Harrell's wishes droning on from one line to the next, only looking up every once in a while to gauge Roy's reactions to what he was reading. Roy didn't interrupt as he would frequently do when in a contest.

John Thomas sat by checking for reaction from all around and finally said, "Mr. Burrell, I don't have to hear all of this. Just have it put on paper and I will carry out my part, I promise."

"John Thomas, goddammit, you are going to have to get used to dealing with white folks outside of the farm!" scolded his Daddy. "Roy is a good one to learn from"

"He won't be learning a goddam thing from me, Uncle Burrell, 'cause I ain't gonna to teach him nothing! In fact, I don't think I want to have anything to do with him or anybody else in that family. I don't believe in this whole race mixing stuff. I'm going my own way." Roy stood up as if to leave. Sweat was pouring from his crimson face. He was mad as hell and he was not faking it this time. His eyes reddened and his blood vessels were protruding more than ever on his neck and forehead.

"I thought I told you to sit down, boy, and that means stay down until we finish, Roy! Goddammit!" Uncle Burrell was beside himself again. "Let's don't make this no harder than it really is. I ain't asking you to teach him a damn thing. He can learn from you just by looking at the way you clown and how you carry yourself especially when you making a fool of yourself just like you're doing right now. Go ahead, Simon!"

"Mr. Harrell, I'm just going to read from notes," Simon said. "It will take too long if we want to get out of here anytime soon. So here goes. Well, just to refresh anybody who needs it, sister May gave her share to Mr. Harrell. The Will must state this. Now everybody agrees that Mr. Harrell owns the entire place called 'Rose Hill Place.' It was conveyed by warranty deed listing Mrs. C. A. Harrell, Grantor, to B. F. Harrell, Grantee. That was recorded on February 10, 1915 and it was noted, 'Love and Affection.' The description of the property was as follows: "All that part of the land Number 235 and 224 as lies south of the old Columbus Road (now Chipley) better known as the 'Rose Hill Place' in the 5th District of Troup County containing 253 acres, more or less. That's where he and his family, I mean where his family lives."

The subject of race in America is not an easy one. It can have a socially constructed meaning, or it can be considered a biological construct. But which is correct? It is probably safe to say that a great many people believe that there are only biological races among humans; for example, some believe that if a "white" and a "black" produced an offspring, that offspring would be a biological "black;" however, it has been proved conclusively that there is no such thing as a scientifically constructed biological race; therefore, race, per se, is a nonentity and does not exist among humans. On the face of it, it really does not make good sense to believe that such an admixture could be characterized as one or the other races.

Now was the time that a white Harrell descendant, Roy, with witnesses, especially family, had to recognize the "Winstons," although "non-white," as a family element associated with them even though it was through Uncle Burrell. The Harrell family's face to the white community was that Burrell's family did not exist although it was widely known that Burrell had "colored children." Within the family, Burrell was castigated for his having been a "wrong" doer, but who was so direly needed for their own well being that whatever Burrell did or said was gospel. Among themselves, they could not accept Burrell and Rosa's relationship as a "husband-wife" affair and accused Burrell as taking advantage of that "colored" woman, "shamefully by giving her all of those babies."

"Mr. Harrell wants Rose Hill to go to his boys," Simon droned on. "There were two properties that were acquired from the Hoggs by Mr. Harrell. It didn't matter how he acquired them, it's legal. One is to be given to Roy and his family and the other is to be given to Mr. Harrell's girls, Rosa Belle and the rest of them. Miss Verne was next. She willed you her share, Mr. Roy," calling him by name to keep his attention from straying.

"You know damn well that that's not the way it was!" Roy clamored. "I was to be given Rose Hill. Uncle Burrell, speak up!"

"Roy, have some damn sense. Stop making a fool of yourself. Does it really make any kind of sense to you that I was leaving nothing to my family?" Uncle Burrell thundered. "You didn't understand what you were to do or you didn't want to understand it."

"I'll just sit here and be quiet then and do whatever in the hell I'm told if that's OK by everybody. OK? And especially if it's OK by you, Mister John Thomas?" spoken with so much rage and venom as to splatter sputum across the table, expressing utter contempt for John Thomas. Then he slammed down both hands on the table with such force that the windowpanes rattled.

John Thomas pondered how should he respond to this tirade, or should he just keep quiet. He knew either way he was going to be attacked by Roy in some manner, so he had better head it off at the pass right now. He stood up, dwarfing everybody at the table and said, "Roy, I am your Uncle Burrell's own flesh and blood. By rights, I should be the executor and sole beneficiary of his estate and I should shoulder the responsibility to see to it that my father's wishes are carried out in the way he wants them to be. Right now, everything is in his name. Now we can work together if you want or we can leave it to a court to decide. In addition, you have been disrespecting him. That's got to stop, right now! He's still the head of our family. Now if you want to make something out of it, why don't you step outside?" John Thomas was really asking for it. He had just lumped Roy into the family with him by saying "our family."

Roy was fuming by having, in his own mind, a "nigger" talk to him like that.

"First of all, don't you call me 'Roy', boy! It's 'Mister Roy' to you! You understand me?"

John Thomas coolly responded, "I shouldn't have a problem in returning the respect, just a few minutes ago, you called me 'Mister John Thomas.' I've already invited you outside to settle this; the invitation still stands, Roy. Or should I say "Mister Roy?" Understand, you are just a nephew. *I* am a *son*. I've got more Burrell Harrell blood in me than you."

"Just where in the hell do you think you are, boy?" Roy said fuming. "This is the Ol' South boy, goddammit, and you are a bastard and therefore, you don't count, and speaking of the courts, every court in this here land would side with me."

John Thomas bristled at being called a "bastard" and was really ready to settle the score right then and there. He was furious. "For your information," directing his comments to Roy again, "Georgia law recognizes so-called 'bastards' or illegitimate children. It makes me no less a relative than if my mother and Mr. Burrell had a marriage license. Get your facts straight, boy!" Calling an adult a "boy" was always insulting no matter who delivered it. "I don't consider myself a bastard," said John Thomas. "My mother and father live together as a family with their children. All of us are whole. We are all OK with ourselves."

Simon, the lawyer decided that he had better jump in at this point before things really got totally out of hand. Mr. Burrell was just sitting by being amused. He was proud of his boy. He didn't realize that John

145

Thomas could be so forceful. He didn't take into account that John Thomas didn't know really how to be afraid of "white folks." He had been shielded from so many of the ways of the Ol' South by his Daddy that he didn't have a clue that he was putting his life in grave jeopardy, blood relative or not, without the sanction of the law.

"Gentlemen," said Simon, "please calm down. Pretty please. I am doing this job not just for family but I am the one who is to see to it that the revised Will, the codicil, is legal and I will put it in final form, as I know Mr. Harrell wants it. Mr. Roy, I am still going to keep you as the executor but I would like to suggest that you maintain a very cool head from now on. I know that you really don't want it done this way but it's the only practical way for it to be. That's what the man wants, why continue to fight it. We don't want to get the ladies involved especially with these kinds of outbursts. This kind of carrying on can tear up your whole family. Mr. Roy, again, you should to go along with this if you want anything for your own family or yourself other than what your Aunts are willing to you now. Your Aunt May has now put everything in Mr. Harrell's hands. He may want to leave you something extra, too. Remember your Dad didn't have a share or stake in any of this. He really gave up his rights to everything based on his mother's, your Grandmother's insistence because of the large debts he ran up. She paid them off and he gave up his share of the inheritance for that. I have my instructions. It had nothing to do with his character. Do you want to remain as the executor and be willing to maintain a calm stance or shall we force the system to deal with John Thomas? It'll be wild but you know things are changing all around us. We are about to move into the '60's. So let's get back to work," Simon pleaded being just about spent and at his limit of patience and forbearance. Then again, he wanted to be paid.

"And oh, Mr. Roy, I have a piece of paper here that you may not be aware of. I plumb nearly forgot it, that's the way y'all say it, right? How am I doing with the language of the South? Pretty good, huh? It was kind of surprising to me when I first saw it. It's a Quit Claim deed where your father, Tom, granted to your grandmother. It says he relinquished his "entire interest in the estate of B. W. Harrell late of said county, deceased, as one of the heirs of the said B. W. Harrell, the interest herein conveyed being all of my right, title and interest, claim

146

and demand on said Estate of whatever it may contain and where ever found." It was dated November 30, 1901 and recorded on December 29, 1901. There were no conditions stated. It appeared that there was no coercion or anything of the sorts. The consideration was for the value received, money or what? It's puzzling. Is this how he was cut out of the properties? What else did 'Mama' hold over him? This had to be the act of 'disinheritance.' It was well before Uncle Tom was killed. In fact, before you were born. So the talk of her thinking that his issue had been sufficiently rewarded by the amount of money she spent to prosecute George Cummings was just a fabrication. Interesting though."

"I want to say this," Roy said rather coolly for a change, "I may be the hothead here but I have taken a hell of a lot of crap and abuse from this entire family. I don't intend to keep taking this crap. Goddamit! . . . . . . Aw, what's the damn use? Wrap it up! I am sure that I can work with this here boy or anybody else except that crazy, uppity, tall ass sis . . ."

John Thomas was still standing and stared menacingly at Roy. Roy was about to speak disparagingly of Rosa Belle, Uncle Burrell's eldest child, and John Thomas was ready to defend her honor on the spot. In spite of all of this, Roy had already prepared himself as to how he was going to carry out the probate when the time came. In the end, he would be the one to tell this lawyer what to do, as he would be the senior Harrell male surviving his Uncle Burrell. Now having the necessary power, the big drawback on his new found joy was that it was he who would have to support and see after the welfare of his Aunts. That's how things should have been done in the first place. It never should have been seen as a problem in his mind in the first place, he had now come to realize. All he had to do as to keep his nose clean, and mouth shut, go along with things that didn't matter for who was going to challenge him after Uncle Burrell died? He felt relieved. He now had a strategy and was almost in charge of everything at this very moment. He felt good. The air had been cleared literally, seemingly only because he had just taken a very deep breath. Roy continued to muse for the rest of the session.

"It's a good day, Uncle Burrell. A very good day!" Roy sighed, but smiling. The others looked at one another and wondered what in the world had come over Roy. Now they really had cause for concern, but what?

Roy's distaste for Rosa Belle went back to the time when her husband, Walt, was having a rough time making ends meet. Roy in his "kindness" had offered Rosa Belle a job working for him. She thought that it would be a position in his real estate business but it turned out to be as a maid to his family. Who had ever heard of any colored working in a real estate office no matter how white they looked? Rosa Belle was quite incensed but took the job as the funds, though a mere pittance, were sorely needed. She had nothing but trouble working for him as she would have had working for any white, especially because he was a first cousin and she looked just as "white" as he did.

Their encounters were frequent. One day she opted to "sass" him. Her very presence irritated him. She was tall and with strikingly keen features of the upper class, well-bred white ladies, yet she was just a farm girl and a "colored" one at that. He was eight years her senior. She had the audacity to call him "white trash." This hurt, coming even from her. Roy hauled off and tried to strike her but she bristled and dared him; furthermore, she declared that she was going to tell Mr. Burrell and get him cut out of any inheritances. Their paths deliberately never crossed again for several years.

"Well done, Simon," his Mr. Harrell said, as he was quite pleased with the outcome of the meeting. "Simon, I just want you to make sure that John Thomas has a true copy of this, probate it if he wants to, so he can pass it around to his brothers and sisters so they can know what's coming to them."

"I'll certainly do that," Simon said. With that Simon handed the will to Mr. Harrell and cousins, Roy and John Thomas, and said that it should be notarized and filed. It reads as follows:

ITEM ONE

It is my will and desire that my body be buried in a Christian-like manner, the place and details I leave to my family.

ITEM TWO

It is my will and desire that all my just debts be paid as soon as practicable after my death.

ITEM THREE

I will and bequeath and devise all of my property both real and personal, to my Nephew, Roy Wallace Harrell, and my sons, John Thomas Winston, Gaines Tyrone Winston, George Frank Winston, Alfred Gordon Winston, and James Floyd Winston, and to my daughters, Rosa Belle Winston Parker, Marguerite Winston Adams, Precious Winston Brooks, and Mary B. Winston Fannings to be theirs for and during their natural lives and at their death the remainder to be distributed as hereinafter directed.

More specifically, I will that the remainder of the property known as "Rose Hill Place" not previously conveyed and occupying so much of Land Lots 235 and 224 in the 5th Land District, Troup County, Georgia, to my sons as listed above. This property is fully described in Plat Book 9, Page 122. I will to my daughters as listed above that property known as the Hogg property, south of Georgia State Highway 18 occupying Land Lot 224 and divided by Georgia State Highway 103. The remainder of my property, I will to my nephew, Roy Harrell and to be distributed as indicated below.

It is also my will that my sons, John Thomas Winston and Alfred Gordon Winston, provide care for their mother and my life long companion, Rosa Rutledge Winston, with proceeds heretofore provided.

ITEM FOUR

I will and direct that my nephew, Roy Wallace Harrell, shall have the full right, power and authority to sell any portion of the property of which I may die seized and to use the proceeds thereof should it, in his judgment, be necessary that such be done to resolve any outstanding matters which require settlement.

ITEM FIVE

I, will, bequeath and devise the remainder of the property, after the death of my nephew, Roy Wallace Harrell, to be his in fee simple, directing however, that he retain the interest in the Harrell Plantation and that the plantation be kept together and carry out my wishes known to him.

ITEM SIX

I hereby make and appoint Roy Wallace Harrell, executor of this will. Should he be unable or unwilling for any reason to act, I appoint John Will Johnson, Jr. who shall act with the full power and authority granted herein. They and neither of them shall be required to make any inventory of my property and appraisement, or from giving any bond, the only requirement being that this will be probated, and they are further relieved from making any returns of their acts and doings to any court whatsoever.

This the 15th of September 1959.

The Will or codicil was signed typically in Burrell's flowing cursive signature: "Burrell F. Harrell"

Declared, published, signed and sealed by Burrell F. Harrell, as his last will and testament, in the presence of the undersigned as witnesses, he first signing in our presence, and we, then, at this special instance and request, signing in his presence and in the presence of each other.

This the 15th day of September 1959

Signature blocks for the following persons were affixed:

/s/ Loeb C. Ketzky

150

Courtesy, Troup County Historical Society

The Rutledge House

Courtesy, Chattahoochee Valley Historical Society

Maull-Harrell House

West Point High School.

HIGH SCHOOL
West Point, Georgia

Courtesy, Chattahoochee Valley Historical Society

West Point, Georgia Circa 1930

Troup County Court House LaGrange, Georgia

and Confederate Memorial   - circa 1890s

Lillie Rutledge

Belle Rutledge

Lovett and Belle

Winston circa 1920

Thomas Gordon Harrell 1879-1920

Burrell, Ethel, and Verne (circa 1890)

Rosa Rutledge Winston   (1891 -1977)

Samuel Cheatham Harrell   (1892 -1925)

Belle's 95th birthday celebration with daughters Rosa, Lizzie, Caroline, Martha and great grand daughters.

Rosa Belle as "debutante" circa 1920s

Rosa Belle circa 1980s (1911-2003)

George Frank (Sug) Winston-Harrell at the Helm
(1916 - 1970)

Marguerite Winston-Harrell Adams
(1919-1991)

Marguerite with son, Ray and daughter, Brenda 1950s

Precious as school girl to College Freshman

Precious escorted by Nephew, Pearson

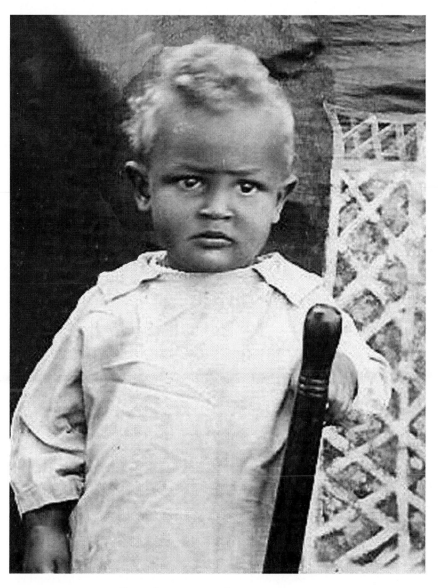

John Thomas at three years old

John Thomas in school "uniform" of the day

John Thomas as star basketball player
and Graduate -- TSHS -- 1944

John Thomas Winston-Harrell
(1923-2002)

Mr. and Mrs. John (Ardell) Thomas Winston

John Thomas

Alfred Gordon   James Floyd
(late 1920s – early 1930s)

Master Sergeant Alfred Gordon Winston-Harrell
(1924-1969)

James Floyd Winston-Harrell
(1926-1968)

Belle and Bob Rutledge- siblings (circa 1960)

Mary Bessie Winston as a teen

Miss TSHS, Mary, with attendants; l-r, Mary Alice Hunter,
Dorothy Wright, Minnie Tatum and Hettie Lou Canady

Mary and Jim Fannings

Mary with daughter, Beverly, and son, Jim Jr.

Jim and Mary flanking CME Church Members

Mr. and Mrs. Jim E. (Patsy) Fannings (center) and parents,
Elbert and Nanny Fields (left) and Mary and Jim E. Fannings Sr.

Miss Eberhardt, Z. Carr, A. Billingslea, R. Chappelle, R. Canady, J. Wright, E. Johnson, C. Winston, D. Hodo, M. Burton, H. Canady, E. Weston, J. Davidson, F. Canady, J. B. Phillips, **Mary Bessie Winston,** E. Johnson, C. Parham, **Gaines Tyrone Winston,** A. Pittman, N. Schell, *Rear:* G. Thomas, G. Bonner, Mary Davidson, K. Billingslea, D. Wright, J. Brooks, L. Hatchett, A. Williams, Forrester Davidson

Mr. Elmer Gould, Prin., Elzatie Johnson, James Schell,
Pearl Lee, Charles Winston

Class of

Ola Lea Hodo, **Alfred Winston**, Louise Summers, Miss Ann Johnson, Class Advisor, Alzora Johnson, Calvin Brown, and Julia Pearl Davidson

1945

Rear: Elmer Gould, M.A. Hill, E. Parham, F. Canady, E. Billingslea, **Mary Winston**, Lilla Winston, Emma Johnson, Mrs. C. Gordon
Front: A. Ransom, C. Parham, H. Lee, N. Schell, B. Hudmon, E. Johnson, C. Lovelace. W. Burton, **Jim E. Fannings**

Class of 1947

Master Sergeant Gaines Tyrone Winston -- 1960's

Gaines and Drinking Buddies at Ft. Jackson, SC - 1951

/s/ Annie Jane Davis

/s/   Mrs Otis Williams

John Thomas also looked over the Will that had been passed on to him at the end of the meeting. "Remember, John Thomas, you can have this one probated if for no other reason than to get it on the record. That's what Mr. Harrell said. You heard him," said Simon. John Thomas did not recall that Mr. Burrell said that but that was OK with him. After his review, he thought that this was not only good but also guaranteed them some of the property that Mr. Burrell was going to distribute.

Alfred had talked with Roy from time to time as to how the land was to be issued to the heirs including him and his brothers and sisters. Alfred and Roy got along quite well and Alfred trusted him implicitly. Roy swore that he would always do right by them. John Thomas demurred but told Alfred that it would be his responsibility to get the new Will probated. Alfred was a peacemaker and saw to it that all of the sisters and two other brothers knew what was coming to them.

From all indications, this will was never notarized, filed, nor probated, and none of the properties was ever conveyed, leaving only the 10.4 acres more or less as previously conveyed to the sons. It was said that John Thomas had kept his copy of the Will and never brought it forward but retained it among his papers. John Thomas even concealed important papers from his wife. A thorough search of John Thomas' files turned up no papers of this kind. Any formal demand by the family would not be heard if these papers were not found. Daughter Mary declared that she had had the will in her hands written in longhand by Mr. Burrell himself. She herself had reviewed it because Mr. Burrell wanted to know if she thought the parcels of properties being left to the girls was fair. She thought so. John Thomas, as the story goes, was supposed to be coordinating all of this documentation but somehow it disappeared never again to be seen by the light of day.

151

Chapter 12. The Interchange at State Road-18

"Uncle Burrell," Roy said rather cordially and respectfully but playfully for the first time after the meeting adjourned to Bubber Johnson's office. "I hear that the State's done got in touch with you to buy some of your land to finish up the Interstate that's connecting us to Alabama. That's going to be a big deal, you know that?"

"Roy, where do you get all of your information? Have you been poking your nose in to my business again without me asking you to?" Uncle Burrell demanded.

"Well, you know I am following in your footsteps, Uncle Burrell. I want to be a big land baron just like you. Seeing as how they need to come through your lands, you are going to need a lot of help on your side. I can provide that, and you need me. You know also that the Federal Government is involved and it takes them a helluva long time to get everything done. The Feds provide about 90 per cent of the money for these here projects. You know how many years they been hung up with that stretch between West Point and the Alabama state line? Well, the word is out that you are the holdout; you bucked them, and the cause of that delay. They may be out to get you. The State may even condemn your land and give you next to nothing for it."

"Roy, I'm not worried about that part but while we're all here why don't we talk about it," Uncle Burrell said. "Let me just tell you up front Roy, your cousin, Bubber Johnson, has already agreed to be my lawyer on this project. Word's out that some young thing up there in the LaGrange office feeds you everything you want to know. You might just be good for the team with that kind of connection but you better be careful."

"Nothing of the kind, but I do have my connections," Roy admitted. "And they're all reliable."

"You may as well know, Roy, that my boy here, John Thomas, is already in on it, too. We must get along, you hear?" Uncle Burrell knew that he needed Roy what with all of the responsibilities he would soon be unable to attend to.

"Bubber. Why don't you start out by telling everybody what we learned so far?

"But before you do, Bubber, why don't you have one of them dollies in there to go over to Nader's Café and get us some sandwiches and Co-Colas. You can add this to your tab," Uncle Burrell chuckled.

"Yes Sir, right away."

"Hold on," Roy said. "I've got to go over to see about my property."

"You can't go," Uncle Burrell said. "And if you want to get involved in this Interstate Highway thing, you'd better hang around. I admit that they have waited too long already."

"Uncle Burrell, get smart. They have no choice but to come to you. Alabama has already finished up its part. The State of Georgia itself has been stalling. The politicians in Troup County are trying to get in on the act and if we are to get our share out of this we must get the ball rolling. The bridges across the Chattahoochee and the Long Cane Creek need to get built and connected; that will cost a mint. These by themselves involve hundreds of thousand of dollars. One of the biggest items is that the interchange is right on your property and they have to buy right of way and a lot of it. The State and the Federal Government have budgeted over $5, 000,000 for this stretch of the Interstate." Roy comes to realize that he is talking too much.

Shortly afterwards, the sandwiches and Coca-Colas arrive. Roy excuses himself for a moment and this gives Bubber a chance to advise Uncle Burrell on including Roy in the Project.

"Uncle Burrell, Roy has been passing himself off as a principal in this project and for the good of all why don't we reschedule this meeting so that Roy can go and attend to his business. We may not be able to include him at all and certainly not at this time."

153

Roy returns quickly, sits down and starts to eat his sandwich. The other three look at each other and Bubber says, "I guess we had better get on with it. Here is what they want in general. Uncle Burrell, they are not sure how many acres of land they will need. It must be close to 500 maybe even more. The big problem is that the Long Cane Creek meanders all over the place and they are thinking that the course of the creek will have to be changed. That's where the cost of the project is going to skyrocket. Now as you know, that creek is pretty valuable to you and the others around here because you use the waterpower to run your gristmill and the cotton gin. You could be put out of commission from months to years. This is where most of your current cash is coming from. You have the opportunity to get a whole lot of money for the property that they will have to dig up, to say nothing about the loss of revenue from the mill. We are talking about in the hundreds of thousands of dollars. Maybe up to a million. We are going to have to play it cagey and start operating like them damn Yankees.

"Roy, I hear that they have already made you an offer for your land. What's happening? Can you tell us anything?" asked Bubber.

"Not really, Bubber, I'm not supposed to talk about it until they settle with Uncle Burrell."

"Sounds to me like they already decided what's what. You not selling us out, are you boy?" Uncle Burrell demanded.

"Uncle Burrell, with all due respect, don't ever accuse me of selling out the family's interest to nobody in no way," Roy's sounding conciliatory. "All I was trying to do was to get a good deal for me once you guys settled. I already knew that they had started talking to you. I was hoping that you would let me in on it so that we could work together. And we still can, can't we?"

"Roy, I just wish that you would stop going off so half-cocked. And about 'selling us out,' are your interests the same as the family's?" asked Uncle Burrell. "It seems to me that I determine the family's interests, not you."

"OK, let's look at these drawings and specs." Bubber laid out scads of maps and specifications on the conference table. "We all need to study these and understand just what they are after. We know what they are demanding, so why don't we fold our tents and meet at Uncle Burrell's at seven o'clock sharp tomorrow morning. This way, we can walk the property and discuss at the same time anything that will be bothering us. John Thomas? You coming with us?" Bubber asked.

"Wouldn't miss it for anything in the world," John Thomas said. "I recommend that you wear long sleeves, some ducking pants, wide brim hat, and brogan shoes. There are lots of thorns and briars out there. It's not much more than a big briar patch anyway. You city boys may not survive it."

"John Thomas, don't try to tell me what to do! If I ever need anything from you, I'll ask you, you understand?" Roy shouted angrily.

"Roy, you promised to work together with me just a few minutes ago. Please," begged John Thomas. "Please."

Mr. Burrell smiled. "All of these disagreements can't be good for a 71-year old heart."

John Thomas was the one to take the road drawings and specifications home with him that evening. Right after supper, John Thomas invited his brother Alfred with his encyclopedic mind to come over to review the drawings and specifications and the Government's proposal to Mr. Burrell with him. After they fully understood the project, they would be ready for the morning meeting.

It was September of 1961. The State was no longer waiting for Mr. Harrell to do his thing. It had already seized the land it needed. The only real actions left were to settle on the price of the land. The local sheriff had already served papers on Mr. Harrell to appear for trial and allow a jury to fix the payout.

The Federal Interstate Highway System was revitalized in the Eisenhower Administration in 1954. It was devised in the beginning because more and more drivers were taking to the road to include even pleasure driving. Some was for business but more for casual travel and vacations. The old, existing Federal highway system was no longer adequate to accommodate modern travel. The long haul travelers didn't want to slow down for every little town around the bend or to buy gasoline and other articles needed when traveling. And the big rig trucks, the eighteen-wheelers, had taken to the highway in competition with the freight train haulers. Just because so many little towns would be bypassed by the new highway system was ground for big battles in the Congress to allow the old roadway system to remain as was. The railroads were into the fray as well because the truckers were now becoming strong competition for moving freight across and around the country.

Interstate 95 initiated this massive national highway construction project in New England, down the East Coast to Florida and ending up in Miami. It was an instant success. Interstate 5 on the West Coast extended through California, Oregon and Washington from Mexico to Canada. Of course there were cross-country interstates but nothing to rival these two extremities. Interstate 95 was seen as a vacation stretch from New York to Florida. What about the interior and all of those cities that were being bypassed in Virginia and the Carolinas, Georgia and other Southeastern states? Their delegation was powerful as its representatives were the ones who had seniority – the key to the control of the Congress. Two powerful Democrat Senators from Georgia, namely, Russell and George, lobbied to get Interstate 85 going. Interstate 85 was designed to head out of Richmond, Virginia and to land in Montgomery, Alabama. This stretch of the highway had already been completed from Montgomery to the Georgia state line at the west bank of the Chattahoochee River. The highway would not have been completely finished until the Georgia segment was done. The construction plodded along from the north and finally reached Georgia. The Georgia Highway Department took over the construction, moving it rather rapidly. Land acquisition was rather easy because the right of ways needed for the highway were mostly rural and could be bought on the cheap. Not a lot of land was needed anyway, as only a three hundred foot-wide swath of land throughout the length of the roadway was required, even though it rearranged the countryside, particularly where there were cattle crossings and service roads were to be maintained. Interstate 75 was being built at the same time as I-85, providing a big drain on the State's budget. Both of these interstates intersected at Atlanta, now unmistakably the hub of the region. The trucking industry was clamoring for interstate bypasses around Atlanta, or at least to have

156

them laid out for future consideration. Although the states were required to provide only five percent of the budget, the till was being drained and local initiatives were suffering. The Feds threatened to withdraw funds if Georgia didn't continue to move forward at the agreed pace.

The local and small town politicians were becoming concerned now that it was very clear that the completion of Interstate 85 would have a severe impact on the local economies. Resistance to kill new bond issues was being instigated until the Governor threatened to withdraw support for projects in the areas affected. That notwithstanding, it was clear that Alabama economies would be stimulated with the completion of the Interstate, and Georgia would suffer as a result. They need not have fretted. All the State had to do was to acquire a relatively small parcel of land to secure the right of way.

The highway had now been completed through LaGrange in Troup County to the then Exit 2. Big black and yellow-striped barricades halted any trespass. "DETOUR" was posted all over the place. Route US 29 was still the King of the Roads! All traffic through to Alabama had to pass through Gabbettville and downtown West Point, the textile capital of the world, and then on to Alabama and points south. This was a slow grind as it was only two narrow lanes, many curves, and local farm traffic used it all day. West Point was probably worth the delay as the entrance to the City on US29 was beautiful. The classically designed West Point High School, completed in 1930, sat majestically atop the highest hill in the area, called "College Hill," in the City overlooking Eighth Street, which had the appearance of a beautiful French boulevard. At the foot of the hill stood a classically sculptured obelisk commemorating the Confederate soldiers whose lives were lost in the Battle of West Point. With your eyes shut, you could imagine a tree-lined thoroughfare channeling into a two-lane steel trestle that spanned the rapidly flowing Chattahoochee River.

There sat downtown West Point, a progressive and prosperous little city of opportunity in the textile industry. Almost everything you needed that was made of cotton pretty much had its genesis right there. This little city was going to be bypassed, and sacrificed for progress. Its savior was going to be none other than one Burrell Floyd Harrell. This never occurred to Burrell, because his only interest was to save the land of his birthplace and keep those carpetbaggers off his land. If he were

157

ever forced to give it up, the authorities would have to pay him dearly. He had already staved them off far too long and he knew it. He often wondered what were they made of. It was time. The time had come for his final thrust, bayonet affixed! Burrell was a "soldier." He would often recall the stories that his father told him about the battles during the War Between the States. He imagined himself defending Fort Tyler to the bitter end.

The partners in contention met up at the Big House in Burrell's room the next morning as planned and discussed a few minor points to orient and brief them as to the lay of the land. Alfred spread the drawings out on that solitary table in his father's room and went through painstakingly each detail he thought was of interest to the State. He pointed out where the project was to start:

"We are talking about a project whose road's length is a little over two and one-half miles. Part of that is the length of the bridges over the Chattahoochee River and the Long Cane Creek. The other bridges over State Highway 18 are overpasses on 'our' property." Alfred's reference to "our property" was a signal to Roy and Bubber that he considered that he was already an owner of the land or at least in line to inherit this property after having been freshly informed by John Thomas as to the contents of the new Will. "The State's only concern is to get enough right-of-way for the road itself and the interchange. They only need 150 feet from the center to each side of the highway, a total of 300 feet across. The total land needed for the overpass and the roadway comes to a little over 24 acres. There has been some talk that the land over to the river is ours too, but Skinner, Beall, and others own the land in between. We have to show that our property is valued a whole lot more than the State has offered. Mr. Burrell, if you are ready, let's go!

"Not so fast," Mr. Burrell said. "Where's that lawyer fellow? Wasn't he supposed to be here, Bubber? He's the one who needs to be filled in on all of this."

"I'm right here Mr. Harrell," answered James R. Lewis, of the Law Firm of Sims & Lewis, LaGrange. "You had a couple of right mean looking dogs daring me to come on your property, Mr. Harrell."

"Don't pay them no mind, they'll only take a big plug out of your behind. Boy, what I want you to understand is I really don't want to part with this here land at all. I know that I am going to have to do that now. Everybody is against me. After I was served them papers, I knew that it was all over. My father handed me down this land. I was born on it. He told me to take care of it and by God, that's exactly what I intend to do. Understand me good now, boy. I don't care how much or how little they take, I want to squeeze every dollar out of them that I can. I want them to pay and pay and pay! Don't try to bamboozle me with all of that legal mumbo jumbo stuff about it's the value of that land that counts. How can they say there's a different value for land? Ain't no more being created, right? So it's all very valuable. It's a scarce commodity. You been to college where they teach you all that shit. Commodity hell. It's all the same dirt. When I first heard that I almost laughed my ass off. You read the file and you know they paid up to $2,000.00 per acre up in there in Coweta County. I'll take that. Get it for me! That's your job, boy!"

"My firm will pull out all stops to get you every penny it's worth."

"Here I'm talking about dollars and you're talking about pennies. Are we on the same track, boy?" Mr. Harrell demanded. "Can't accuse us of thinking big, huh?"

"Y'all ready?" Mr. Burrell Floyd yelled. "Then, what the hell we waiting for, let's go! Charge! Y'all heard the man. Move it!"

Alfred headed the group by leading out with Mr. Burrell. Everybody dressed as John Thomas suggested the day before except for Bubber. He was really a city and a college boy. Never really got his hands dirty. Had been off to the University of Alabama and got himself a law degree. His immediate family was more polished than the rest of them. His Daddy was a merchant and banker in Langdale and more inclined to the finer things of life. His everyday clothes were the "Sunday-go-to-Meetings attire" for the "country" boys. Alfred was familiar with the entire property as he was the "keeper" of Mr. Burrell's records, what few there were.

It was already swelteringly hot at half past seven. Ol' Sol can be very mean in Georgia even in the late spring. "We must make note of all of our access roads and rights-of-way that we need so we can continue to run our businesses out here. Anywhere they need access will be a point for us to get more money for the property. We know that they are going to try to low ball us and try to beat us out of our due wherever they can," said John Thomas. "Like Bubber said yesterday, we'd better be on our toes, otherwise they gonna take us to the cleaners." The camaraderie had grown in the last few days of association. John Thomas no longer addressed John Will as "Mr. Bubber" anymore. Bubber didn't care.

Mr. Burrell was more and more delighted to see how his boys were picking up the reins. But it didn't matter, he realized, because they had no power. He felt that he had prepared them for life after he passed on. Maybe he should have done more. He was right proud of himself. He wanted to caution John Thomas for the way he handled Bubber by not calling him "mister" like the other colored did. But what the hell, he was getting away with it. Things were going to change one day, anyway. Everybody in the pack was now bushed from the walking except for Mr. Burrell and his sons. Roy remained silent. He was taking it all in after he came to the full realization that he was the real power and everybody else were peons and eventually would dance to his tune when the right time came.

As they continued to walk, cockleburs clinging to their pants legs, bramble bushes impeding their progress, each noted that some building, shed, barn, feeding trough, and the like on the property were not included on the drawings. Some access roads were going to be blocked, or that access to the rest of the property would be limited or impassable once the construction got started. Mr. Lewis took copious notes. It was not how much land they took but how they would destroy its value for farming.

"Dadgummit! I didn't think to have water or sodas out here for us when we got to this point. I must be slipping," Mr. Burrell said.

"I got you covered. I already took care of that, Mr. Burrell," John Thomas said. "I guess we're ready to take a break, Sir. We can go over yonder to that shade tree and sit on them benches. We got water and sodas waiting for us. There're some sandwiches, too, for you who missed breakfast. Maw fixed them for us." "Maw" was his mother, Rosa.

160

Mr. Burrell was a leathery cuss. His skin was now deeply tanned from his being constantly in the sun and perhaps by not sparing the bottle. Even now in his mid-seventies, he was still robust though not the man he used to be; however, his muscles were still bulging and taut, his fists as big as cantaloupes. His voice was hoarse now but husky and could still outcuss any sailor. Every now and then he would call for the city boys to keep up. "This ain't child's play", he would say. His khakis and wide brimmed straw hat were the "uniform of the day." Roy, John Thomas, Alfred and Lewis were dressed similarly. Bubber just put on his worst clothes with no headgear but they were still "Sunday-go-to-meetings" insofar as the others were concerned." Alfred was also the scribe. He was full of notes and information that may have been needed for any negotiations between them and for the State and Federal representatives, if need be.

Some items that were found during their walkthroughs around the plantation were not to be noted but cleared out before the state officials came in for their inspection. A few abandoned white lightning stills were found in several areas on the plantation. Some were still functional.

"Have them goddam things cleared out of here before them revenuers come by," Mr. Burrell ordered. "Who knows how long I can keep them away? All of y'all know that since that Federal agent got shot at out here last year, they've been coming down hard on us out here and all around. Any of these stills belong to you boys?" Mr. Burrell asked directing his question to John Thomas and Alfred.

"We can find out who put them here, Sir, and we'll see to it that they be cleared out, Mr. Burrell," Alfred's answer was rather cagey as if he didn't already know. These boys were pros in the moonshine business and quite enterprising themselves for they permitted the use of the land by others for a cut of the profits but never directly involved themselves except for James and Sug. The four cousins looked at each other rather sheepishly as this venture was very common in the area where there were so many branches of water and other small streams. And moonshining was a very good cash business as long as the revenuers could be held at bay. "Sealed" whiskey or "store bought" liquor, was not allowed as the ultra conservative Southern Baptist moralists were dead set against drinking whiskey and home brew, although practically everybody did, even the parishioners, but you have to profess to some scruples.

Alfred reminisced about the "good old days" when the times were so good. The making of moonshine was not difficult, but it was an art. The ingredients were not hard to come by. The fact that moonshining was illegal kept the makers very wary because Federal agents and the sheriff's police force were always on the lookout or prowl for violators and would arrest them on sight. Old folks and women were not allowed, for when a revenuer happened in the vicinity of a still, one had to be fleet afoot, otherwise, he would wind up in the calaboose for a lengthy stay. Even with a good lookout, many distillers were caught. Everything needed for the still was easy to come by as well as the ingredients. It was a business – a big business. Some of the most reputable citizens bankrolled many of the operations. They were the venture capitalists of the day. It was dirty money but easy. The seed and feed stores, P. O. Myhand, and Zachry Brothers, sold all of the right kind of ingredients necessary to make "white lightning" to suit the very discriminating tastes of Troup, Harris and Chambers Counties. There was nothing illegal about the selling of the grains. The wagons would be loaded to the hilt with the necessary grains in 100-pound croaker sacks for processing and headed for home. Of course, the farm animals ate these grains as well. The best stuff was made with corn, corn stalks, sugar cane stalks, and such other non-fruity vegetation that was in the vicinity of the still. Sometimes sassafras roots were tossed in for good flavor, but corn was it. The big time operators used 55-gallon drums as the mash unit. Charcoal was the heating fuel, as it burned hot and long. The heads of the drum were sufficiently sealed to allow steam to escape through the piping or coils, which ran through the cool branch water, condensed, and distilled into a collecting container. These were not fly-by-night operations, and it took days sometimes to produce a sufficient amount of "good" booze for distribution. This was a cash product, from distillation and wholesale to distribution and retail – sold on a "shot" basis. The biggest amount of money was made during World War II. Everybody prospered. Mr. Burrell made a killing at the production end of the business. A review of the Chambers County Superior Court records in the 1920's and 30's showed that 90 per cent of the prosecutions were due to "illegal distillation." Perhaps the worst thing that would happen was for the still to be located by the revenuers and

162

when discovered, they would destroy the entire operation. Moonshining truly was part of the culture.

The troops had just about finished their walk through the fields and now was the time to consider strategy. Eyes turned to Bubber. His practice at the time was limited to insurance matters and claims, local issues in the textile industry, and real estate in the region rather than dealing with State and Federal officials in governmental matters. It was he who thought it best to call in a law firm out of LaGrange that was more familiar with government condemnation proceedings; however, Bubber remained Attorney-in-Fact. James R. Lewis arranged for the meeting to be in his downtown LaGrange law office's conference room. The law office is still located on LaFayette Square in the heart of the City of LaGrange, which is now Duncan, Thomasson et al. The square is beautifully laid out, with water fountains surrounding the inner arboretum, varied flora native to Georgia, with its centerpiece being a statue of the Marquis de Lafayette, the French patriot whose military prowess and contributions were recognized in naming the park.

Lewis opened up the meeting by introducing John Will as the lawyer representing his uncle, Mr. Harrell's interests. John Will in turn introduced his Uncle Burrell and his cousins, Roy, John Thomas, and Alfred. He made special mention of John Thomas and Alfred as sons of his Uncle Burrell who would pursue their father's interests if need be, suggesting that the State should not expect quick resolution of the issues involved if they anticipated Uncle Burrell's imminent demise. Mr. William P. Trotter, the State's counsel for condemnation, acknowledged their presence and shook their hands vigorously and extended the utmost in cordiality. Had Mr. Trotter been aware that the sons were mulattoes, he perhaps may not have been so cordial. He then requested that he be permitted to explain the State's position on the condemnation.

Mr. Trotter warily indicated, "There was perhaps some misinterpretation or misunderstanding, willful or not, as to the State's proposal. It was only an offer, as the State intended to condemn the land by taking only what was minimally needed, and offering what it considered to be a fair price for the land of interest. After all, this was a project in the best interest of the public. So the condemnation is based on its powers of eminent domain. The State in such an instance had preeminence over personal or individual rights." He tersely closed by declaring, "The

State would proceed immediately toward completion of the condemnation, with the settlement determined by the jury through the court system of all properties being sought!"

Mr. Burrell was horrified. "Over my dead body!" he shouted. "These lands have been in my family since the mid 1800's and nobody but nobody's gonna take them from me. Get the suit ready boys. This will never happen. Never!" With that tirade, he stormed out of the meeting. Alfred quickly followed him to keep him as calm as he could. He knew that the discussions would go on without Mr. Burrell.

Now being a bit exasperated, Mr. Trotter said, "the State would proceed to condemnation and forcibly maintain the seizure of the land, as necessary."

"Please don't talk in those terms," John Will said, "as I believe that we can get him to come around. Also, please don't offer these kinds of ridiculous foregone conclusions if you expect cooperation to get things moving rather swiftly toward completing the project. We all can still hang you up."

"He has sat on this proposal for months, Mr. Johnson!" Mr. Trotter exclaimed, still irritated. "Every day, this project is costing tons more money because of his stubbornness and refusal even to consider our fair and reasonable offer."

"Perhaps you should tell us what your "fair and reasonable" offer is, Mr. Trotter," John Will retorted.

"We are offering $145.00 an acre," Mr. Trotter said.

"What!! Only one hundred and forty-five dollars!" John Will, John Thomas, and Roy exclaimed at the same time.

"You have got to be kidding!" John Will said in the manner of an English barrister. "We happen to know that you are paying $2,000.00 per acre up in Coweta County. Perhaps you can tell us why land less than 30 miles away through this same type of scrubby pine, woodsy thickets, and scraggly fields that we see here are worth so much more.

164

Why? You will have to prove to us that your valuation is fair. This is either incompetence or favoritism."

"We don't just make up the numbers, Mr. Johnson," Trotter said. "We have appraisers who are experts and have legions of experience and they have been on this job from the very beginning. In addition, land recently sold in that very same amount."

"Then, therein lies your problem. Who do they work for? The State or is this a private club? The numbers are obviously contrived. All you are trying to do is save the State money at the expense of a little farmer."

"The State," countered Trotter rather meekly, "No, I am not going to answer your questions or respond to your insinuations, Mr. Johnson. We have established procedures for resolving these kinds of issues. My advice to you is to have Mr. Harrell take the monies offered so that we can get on with the project. We all would be the ultimate benefactors. We'll see you in court."

"Thieves," Roy suggested loudly. He was about to become more actively involved in the negotiations until Bubber cautioned him that it was either his or Uncle Burrell's place to speak. Roy became a little put out that Bubber, 17 years his junior, although a lawyer, was trying to chastise him. In the Grand Ol' South, this ain't the way it's done. It shows lack of respect for ones' elders.

"Then, we better get Uncle Burrell back in here," countered Roy. John Will let it go.

"Mr. Trotter," John Will said, "We need to have a session between us before this continues. In addition I want to try to get my Uncle back in here."

"Very well," Mr. Trotter said. "Take all the time you want. This won't be settled in a day, I promise you, although the courts have been very fast on this overall project of late, probably because the Feds have a tendency to pull back monies already allocated. Your Uncle must realize that this project is good for the State."

"If it ain't good for West Point, it ain't good for the State," said Roy. "This proposed roadway will bypass West Point altogether. The City will die. It's the Hub for the Textile industry in this area if not the nation. This is our economic center. It will be a disaster. Business will be taken away and centered farther south in Alabama. I am surprised that you got this far without incurring the wrath of the West Point Manufacturing Company. They're the power in this area."

It could be that the West Point Manufacturing Company would hardly be affected because its interests in Alabama and Georgia were complementary and it saw no distinctions across state lines. It was the community of interests that was the power here.

"Oh, we have heard from them, too often as a matter of fact. You forget, Sir. This is a Federal Project, so we don't make these kinds of distinctions between the States," Mr. Trotter said. "This project has already been delayed with the State's having to withdraw its own allocation as so much difficulty has been encountered by you people here in Troup County.

"Mr. Johnson, perhaps we should wrap this up for today and meet back here tomorrow morning to see if we can't make some headway. Frankly, I am about ready to start another case as this seems to have no genuine local interest."

John Thomas, Alfred, Roy and Bubber tried in vain to convince the old man to lighten his stance. He had previously agreed that he would not raise his hackles anymore. That lasted only minutes. The State was eventually going to have its way. Perhaps the best thing to do was to try to get the politicians to deal with the issue. Burrell came up with the poignant idea of the day. He was going to write Senator Herman Talmadge and tell him that the State was trying to gyp him out of his land. He believed that the Senator owed him a thing or two for his support when the Senator was running for Governor and also in the last major state election.

The Senator dispatched an aide to see Mr. Burrell Floyd Harrell and to find out how he was being "mistreated" by the State. The aide was only to do fact-finding and report back to the Senator. A response in short order was sent back to Mr. Harrell over the Senator's signature

166

promising that he would look into every avenue in trying to save the property, and as soon as that determination was made, the State would contact him with the result of their findings and what action needed to be taken. This bit of news raised Mr. Harrell's spirits somewhat, as he began to realize that he would not be able to stop what these intruders called progress. Senator Talmadge did not respond directly to Mr. Harrell. His answer went directly to the State, resulting in the Department of Transportation's sending the following letter to Mr. Harrell:

EXHIBIT I

October 23, 1961

Mr. B. F. Harrell

West Point, Georgia

Dear Sir:

Mr. Jim L. Gillis, Sr., Chairman of the State Highway Board, has asked me to write you concerning the right-of-way, which it is necessary that the State acquire from you in conjunction with the construction of Interstate Route 85 in Harris County. I also have in hand, your letter to Senator Herman Talmadge wherein you outline your problems, together with a copy of his reply to you in which he stated he was requesting Mr. Gillis to investigate the matter. Since the plans were prepared for this project in my office, Mr. Gillis felt it best that I reply directly to your questions.

It is unfortunate, but nevertheless a fact, that a project of this magnitude cannot be constructed without inconveniencing some of the citizens who own the land it must traverse. In preparing our designs we make every possible effort to minimize the damage to the property we must cross. We realized in crossing your land, the project split the large pasture and farming area into two sections. The majority of your land is located in the Long Cane Creek bottom and the drainage problems in that area are very severe. It is true that a portion of the creek channel must be changed in order for the Interstate Highway to have proper alignment. I can assure you that we will provide sufficient new channel for the creek, to assure you that no land that was not previously inundated by the creek, will be flooded by the construction of the new highway. I can also assure that the twin barrel 8' x 8' concrete box culvert will be constructed north of State Route 18 and can be used by you at low water periods to move cattle back and forth under the new highway. Similarly, a 5'x 4' single barrel concrete culvert will be constructed south of

168

State Route 18. This culvert is also large enough to pass cattle under the new highway at low water.

I understand that, although we have taken title to the right-of—way that we need for the construction, no settlement has been reached with you as to the total amount of money that will be paid for your land. While my office has nothing to do with the negotiations for rights-of-way, I know from previous experience that the men who are in charge of this phase of the work will make every effort to be fair as possible in arranging final settlement with the property owners.

I am enclosing a print of the plan sheet taken from the construction plans on which I have circled in "red" the location of the two culverts I referred to above.

I trust this information will clear up the questions in your mind about how the new Interstate Highway will affect your property. If I can be of further assistance, please do not hesitate to advise me,

Yours very truly,

John M. Wilkerson, Jr.

State Road Design Engineer

JMV:cs

Attachment

Cc:Mr. Jim L. Gillis, Sr.

    Mr. C. A. Curtis

    Mr. J. W. Wade

    Honorable Herman E. Talmadge,

    United States Senator

Mr. Harrell had all but resigned himself that all of his land would be kept by the State, when the State really was only interested in right of way. He thought that he would lose control of his land, and that would be the end of the family's legacy. It was just he and his two sisters left, and what could an old man do to hold back this onslaught on his personal freedom and individual rights. He spent hours poring over drawings and maps of the proposed interchange He was looking for flaws. The letter boosted his resolve so much so that he became active in the preparation of the law suit that he was going to file against the state protesting the outlandishly small amount of money offered for such pristine lands. Three suits were filed.

The day of the trial had rolled around. It was a festive day. Trials of this sort always attracted large crowds particularly when the principal defendant was popular. Mr. Harrell had a tough time keeping up with his entourage on the way to the courthouse. He knew that he should have been leading his troops, but he was now just an "old swashbuckling" codger of 77 years. But he was picking up one foot and putting down the other and somehow he managed to stay abreast of his lawyer. He hadn't been to LaGrange's Courthouse in many a moon. Insofar as he was concerned, the world revolved around his plantation. When he finally looked up to see where he was going, he was startled to see that the beautiful, domed courthouse was no longer there. He asked his lawyer: "Say, boy, what in the hell happened to that fine old building that was standing here?"

It burned a few years ago," Mr. Lewis said. "In 1936 to be exact."

"Hell, that was a long time ago. And this was what they replaced it with?" Mr. Harrell asked unbelievingly.

"Things cost a bit more nowadays, Sir, so they put up a very efficient, modern building. All of those windows let in plenty of light. Saves on energy. Lots of storage space what with all of the records that need to be kept."

"By the way, did they manage to save all the records?" Mr. Harrell asked.

170

"Yes Sir, they did indeed. The citizens banded together and went into that building and saved everything. I'm told that that was really a sight to see," Lewis said. "LaGrange was very dear to them."

"John Thomas, stay close to me now. I may need a little help getting up them steps," Mr. Burrell said. "This old man's 77 year-old legs have walked many a mile and they can still go a few more but these here steps do take their toll."

Chapter 13. The Trial

The State was unable to extract any concessions from Burrell Harrell. He was determined to bring the State to its knees. It had encroached upon his rights and he would not stand for it. He had been done wrong and he would get just compensation no matter the situation. The "Moment of Truth" had arrived.

On August 25th of 1961, the County Sheriff attested as follows:

Georgia, Troup County:

I have this 25th Day of August 1961 served B. F. Harrell personally with a copy of this order.

L. W. Bailey, Sheriff,

Troup County, Georgia

The order read as follows:

IN THE SUPERIOR COURT OF

TROUP COUNTY

GEORGIA

STATE HIGHWAY DEPARTMENT OF GEORGIA

VS.

24.700 acres of land; and **B.F. Harrell** (the names of R. W. Harrell,

Federal Land Bank, and Greenville Production Co. were handwritten on the order.)

TO THE NAMED DEFENDANT-CONDEMNEE AND TO THE PERSON IN POSSESSION OF THE PROPERTY DESCRIBED IN

THE PETITION FOR CONDEMNATION AND DECLARATION OF TAKING IN THE ABOVE STATED CASE; AND TO ALL AND SINGULAR THE SHERIFFS OF THIS STATE AND COUNTY AND THEIR LAWFUL DEPUTIES:

The plaintiff-Condemnor, State Highway Department of Georgia, in the above stated case having brought and filed in said court its petition in rem to condemn the property therein described: and

Having made and filed in said court its Declaration of Taking against said described property, and having deposited with the Clerk of the Superior Court the estimated just compensation for said property in the sum of $7,913.47, all as provided for by that certain act of the General Assembly of Georgia of 1961, approved April 5, 1961, Georgia Laws 1961, approved April 5, 1961 et seq.: and

It appearing to the court that service of such petition and Declaration has been had on the person in possession of said property: and that a diligent and reasonable effort has been made to cause service to be had upon all other persons having any interest in or claim against said property; and

It being provided by said act as follows:

"Upon the filing of declaration of taking, the Court shall have the power to fix the time, the same to be not later than sixty days from the date of the filing of the declaration of taking, as herein provided for, within which and the terms upon which the parties in possession shall be required to surrender possession to petitioner"; and, the plaintiff-Condemnor having applied to the court for immediate possession of the said described property: and an order having been made, requiring the person in possession, and the defendant-Condemnees, as well as all other interested persons, to show cause at the time and place set out in said order why such prayer for immediate possession should not be granted; and such hearing having been had before me on this date,

It is Considered, Ordered and Adjudged that B. F. Harrell/R.W. Harrell, Federal Land Bank, and Greenville PCA, being shown to

173

be the person(s) in possession of said property, do deliver up to the state Highway Department of Georgia not later than the 5th day of September 1961, the full, peaceable, lawful and quiet possession of the said premises described in the Declaration of Taking.

Upon the fail of such persons to do so, the Sheriff of said County and his lawful deputies are hereby commanded to proceed forthwith to put the said State Highway Department of Georgia in full, peaceable, lawful and quiet possession of the said premises.

It being further provided in said statute that: "The court shall have the power to make such orders in respect of encumbrances, liens, rents, taxes, assessments, insurance, and other charges, if any, as shall be just and equitable."

It is further considered, ordered and adjudged as follows:

This the 25th day of August, 1961.

Signed: Lamar Knight

JUDGE SUPERIOR COURT

Carrolton Judicial Circuit

ATTEST:

Jno. A. Corley

CLERK SUPERIOR COURT

Troup COUNTY

Similar orders were issued for the other three properties whose values were contested by Mr. Harrell.

"I want to appeal all of this. Take your time," Mr. Harrell said.

"I am afraid that you are no longer in charge, Uncle Burrell," Bubber said. "The court has spoken. We only have about a week to file the appeal."

"Then, get on with it," Uncle Burrell scolded in a near rage. Roy was enjoying what he was witnessing. Uncle Burrell is handling this matter just right. Everybody else is wrong including the court, he mused. He kept his own counsel now that this whole battle was nearly over as to who owns what is about to be finally settled. He realized that Uncle Burrell would not be pleased with any settlement because a little bit of his soul was about to be taken along with his land.

"No use of scolding and short tempers, we own it, Sir, and we'll win it, just watch us. We'll get more than they are offering," said Bubber. "Request for appeal will be filed tomorrow. You see any problems with that Mr. Lewis?"

"None whatsoever."

Notice was issued the next day. It iterated the State as the plaintiff versus the defendants namely the acreage under consideration and the Harrell party as defendants. It read as follows:

"The defendants named in the foregoing condemnation in rem filed under and by virtue of the provisions of an act entitled "Procedure for the Exercise of the Power of Eminent Domain" Georgia Laws 1961, page 517, et seq., being dissatisfied with the sufficiency of the amount of the estimated just compensation fixed by the Condemnor and determined as follows:

"The amount of $7,913,47 being an average of the appraisers, to wit:

Will E. Morgan ---- $7,886.18

A.J. Jarrell ---------- $7,432.11

Richard Mallory --- $8,422.11"

Do hereby within 15 days following the date of the last advertisement of said cause, to wit: September 1, 1961, in the LaGrange Daily News, the

175

official Newspaper of Troup County, Georgia, file this their Notice of Appeal in accordance with Section 10 of the aforementioned act to the end that the issue thus formed, that is, the value of and the just compensation for the damage done to the remaining lands of the defendants by virtue of the taking, may by fixed and determined by a jury in the Superior Court of Troup County in the State of Georgia.

Signed: Lamar Knight

JUDGE SUPERIOR COURT

The trial was set for November 15, 1961.

On this date, a large crowd gathered at the courthouse steps to witness if Burrell Floyd Harrell would win this one, too. Burrell was a winner and was generally liked by most except the ones he had bested over the years. The gallery was packed mostly by the colored as so many of them were quite fond of Mr. Burrell. The gallery was where they were required to sit during the days of segregation and now this just represented conditioning because they were free to sit wherever they pleased. He was thought to be fair and just and had helped many of them no matter their problems. The courtroom was friendly as determined by the chatter going on. When Mr. Harrell walked in, a hush came over the courtroom. He was no longer that real robust man who could take out anybody without really trying, but he did appear somewhat fit, however, for a man of 77 years and in the 1960s, too. But he was a bit stooped, that full head of hair was thinning severely and completely white. His nephews, John Will (Bubber) and Roy as well as his sons, John Thomas and Alfred, accompanied him. Mr. Harrell sat at the defendant's table with his lawyers (John Will, Jr. and James Lewis) flanking him. Roy, John Thomas, and Alfred sat immediately behind them.

The bailiff announced the Judge: "All rise. "The Honorable Lamar Knight, Judge of the Superior Court, Presiding."

The judge seated himself, after which the courtroom spectators were told: "You may be seated."

The Jurors marched in and took their seats. Not a single female -- no blacks.

Mr. Harrell glanced over at the jurors. Although his eyes were very weak, he recognized some of them. *"They are supposed to be my peers,"* he mused. *"Not by a long shot,"* he shrugged. *"I know now that I am going to be railroaded. Look at 'em. They're just itching to take me out. Maybe a few friends there will keep them from wiping me out completely. Ain't this a bitch? Damn!"*

Judge Knight called on the state to make its charge. Mr. Trotter, counsel for the Condemnor, charged the Jury as follows:

"I charge you that, under the provisions of Section 10 of this Act, this is a de novo investigation, meaning that it is a new investigation, and the amount of your verdict is to be determined solely from the evidence presented on the trial of the case, under the rules of law laid down by the court in this charge.

"Under the provision of the said Section, and under the rules of law laid down, of the said Act, you are first to determine the fair market value of the property taken, and you will do this from the evidence as produced to you on the trial of this case, and under the rules of law laid down to you by the Court in this Charge.

"You will then turn to the questions of consequential damages and consequential benefits. I have, heretofore, defined for you both consequential damages and consequential benefits, I now charge you that it is your duty to consider both consequential damages and benefits to the remaining property of the Condemnees, by reason of the taking and use of the property condemned for the purpose described in the Condemnor's petition, insofar as the same may legitimately appear from the evidence produced to you on this trial. I charge you that, in arriving at your verdict that you may offset consequential benefits against consequential damages and the final amount of your verdict should represent the fair market value of the property taken plus the consequential damages to the property and may be determined by you under the rules of law laid down for you by the court, and as the latter figure may be offset by or diminished by such consequential benefits to such remaining property.

"The Condemnor respectfully requests the above be given in charge to the Jury in this case."

"The request is denied and is to be filed this date November 15, 1961," Judge Knight ordered.

"Counsel for the Condemnee, please present your charge to the Jury," Judge Knight said.

"If it please the Court," opened Mr. Lewis:

"I charge you, Gentlemen of the Jury that the amount of just compensation which the Condemnee in this action is entitled to recover shall include not only the value of the property actually taken, that is, the value of the acreage actually condemned, but shall also compensate him for the consequential damage of the remaining property not taken.

"The measure of damages for the taking of part of a tract of land belonging to the Condemnee is the value of the land taken plus the depreciation in the value of the remainder of the tract. Such depreciation is what is meant by consequential or severance damage to remainder of the property not taken. Georgia Power Co. v. Pittman 92 Ga. 92 App. 673, 675.

"In determining the decreased value of the part of the Condemnee's land remaining, it is proper for you to consider the hindering of the enjoyment of the Condemnee of his remaining land caused by cutting off or limiting his access; limiting his access from one portion of his property to the other, or from one pasture to another; the inconvenience and expense to the owner in having to travel and to transport livestock, supplies, and equipment, to the other portions of his land; State Highway Department v. Irvin 100 Ga. 624. 626.

"I charge you further that in determining the amount of consequential damages, it is also proper for you to consider expenses incurred in minimizing the damages to and preserving the land remaining such as the expenses of constructing necessary fences, road and bridges on the land remaining. That is to say, Gentlemen of the Jury, consequential damages include any special damage suffered by the Condemnee, which results in the diminution in the value of his remaining land."

178

Respectively submitted,

SIMS AND LEWIS

/s/ James E. Lewis

Attorneys for Condemnee

Given,

This Nov. 15th, 1961

/s/ Lamar Knight

Filed Nov. 15, 1961

/s/ JNO A. CARLEY, CLK

Witnesses were called both for the defendant and the plaintiff, Testimony was given and taken and the jury deliberated and found for the defense.

"Counsel for the plaintiff, call your first witness," ordered the Judge.

"Your honor, I call Mr. Will E. Morgan, Senior appraiser for the State of Georgia," Mr. Trotter said.

"Mr. Morgan, place your right hand on the Bible. Do you solemnly swear to tell the truth, the whole truth, and nothing but the truth so help you God?"

"I do," Mr. Morgan swore.

"Mr. Morgan, please tell this court of your experience as an appraiser in the State."

"Oh, I have been a land and building appraiser for the better part of 40 or fifty years."

"Has your appraising experience been limited to rural areas?"

"Nope, it's been all over."

"Mr. Morgan, let's get back to your experience. How did you come to be an appraiser?"

"I worked with my Daddy. He was an appraiser and a darn good one at that."

"How long was he an appraiser, Mr. Morgan?"

"Oh, about forty or fifty years."

"What specific techniques do you use in arriving at your appraisals?"

"Mr. Trotter, I try not to give out the secrets of the trade so to speak, but just let me say that the one thing that's overriding in all of this appraisal business is: location, location, location. Sure you check to see if there's been any property sold in the area under consideration, but this is real rural, downright country. Ain't nothing been happening out there for a long time. There is no commercial activity going on for miles around and it seems to me that there is less and less in this region for whatever reason. But right now, this property ain't worth much, it's that creek, the Long Cane Creek, which winds all over the place. When that thing floods which is about every time it rains, it take months to dry out and you can't do nothing with that land. And furthermore, ..."

"Thank you, Mr. Morgan, that will be all."

"Wait a minute, you didn't let me finish," Mr. Morgan interjected. "You do want the Jury to know the process, don't . . . .? I have more to say. The judge told the jury that they are going to be the ones to decide what a fair price is in this case. If that is the case, then they need some schooling. Now this is a one-crop economy here. It's cotton. The processing plants are still here, but the growers, the choppers, and the pickers are gone. Ever since the mechanized cotton picker came into being in 1944, it was over for the locals. California grows more cotton than all of the South combined. Then them foreign countries get in the act, like Egypt.

"Thank you again, Mr. Morgan, I may need to call on you later. Your witness, please."

"Mr. Morgan, you look like a rugged outdoorsman. Do you particularly like your work?" Mr. Lewis asked.

"I do, very much so. In fact, I love it."

"Have you appraised many areas like this on this project, meaning in Georgia and along the planned route of Interstate 85?" wondered Mr. Lewis.

"I can't say that I have. You see it's that river, too, the Chattahoochee, and all those tributaries, creeks and branches and things. Most of the areas elsewhere are kind of high and dry, but not this one," Mr. Morgan offered.

"In other words, Mr. Morgan, if you had been consulted you would have advised the planners to pick some other location for this road, wouldn't you?"

"Objection!" thundered Mr. Trotter.

"Mr. Trotter, I am going to allow this bit of testimony if for no other reason than it's entertaining, but please hold down the speculation. Overruled!"

"Yes, your honor," said Mr. Lewis and turning again to the witness. "Mr. Morgan, what you are really saying is that because the Alabama portion of the highway has been completed, the Federal Government and the State of Georgia have painted themselves into a corner, and have no choice but to continue the project, and had no choice but to take Mr. Harrell's land."

"Your honor, leading the witness!"

"Mr. Trotter, the area that we are in is highly speculative and we are here to determine the value of this land under consideration, aren't we? Many areas influence the value of land, is that not right?" Judge Knight said.

"May I continue, your honor?" Lewis asked.

"Yes, go ahead."

"That would make the land under consideration more valuable not for farming cotton but other considerations such as modern highways, and therefore commanding more money, wouldn't it, Mr. Morgan?"

"You might say that, but since this is all soggy dirt and bottom land, it's harder to work with and would be more expensive to get in the right condition, but dirt is dirt, soggy or not."

"Mr. Morgan, looking at the affidavit submitted to the court, your appraisal is the next lowest in terms of dollars. I have checked many of the others where you are also an appraiser, and it appears that you are consistently the low appraiser. Do you characteristically low-ball all of your estimates trying to seek favor with the State?"

"Objection!"

"I withdraw that question, I apologize, your honor. I have no further questions for this witness."

"Redirect!"

"Mr. Morgan, have you ever had any of your appraisals thrown out or debunked as Mr. Lewis is trying to do? How do you stand with your peers in this business?" asked Mr. Trotter.

"Well, all of them boys kinda look up to me because they appreciate my work and honesty. I teach them as much as I can. Sometimes, they tell me that I have no peer. I'm not always sure that they are not pulling my leg, but I have had a good and satisfying career."

"Your honor, the record shows as I have submitted it in affidavits and exhibits to the Jury and the testimony presented here that the State has exercised every reasonable means to compensate the Condemnees for their property in spite of all of the delaying tactics pulled to frustrate the progress of the highway. We have taken every reasonable action to preserve the integrity of the land while at the same time trying to enhance the environment. We have been very generous in our appraisals to be as fair as we could have possibly been. I don't know what else the Harrells would have us do?

"I have nothing further at this time, however, I reserve the right to further challenge the defense as necessary," Mr. Trotter said in closing his argument.

"Counsel for the Defense, call your first witness."

"Your honor, I call Mr. Burrell Floyd Harrell, a prospective Condemnee," Mr. Lewis said.

Mr. Lewis deliberately didn't tell the defense table that he was going to call Mr. Harrell as a witness. Mr. Johnson would have sternly objected, as they would figure that Uncle Burrell would become emotional and so mad as to destroy the whole case. Mr. Harrell was surprised himself but he was confident. He hadn't been in a courtroom since the early nineteen hundreds when he was in his twenties. He raised himself up ever so slowly. The spectators watched with great anticipation for Mr. Harrell was always a scrappy old contender and he knew he was a winner. His eyesight was none too good anymore, so John Thomas gave him an assist and guided him across the courtroom to the witness stand. Mr. Harrell looked around and tried to make out some of his friends, faintly recognizing only a couple of spectators outside the jury and realized that none of his close friends, his gambling buddies, were anywhere around anymore. He took his seat while continuing to survey the audience.

"Mr. Harrell, do you swear to tell the truth and nothing but the truth, so help you God?"

"Of course, I do."

"Before you start, Counsel, I want to chat with Mr. Harrell for a moment," Judge Knight said.

"Mr. Harrell, is it clear to you what the State is trying to do with respect to your land?"

"Judge, I am not at all clear as to why they have taken my land and I will never accept it. This is my land. Inherited it from my father, Burrell Whatley Harrell, and he from his father, Alfred Lee Harrell. I hear all of this eminent domain stuff, but I just don't buy it. But if you are asking me if I know what's going on, you damn right I do. It says that I am no match for the State. My personal freedom has been trampled on. My boys and my nephews here have talked to me about the whole thing, especially Bubber. He's my youngest sister's son. He's one of my lawyers, too. A damn good one too. But could I tell you this, them State workers showed me no respect when they messed up my land with all of them dirt-moving machines and scared the hell out of my cattle. And I looked at them drawings, them plans that they have and they show how the State plans to rape my land and don't even want to give me a fair price for it. They left out those culverts as they call them and the pass-through for my cattle. They left barns and stables off their drawings because they didn't want to pay me for them. That told me that they didn't give a damn and thought that these things were worthless. How can I appreciate what they are trying to do for me when they do things like this to me? It seems that they are trying to do things to me rather than for me. If all of these ladies were not in this courtroom, I would tell you exactly what they are doing to me. It's the same thing that Will Rogers said what Standard Oil was doing to this country. I am left holding the bag. That highway is cutting my land into two sections. I can't drive my cattle through them little holes they call culverts. They're too narrow. A cow with calf won't make it. They tell me that they are going to fix up the creek's new channel so it won't flood the area but will do nothing about the previous flooding. I just know it will make things a lots worse. When did the government ever do anything to help the people? I want to get something out of this too. Nobody said that a highway had to be straight, but they want it to be convenient for them. They are scarring god's creation, my land. I am sickened by it. I am sorry your honor, I am just a beaten old man," he raised his head ever so slightly to see how the jury was reacting to his testimony. He was satisfied. He sat up straight and took a deep breath. The morning sun had just broken through the clouds and cast a narrow beam of light through the upper windows in the courtroom shining directly on him at the witness stand. He took that as a good sign that God was on his side.

"Mr. Harrell, thank you," Judge Knight said. "This court has convened to see to it that the State and other entities of the Government and others do not exceed their authority when dealing with its citizens. Justice will prevail in this court, I can assure you that."

Mr. Trotter, Counsel for the State, wanted to object to what appeared to him to be a charade definitely siding with Mr. Harrell, but he didn't dare. The whole courtroom at this time was on Mr. Harrell's side. The State had been made the villain by the defense. Trotter was going to lose this one, big time.

"Mr. Lewis, do you care to cross examine this witness?" the Judge asked.

"I do believe that will be all unless Mr. Harrell would like to add to what he has already said . . . ." Mr. Lewis indicated looking over at Mr. Harrell.

Mr. Harrell shook his head and tried to stand up. He staggered just a bit. John Thomas sprang like a cat to his father's side and quickly assisted him to his feet. He had stayed close to his father during his giving testimony.

" . . . . But I would like to call Mr. John Thomas Winston to the stand, your honor."

John Thomas beckoned for Alfred to come forward to assist Mr. Burrell back to his seat at the defense's table.

State your name please.

"I am John Thomas Winston."

"Do you solemnly swear . . . . .?

"I do."

There was a stir of activity in the gallery where the great majority of the black spectators sat. Segregation was no longer legal and in force but this was where the colored were relegated to sit when segregation was in vogue and enforced. There was no real trouble but there was chitter-

185

chatter among them as they marveled over the courtesies that John Thomas was accorded and as how he and Alfred asserted themselves in public as if they really belonged to the other side. They were really "acting white." The spectators had never seen this before but then they had never witnessed the likes of a John Thomas or an Alfred testifying in public. They did not see the young men as mulattos or white-looking folks; they saw them as black no matter how light their complexions. So the apparent color did not matter. The brothers never had any trouble knowing or feeling who they were or what they could do except they were not yet ready to abandon their being black to enjoy the courtesies and privileges accorded to whites as a matter of course. They, too, were very reluctant to challenge the "white establishment" and seldom, if ever, did. Things settled down after the contingent in the gallery realized that their inattentiveness and the commotion they created were disrupting the proceedings; in addition, the bailiff was headed in their direction to quell the activity.

"Mr. Winston, will you just tell the court in detail some of the things that your father was indicating while he was on the stand," asked Mr. Lewis.

"I'll be glad to," John Thomas said.

He reeled off a litany of items that he and Alfred had prepared just in case such a question was put to him. The Judge seemed to have been puzzled at the proceedings as to how they were progressing and called counsel to the bench.

"Gentlemen, what's going on? There was a reference to John Thomas Winston's father's testimony. Just why does John Thomas not share his father's last name?" Even though both counsels had worked with John Thomas and others through the preliminaries, there was never any reason to call into question John Thomas' father; all they knew was that it was Mr. Harrell, as John Thomas' last name was assumed. But the contingent in the gallery was well aware of the situation and giggled a bit over the confusion on the floor.

"Let's go on. No, better yet, I want to know why Mr. Winston's last name isn't Harrell." The Judge had not directed his question. Nobody responded. It seemed that everybody knew but the judge.

"Mr. Winston? Suppose you tell me."

John Thomas paused as to how best to put it. "Judge," he said. "My mother, Rosa Winston, and my father, Mister Burrell Harrell, have had a common law marriage, in effect, for the last 50 some years. It is customary for the children of such a "marriage" to take the surname of the mother."

"I see here that her surname was Davidson. Can you explain?"

"Davidson was the name of her husband before Mr. Burrell. He was not our father." The spectators in the gallery stirred a bit as it was generally not known that Miss Rosa had a husband before Mr. Burrell.

"Interesting. You know, Mister Winston that common law marriage is recognized in Georgia and you can assume your father's name anytime you wish. Do you know that?"

"I have no problem with the current arrangement, your Honor. In fact, if I can speak for my family, none of us do." While it was true that he had no trouble with the surname, he had often wondered at times especially when the slaves were freed, why they, the slaves, took the master's surname, but his own "outside" children never did.

"Is there anything else that I should know that you haven't told me, Mr. Winston?" smiled the Judge.

John Thomas is now playing it very cool. Any more disclosures could blow the whole thing wide open. "Not that I know of, Sir." While still on the stand, John Thomas reminisced of the day when he almost deliriously told Mr. Burrell of his good fortune of winning a basketball scholarship to Clark College. He felt that the education that he would have received at college would have averted the mess that Mr. Burrell was into and would have enabled him to keep the farm in pace with modern times and the rewards would have benefited all of the family. It was too late. It was almost over.

The courtroom was still. The gallery was quiet, as was the defense table and the members of the jury who knew Burrell Floyd Harrell.

187

"Mr. Thomas, you may return to your seat. I will have these things on your list entered into the record. Will counsel approach the bench again, please," the judge requested.

"Begging your pardon, Sir. It's 'Winston' not 'Thomas,'" John Thomas said.

The judge looked perplexed; he did not realize that he had used 'Thomas' for John Thomas' surname. The double name, that is, the first name and the middle name was customarily used in the South to identify a person. When an individual did not have a middle name, he was called by the first name and the surname. In a more familiar setting, the individual was called by the first name usually precede by "Miss" or "Mister.

"Boys," said the Judge. "I have heard enough. It appears to me that you with the parties can work this thing out and make a presentation to the jury and see how they find for or against the defendant. I am guessing that you should resume your negotiations and let's bottle this whole thing up as quickly as possible. Maybe tomorrow?"

Counsel assented. The Judge declared that the court was in recess, scheduled to resume at 10:00 AM on the morrow.

After the court was recessed, the principals to the negotiation met in a conference room just beyond the judge's chambers. They spent the better part of two hours hemming and hawing trying to iron out their differences. Their biggest hang-up was trying to put a monetary value on Mr. Harrell's pain and suffering from being estranged from his land, particularly, separating the pasture from the farmland with the highway and the scarring of Rose Hill. Mr. Lewis now was more concerned about his fee. Finally, Mr. Trotter said, "nobody has ever heard of pain and suffering from the sale of land no matter how it is done, so let's forget about that and get the hell out of here. Let's make it an even $10,000 to wrap it up, OK?

The agreement was presented to the jury at the next morning's session. The foreman polled the jury in place and they unanimously accepted the agreement.

The Court made the following determination:

IN THE SUPERIOR COURT OF

TROUP COUNTY, GEORGIA

STATE HIGHWAY DEPARTMENT OF GEORGIA

VS

DOCKET NO. 174/4540   IN REM

37.845 acres of Land; and B.F. Harrell, Roy W. Harrell, Ethel H. Whitten, Evans Harrell, Cordelia H. Johnson, Individually

WHEREAS the above stated action came on regularly for trial before a jury In Troup County Superior Court at the November Term, 1961: and

WHEREAS, on the 10th day of November, 1961, the jury returned its verdict in favor of the condemnees, in the amount of $9,550.00; and

WHEREAS, the sum of $9,550.00 has been paid into the coffers of Troup Superior Court for the benefit of the condemnees for the satisfaction of said verdict; and

WHEREAS, the State of Georgia in laying out and establishing the right of way taken in this proceeding failed to show on said right of way a barn owned by condemnees which encroached on the right of way, and failed to include in the appraisal of said right of way the cost of removing such encroachment and the depreciation in value of the remaining portion of the barn after such encroachment was removed; and

WHEREAS, the parties hereto, after investigation, have agreed that the reasonable difference in the value of the barn before the encroachment is removed and the value of the barn after the

189

encroachment is removed after any severance or consequential damages is $450.00; and

WHEREAS, the additional sum of $450.00 has been paid into the coffers of the court by the condemnor for the use and benefit of the condemnees;

WHEREAS, it appearing to the court that the agreement between the parties is just and equitable and the ends of justice and equity are accomplished thereby;

NOW, THEREFORE. It is considered and adjudged that the condemnees, B. F. Harrell, Roy W. Harrell, Ethel H. Whitten, Evans Harrell, and Cordelia H. Johnson do have and recover of the Condemnor the just and full sum of $10,000.00 with all costs assessed against the Condemnor.

This 14th Day of February, 1962.

/s/ Lamar Knight

Judge Superior Court,

Troup County, Georgia

APPROVED:

/S/ Wm P. Trotter

Attorney for Condemnor

SIMS AND LEWIS

/s/ George E. Sims, Jr.

Attorneys for Condemnees

Chapter 14. The Warranty Deed

The last two days had taken their toll on Burrell. He was drained but somehow relieved, as he knew that there were many other pressing matters to be attended to, and while he was in a most generous mood, he thought that he would heed the advice of his sister, Evans, the incessant diatribes from his lady, Rosa and their daughter, Rosa Belle, and his good ol' buddy James T. Zachry. Zachry was his long-standing friend from way back. They went to school together, played hooky together, played poker together, did business together in the seed and feed markets, and indeed did support each other no matter the situation even when the times were not always good. That collective advice to Burrell was to do something for his children, because there was nothing solid in writing that would guarantee that they would inherit any of his properties and belongings. This had to be his first priority, as he knew his health was beginning to fail rather rapidly.

Among the other things he had to do was trying to get the farm back together. The long pursuit of trying to keep the feds and the state away from his land had diverted his attention away from the business of the farm. He really thought that the farm was running itself. This truly was never the case, especially of late. He was aware that many of the tenant farmers had left the plantation, but he didn't realize that such a large number had left and the impact of their leaving. Many of the crops were no longer being harvested. Some of the cattle were in poor condition. His sons and those tenants who stayed on did their best to keep things on even keel, but there was no boss, no overseer, and very little money. Cattle were stolen and sold by the tenants and sometimes by the sons. The homestead was in a state of disrepair. The business was in disarray. Where were all of those hands that used to take care of that stuff without having to be told? How could things be in such a mess, when it seemed that it was only yesterday that things were running so smoothly? "Yesterday" was many moons ago. Where had all the workers gone? There was the little matter of getting paid and paying the bills. No pay, no work. It had truly been a long time coming. Sometimes things don't wait out of loyalty alone. The few who remained on the farm were the women and children, many of whom could not contribute much even to the maintenance of the enterprise. The tenant houses had become ramshackle and were unlikely to attract any new families.

Now he needed Roy but wouldn't call him. Roy was always waiting in the wings just biding his time, waiting patiently for Uncle Burrell to realize that he was the only game in town. He had to come to him so that he could take full control. That time was almost nigh. Could and would Burrell's sons be able and willing to handle the overall business? He didn't think so and realistically, it was unlikely due to prevailing racial attitudes in the marketplace.

But the biggest concern that Burrell had was the after effects of the trial that was held solely to determine the value of the land that had already been taken by the State. He seemed not to be able to get himself together. Burrell had been hoping for a windfall so large that it would cure most of his business problems, as he had resigned himself to the loss of the land, somewhat. What he did not expect was that the loss would take a great emotional toll on him. Rose Hill Plantation and all of the other land that he had amassed were his soul and his psyche. It really hurt to lose even that tiny bit of land, because he continued to lose so much of himself. He tried to conceal his suffering, but it preoccupied his every waking moment and every action he took. He no longer slept well. He barely ate any more. Then he started to hit the bottle again but more heavily, although he could remain rational most of the time. But he was losing it and he knew it. His worst fears had come true; he was going to have to turn operations over to Roy. The home house, the mansion that is, was wasting away just like its occupants and nothing was being done to restore it. Other priorities came before restoration and there was little extra money for it. Bills were coming due and Roy would have to make arrangements to settle them and from whatever resources were available, not necessarily his own.

But the first priority was to take care of his sons. Burrell took a separate action from the Will to convey some of "Rose Hill Place" to his sons. It was always considered solely his with no one else to share in this little stretch of property. It was just 10 acres more or less out of about a couple of hundred or so, but it was his alone to do however he pleased. He had already given a small parcel to John Thomas as a wedding gift when he and Ardell Davidson married - - the first and only son to do so.

This parcel was the "cornerpiece" of the Rose Hill Plantation – it was where Rose Hill really began. This was valuable corner property for it had frontage on Georgia State Highway 18 for potential commercial development. After this, it was just a matter of taking care of the rest of the boys and in his mind this was sufficient for them to live on. What else they could do for themselves should be their concern, not his.

All of the necessary actions had been taken to draw up the deeds. There was one glaring omission – nothing, absolutely nothing, had been provided for the girls. Apparently, it was the custom of yore to leave property to the sons only as the girls would get married and their interests would be that of their husbands. He was satisfied that the provisions in the "new" will would take care of the girls. Mr. Burrell well knew that the only effective way to convey things of value was through the deed process, yet would he leave this task to somebody else?

Mr. Harrell engaged Grady A. Fuller, Surveyor, licensed in the State of Georgia to lay out the parcels he intended to convey to the boys. Fuller submitted a plat of subdivision of B. F. Harrell Property located in Land Lots Nos. 235 and 224, 5th Land District, Troup County, Georgia, September 3, 1962.

John Thomas's parcel was originally more than an acre, part of which was needed when Roy chose to sell a larger adjacent parcel to complete the deal with the prospective buyer. This left John Thomas with just 0.56 acres on Roy's promise that it would be restored with a whopping 5.0 acres to boot after the transaction was completed. This land sale was necessary to raise cash to pay some of Uncle Burrell's outstanding bills as the proceeds from the state were insufficient, particularly after allocating the "largesse" from the State's payoff for the land that it had taken. These bills ranged from tending the homestead, the business, and farming, to the welfare of the sisters who still occupied the homestead. Burrell still maintained the one room in the rear of the mansion and had begun to spend more and more time there as it was no longer feasible for him to maintain the fiction of sharing his time with Rosa, the children still remaining there, and the farm. Burrell kept a strong box in his room where he hid his gambling winnings – he never commingled his gaming and his business proceeds. This was his emergency fund just in case.

193

The next adjoining parcel was allocated to Gaines, the youngest of the 9 children. This was 2.3 acres. There was no specific order to the allocation in terms of birth order or any other strategy as could best be determined. Gaines' property was by far the most desirable piece from a business viewpoint as it was bordered by commercial property on the West, 240 feet of frontage property on the north bounded by Georgia State Highway 18.

The next parcel was allocated to George Frank, Sug, the eldest son. It was 2.5 acres and the largest of the parcels, suggesting his prized status as being the first-born son. It also had potential as commercial property in that it, too, had 240 feet of frontage with Highway 18; otherwise it was a non-entity.

The next adjacent parcel was allocated to James, the fourth son. It was 2.4 acres. Its boundaries were essentially the same as Gaines' and Sug's in that the frontage was 240 feet on the Highway with lateral boundaries of 400 feet more or less and the southern boundary being a fast moving stream with plenty of fish nonetheless.

Alfred's allocation was the last property listed. It was only 1.9 acres in the form of a triangle, the hypotenuse, the longest side of which was irregularly shaped to provide the easterly and southerly border. This border was to the center of the stream and heavily forested. It, too, was bounded by Highway 18 by more than 300 feet of frontage and reached into Land Lot 224. The next adjacent property was the Old Hogg property as shown on a map (see map) of Troup County in 1910 and now was Mr. Burrell's but unallocated at this time. It was south of Highway 18 and it was said to have been acquired by Mr. Burrell in settlement of a debt of sorts.

This entire action on the part of Mr. Burrell was completed on September 14, 1962. It caused a great deal of consternation among the girls because there was nothing conveyed to them. Miss Rosa had no problem, as she knew that there would always be a place for her in one of her sons' homes. Her attitude was that all problems could be solved in due time; haste always made for trouble. Such homilies still did not satisfy the girls. But they had to understand that this was the first time that there had been any formal acknowledgment or recognition by Mr. Burrell of his family notwithstanding many public displays. With this

194

gift, the boys could move out of the home house in which all were born, the last of which was in 1930. This house had stood the test of time. It was built in the early twenties and had accommodated all of the family rather well. All of the girls were now married off but felt "left out in the cold," so to speak. Neither appreciated that this was not Mr. Burrell's idea of distributing the wealth of land that he had amassed. It was a way of providing a man with his much-needed castle. Taking care of the girls would be done through the will process.

"Home" couldn't be patched up anymore. It had seen its best days. The roof was almost gone. The siding was dilapidated. Even three coats of paint couldn't save it. A good windstorm would save the need to raze it. This old house was left standing and the weather relieved it of its misery over time. It was a well-built house in the beginning that fully provided for the family. Mr. Burrell saw to it. He still came over from time to time to reminisce of the times when he and Rosa sat together in the swing passing the time away oftentimes well into the night. It seemed that through the years anytime one rode down Highway 18 and passed that house, the two of them, Miss Rosa and her Mr. Burrell, could be seen sitting together in the swing on the front porch. Neither seemed to have had a care in the world. They were such lovebirds. That house over the years was allowed to decay by nature's elements.

John Thomas had to build another house because his first one was razed when its land was sold to the gas station owner. It was necessary because Ardell was in a family way again. James' house was smallish but big enough to give him the privacy he needed. Sug's house was adequate for a bachelor's pad but it was Alfred who stepped up to build a house large enough to accommodate his mother. Each of the houses fronted Highway 18 with about 100 feet of setback and they, the boys, were apart for the first time ever, but at the same time were neighbors all by themselves out there in that wilderness called Rose Hill.

In a few short years, the applecart would be upset again over James' death. He left no will and the land conveyed to him by Mr. Burrell was now claimed by his siblings. There were seven of them involved: -- Rosa Belle Winston Parker (Honey), Precious Myra Winston Brooks (Sis), Marguerite Winston Adams (Doll), George Frank Winston (Sug), Alfred Gordon Winston (Bay), at this time, Gaines Tyrone Winston (Foy), the baby girl, Mary Bessie Winston Fannings (Sister). The

195

mother, Rosa Winston, declined a share. John Thomas elected not to be a part of the shares for this 2.4-acre parcel but to act as the mediator and executor. This was the first time that the females had been able to share in the "inheritance" of land from Mr. Burrell but through the benevolence of John Thomas, though indirectly. While saddened by the death of their brother, it was time to rejoice for having something of their own. Each of the siblings received one seventh of a share of the property. But what can one do with 1/7 of 2.4 acres? They wanted to keep the property within the family therefore some family member had to buy it. Nothing happened over the ensuing years until Mary Bessie, baby sister, came forward with an offer for the entire 2.4 acres and any of the other brother's property that was for available.

Chapter 15. The Demise of a Titan

Mr. Burrell had heard about the squabbles between the children over how the land was to be shared. Rosa Belle, the eldest daughter, visited him in his room at the big house. She was just sick and tired of the pretense that had been put on by Mr. Burrell over the years. She wanted to give him a piece of her mind. Although never hesitating in the past, she had been unable to get any action or results from him. His manner of dealing with her was to ignore her – no comment, no recognition of her except through a slighted greeting.

"What is it you want this time, Honey?" his calling her by her nickname.

"Mr. Burrell Harrell, my finally acknowledged father -- the great Mr. Burrell Floyd Harrell! A rich man! The wealthy landowner of our time. Land baron! A skinflint! A miser. A hypocrite! Do you think giving 10 little acres of land to your sons is in any way adequate for an inheritance? There are thousands of acres of land out here and you can only muster 10? Where will the rest of it go? Oh! To your Harrell heirs? Get off it, man! That's always the reason you use when talking to us about the distribution. That it's going to be left to your heirs? Or it's "heir" property. We are your flesh and blood, man, Mr. Burrell -- your own children! Are we not your heirs? It is so small and shortsighted for you hide behind this ruse. The real reason you are not accepting us as your own family is that we are not of your own kind. It must be this race thing. It is, isn't it? You must be of good will as a man and as a father to do the right thing by your children. You got to stand up and be counted! You racist, you!"

Well, he understood that the 10 acres that was conveyed to the boys was hardly generous, but it certainly did not represent his intention about conveying Rose Hill to the boys as a kind of good will gesture.

There, Rosa Belle stood over him, demanding that he do more. Not just the total of 10 miserly little acres that they already received, but she now wanted him to convey all that was left of Rose Hill – to include all 181.8 acres. This is where they were all born -- their own homestead. This was their farm, the most fertile patch of land in all of Georgia insofar as he was concerned. He was being forced to come to terms with his fatherhood and his past. No matter how much he had done for this family, he still had not come around to facing his full duty as a father and therefore to Rosa of and toward his family and their issue. This whole fiasco was of his own making, and he felt that he didn't need his "daughter" to "bless him out" for his shortcomings. But in actuality he did, because he had heretofore refused to face the truth or the consequences.

He was sick now, had had a debilitating stroke, and couldn't quite rationalize all that was happening around him, He was paralyzed down his left side and was hardly mobile.

"Honey, I suppose somebody should have made me aware or made me understand my obligations a long time ago. May Jimmie tried. Even my mother, who was dead set against me and Rosa, tried. Evans wanted to take a couple of y'all down to Florida to be raised as white. I guess it was the times about what I didn't have to do because I was a free white man, but I was not big enough of a man to do what I should have done about my family. I am so sorry. Here I am all laid up and there ain't much more that I can do now, but I will take care of it right away. My original intentions were to convey all of Rose Hill to the boys. But I was talked out of it and that it was sufficient for me to give only those 10 acres. Maybe that is why Roy thought he was owed it."

"Come off it, Mr. Burrell!" "Mr. Burrell Harrell, you never did anything that you didn't want to do." Rosa Belle continued. "You are now making excuses. You must come to terms with yourself before you meet your maker and there is no better time than now. Otherwise, you won't be forgiven. For your own sake, man, and your own peace of mind, do it now," Rosa Belle pleaded with tears in her eyes.

The old Negro spiritual, "Get Right With God," came to her mind; she could hear the congregation singing at their New Harmony C.M.E. Church, just singing:

Get right with God,

And do it now.

198

Get right with God,

And he will show you how.

Get Right with God,

Down at the cross,

Where he shed his blood.

Get right, get right,

Get right, get right with God!

This spiritual was aimed at the bereaved family during the funeral of a loved one.

She had never shed tears for or over him before, in fact, she had felt only hatred for him. She, too, was coming to terms with herself. As white as she was, she was nothing less than anti-white. She now knew that she was wrong, but didn't believe that she could ever come to terms with her whole being until her father could make amends for his wrongs.

"Thanks to you, Honey. Nobody else had the courage to call me down but you. I'll make amends. Have Gordon (Alfred) to come over to see me right away. You come back to see me again, you hear? Will you? Please."

Alfred, the very one that he could trust to carry out any assignment, came in through the back door and into Mr. Burrell's bedroom.

"Gordon," Mr. Burrell said. "Gordon, I want you to get that lawyer fellow up there in LaGrange, and that surveyor, Grady Fuller, to draw up the deeds and a new plat for Rose Hill, so that I can make sure that all of y'all inherit Rose Hill. But you must make haste. I want you to take charge of all of it yourself. Don't let nobody else get involved, you understand? Nobody!" Don't you tarry now, you hear?" Mr. Burrell rasped.

Mr. Burrell knew that his days were numbered. Just how long, he reasoned, not long. He knew that he was not going to recover from that stroke that sent him reeling into outer space.

"Yes, Sir!" Alfred snapped-to as if he had just been given a military order.

"Gordon, before you go, tell your mother I want to see her. She ain't been coming to see me lately," Mr. Burrell slurred. He was paralyzed down his left side from head to foot. He couldn't even wriggle his ears anymore. This had been a great delight for the children. He could barely talk, but his mind seemed to have been fairly clear.

Alfred strode off hastily with the papers and once again engaged the law firm of Richter, Willis & McKenzie in LaGrange on that same afternoon. He was told that everything would be ready in a week. The law firm called him in two days for some clarifications. After changes, all that was needed was to get Mr. Burrell's signature. Alfred promised that he would be in LaGrange directly. This meant real soon. The Warranty Deeds, along with the Plat Plan, were ready on November 15, 1965. The plat referred to in the deeds showed thereon the property that was being conveyed to Gaines, George Frank, James, and Alfred. Still no girls were included. This plat showed not only the original 10.4 acres previously conveyed, but also the remainder of Rose Hill, all totaled 182.4 acres. This included all of the property south of the branch that marked the property line of the first conveyance down to the Troup County – Harris County Line. (Refer to drawing of Warranty Deed.)

For some reason not clear to many, Alfred dragged his feet on this one at such a critical point in time. Time was of the essence and it was running out. Alfred did not seem to realize that Mr. Burrell was in his final days, just how long, who knew? One reason perhaps was that Mr. Burrell had lingered for such long time in this semi-comatose state -- he was in and out of consciousness – which no one thought his end would be soon.

A few old buddies started to come by to pay their farewells. A few other old enemies also dropped by to see if he was really going to go this time. He was a hardy old soul, still crusty and crafty at 79. Burrell smiled at those he recognized but most of them he thought were there just as curiosity seekers. Their entry was through the back door as the parlor and the front of the house were still reserved for select company, most of whom had already passed on. The rear entrance was reserved for servants and undesirables, though it was the best entrance at any rate as Burrell's room was in the rear and was privately accessible from the outside. There he lay in an emaciated state in this bare room that was now furnished with a few extra chairs for those who came around to pay their respects and others who were just simply well wishers.

Rosa waited a few days, and finally came over mainly to see if he was comfortable. She was amazed at how dark, dank and unkempt the room had become. It appeared as if it had not been tidied up in a long time.

"Let's get some more light in this here place," she said. She called in Mattie Kate who had been hired by Mr. Roy to keep his Uncle Burrell cleaned up, fed, and comfortable. Even in his feeble condition, Mattie Kate found his demeanor unbearable. She was uniformed, big, and loud. She stayed as far away from Mr. Burrell as possible, as she was only interested in hearing his call or the bell ring when he needed something.

"I'm sorry Miss Rosa, I was hired here as a caregiver. I don't do nobody's housework!" Mattie Kate thundered. "I'm a private duty nurse."

"Have you been paid yet," Miss Rosa asked. "And who hired you?"

"Why, no ma'm, I ain't been paid," Mattie Kate answered. "Mr. Roy hired me."

"Oh my God, then, you'd better do what I tell you. You got to hound him to get your money, which may be never. I will take care of your pay," Miss Rosa said.

Down came the heavy drapery as well as the blinds that appeared as if they had never been opened, let alone cleaned. Sunlight bathed the room now that the heavy drapery was gone. The trees at the edge of the house had been scuttled to make room for the renovations that Burrell planned for restoring the mansion to its original glory. He had made great plans that were now forever abandoned due to the state's miserly offering for the condemnation and seizure of his property for Interstate I-85 construction. Partly because of this, he had lost his will to do

201

anything more. He had simply given up but face it, he was just days from being 80 years old.

He showed no signs of recovering from the stroke that had put him in a near vegetative state. He was drinking heavily and for the most part he was in a near stupor, plus many of the folks who used to deal with him paid little or no heed to whatever he said.

On this one afternoon, he perked up a bit. He was so glad to see his Rosa. Rosa knew that the Harrell sisters did not want her there, but Mr. Burrell had asked for her and there was nothing that they would do to deny him, as he had been so good and generous to them over the years, at least in his own mind. In Rosa's mind, they were some of the cause of his infirmity resulting from, as she believed, their utter dependence upon him. She would make a poultice dipped in cool water and place it on his forehead to comfort him. At other times, she would hold his hand and stroke it gently. He did the best he could to squeeze it back wherein once a mighty grip was his.

"I'm so sorry that things didn't go better for us, Rosa, but . . . I didn't know how to handle things really in the face of all of the scorn that was heaped on me. I think I weathered it pretty good but it was hard. Sometimes I thought that I would go crazy. I loved you so and I still do," he gasped so hard and his breathing was so labored. "Stay with me as long as you can. I'm slipping away. I know it," he wheezed.

"You just need a little rest, Mr. Burrell. It's been tough for you today to receive all of your cronies. I will stay as long as you want, but Mattie Kate needs to come in and freshen you up and Toussaint, the newly hired hospital orderly, is here to lift you for her. You still too heavy for her to lift as big as she is, and then you'd better get some sleep, too. I'll be back tomorrow."

"Rosa, tomorrow may never come for me," he said. "Can you stay with me till the end?"

"Mr. Burrell, no reason for you to talk nonsense like that. You'll outlive all of us."

"Then just hold my hand tight. Yours are so warm. Do you still love me, Rosa?"

As she tried to steal away from the room, he cried out weakly, "Rosa, please don't leave me. Look under the bed; get that lock box. It's yours. Take it. Don't let nobody see it. Let nobody know you have it. Take care of yourself. I'm not long for this world. I'm still so sorry . . . ."

She bent over and kissed his forehead. "Don't worry about it, Mister Burrell, I wouldn't have had it any other way." Rosa gently slid her hand across his face to close his eyes. A little smile graced his face and he was gone.

The warranty deed and the plat plan were completed. There was inscribed in the center of the drawing the total acreage of land to be conveyed, 171.8 acres, with the names of each son printed on it except for John Thomas.' The Plat plan had printed in the upper right-hand corner, the following: "PLAT SHOWING PROPERTY BEING CONVEYED TO GAINES T. WINSTON, GEORGE F. WINSTON, JAMES F. WINSTON AND ALFRED G. WINSTON LOCATED PARTLY IN LAND LOTS NOS. 235 AND 224 5TH LAND DISTRICT, TROUP COUNTY, GA. SCALE 1" = 200' NOVEMBER 15, 1965 GRADY A. FULLER, L.S. GA. REG. NO.1133." John Thomas was to get the land where the Coca-Cola Bottling Plant now stands. Alfred had that paperwork in hand, too. All he needed was Mr. Burrell's signature and a notary public's OK. Somehow he seemed not to have realized that Mr. Burrell's life's was waning so fast. While Alfred procrastinated, Mr. Burrell passed on in the presence of his beloved Rosa.

After hearing of Mr. Burrell's death, Alfred rushed to LaGrange to get the papers processed and certified less his father's signature. He had just plain messed up. He knew it. "Damn," he declared. "Can't I do anything right anymore? What's wrong with me? What's coming over me? Is it the liquor, or what? I can't even follow simple directions anymore."

He bounded into the law offices of Schicter and Company. No amount of pleading convinced the law firm to process the documents as Alfred argued that this was Mr. Burrell's intent. "You folks write in "X's" all of the time! Why not now?" In his own mind all they had to do was to place an "X" on the signature line. In the lawyer's mind was the question of why wasn't Alfred smart enough to do that himself.

"If you had come earlier, before he died, that is, there would not have been a problem," a law partner said. Ironically, it was Alfred who insisted on having Mr. Burrell sign the deed so there would have been no question as to Mr. Burrell's intentions. Alfred was always the meticulous one, always concerned about perceptions, appearances as to what was to be considered right and wrong, and that the "truth" must always be known and therefore, it shall prevail. He now wondered if he had gone through life with a profound misconception as to how things got done and how things really were. This was the influence of the "black culture" on his being. If he had "turned white" for a moment, these qualms more than likely would not have entered his mind. This is why Mr. Burrell wanted them to work with Roy as he, Roy, had mastered the system.

As fate would have it, the full Rose Hill Plantation was never conveyed to the boys, and as such would be distributed as per the 1941 Last Will and Testament of one Burrell Floyd Harrell, deceased, and to be probated.

Burrell Floyd Harrell was kind of a mythical figure, known by all, loved by some, hated by many, and roundly feared by a few as it seemed that he always meant business even while at play, if he ever played. He stood at the head of a great pioneer family that settled East Alabama and West Georgia. He advanced the cotton industry immeasurably. He was a legendary figure about whom stories abound, many of them true. A man with his bravado could have gone far, except he was inclined to do only his own thing in his own time and in his own way, with little regard towards others, and deny anything else if it impinged on his being. He stood his ground no matter what. He was a man's man.

His body had lain in repose at the Old Harrell Mansion for a couple of days, after which it was taken to the Old Cemetery in Cusseta, Alabama. Cusseta, about 20 or 30 miles down the road, was where the family settled when moving in from the Carolinas and Virginia back in the pioneer days of the late 1700s and the early 1800s. The family was heavily inclined towards religion, although Burrell had little time for such. He didn't want a big fuss made over him but he did want to be buried in the old family plot next to his grandmother, Mahala.

The cemetery, then, was more than 100 years old, although it is now divided between the old and the new. The graves surrounding the Harrell's gravesite property are seemingly ancient, some showing above ground interment methods unimaginable even in New Orleans. They appear as relics out of the distant past. There is currently no plan to restore them.

The family members already interred there were laid out quite appropriately. Alfred Lee Harrell, born in 1808, is first, and next to him is Mahala, and then "Burrell Floyd Harrell," his granite slab simply inscribed "1884 – 1965". The most impressive monument in the plot is that of Burrell Whatley Harrell, Burrell Floyd's father. It was he who spearheaded the family's progress. The plot is impressively fenced off with an attending gate showing that at the time of its creation, the family did not expect to grow so large. As a result, some family members are buried outside of the enclosed compound. Alfred Lee, II for one. Or could it have been that those who are buried outside of the plot did not measure up to the standard demanded by the family? It is rather lavish for the time, showing that the family thought a great deal of itself and how it wanted to be remembered.

Only a graveside ceremony was held per Burrell's wishes, as he was not a man of the church. Legions attended the services. Nearly everyone on the white side of the family showed up, which was surprising as so many in the family decried Burrell's behavior in ordinary life. The showing of the faithful topped those of brother Tom back in 1920. This was a big family. Not just the Harrells, but also the Combs, Floyds, Johnsons, Johnstons, Stricklands, Wallaces, McClendons, Evans, Smiths, and a host of in-laws and distant relatives and friends in search of family. Many of them had never met each other, and they were not all friendly toward one another, but now was a time for solidarity, mourning -- healing. The titular head of the family had just passed on.

George Frank, John Thomas, Alfred Gordon, James Floyd, and Gaines Tyrone, his sons, were all in attendance and what's more stood with the rest of the family. Few knew that they were not white. None of his daughters attended. Rosa Belle still wouldn't have been caught dead honoring this man, her father. One of the girls was not informed of his passing, and the two others were away in Michigan. Rosa, Burrell's life-long companion and mother of his nine children, attended as well, along with her daughter-in-law, Ardell, John Thomas' wife. However, the two of them stood many yards apart from the family at the foot of a knoll, down from the gravesite but close enough to witness the conduct of the ceremony. She, Rosa, had debated long and hard before attending the services but realized that she was a part of that man, not the other side of his family, and he a part of her. He was the father of their children, and the two of them had been one for more than a half century in their brand of matrimony and togetherness.

Cusseta had never seen such a large funeral cortege in its entire 200 years or so of existence.

With Burrell's passing, this whole family, the entourage of family, no matter how intertwined, was relieved. No tears were shed, although most were still so attached to him, even though he had not been the Spartan force in most of their lives for some years, but his legacy remained. A few lingered after the burial, and some of them came over to his boys and greeted them, those members of the family of whom they had only heard but never met. One of the younger ladies, a second cousin to Burrell's children, walked over to Rosa, embraced her and acknowledged her presence while offering her condolences. Rosa added, "We had to come because we couldn't let 'them' put him away without us saying goodbye." Finally, all drifted away after paying homage to the Titan of their times.

Chapter 16. The Probate

It's always difficult to get a family together in the dead of winter except for funerals and the reading of wills. It was December 10, 1965, a bleak day, barely a week after Burrell Floyd Harrell had been laid to rest. The following notice appeared in the LaGrange Daily News, LaGrange, Georgia:

"GEORGIA, TROUP COUNTY, IN COURT OF ORDINARY, SAID COUNTY.

ORDER FOR SERVICE BY PUBLICATION GRANTED DECEMBER 10, 1965.

ESTATE OF BURRELL F. HARRELL, DECEASED.

NOTICE TO: Ethel H. Whitten, 225 Coconut Street, Sarasota, Florida;

William Lee Harrell, Childersburg, Alabama;

Thomas W. Harrell, 466 La Prenda Road, Los Altos,

California; Evans C. Johnson, 307 Cumberland Road,

DeLand, Florida; Marie J. Cunningham, 1029 North Pine Street, Florence, Alabama.

Application having been made to probate the Will of Burrell F. Harrell, deceased, in Solemn Form, and for Letters Testamentary to issue to Roy W. Harrell in terms of the law, and an order for service by publication to the above named parties having been granted by the Court of the Ordinary on the 10th day of December, 1965, Ethel Harrell Whitten, William Lee Harrell, Thomas W. Harrell, Evans C. Johnson, and Marie J. Cunningham, being heirs at law of such deceased residing without the State, and are hereby ordered to be and appear before the Court of

Ordinary to be held in and for said county on the first Monday in January, next, then and there to show cause, if any exist, why the paper offered for probate by Roy W. Harrell, Petitioner, as the Last Will and Testament of Burrell F. Harrell, late of said County, deceased should not be proven in Solemn Form and admitted to the record as the Last Will and Testament of said deceased.

By order of said court, this 10th day of December, 1965."

It is instructive to note that the natural children of Burrell F. Harrell were not listed. But this order did appear in the local newspaper, the LaGrange Daily News, a newspaper published in LaGrange, Georgia, in which Sheriff's sales are advertised once a week for four weeks immediately prior to the court's session. Burrell's children were not only aware but also, in effect, legally notified. Each of the heirs at law named in the advertisement was required to respond to the notice and each did.

The petition to probate the Will was issued and the heirs at law were ordered to appear on the first Monday in January 1966. The Attorney for Petitioner was none other than John W. Johnson, Jr., a nephew, a first cousin, and an heir at law, his mother being the youngest sister of his Uncle Burrell.

Before the petition could be ruled on, an amendment to it was received by the Court of Ordinary. It read as follows:

ESTATE OF BURRELL F. HARRELL, DECEASED

IN THE COURT OF ORDINARY

GEORGIA

TROUP COUNTY

AMENDMENT TO PETITION TO PROBATE WILL OF BURRELL F. HARRELL, DECEASED, IN SOLEMN FORM TO THE COURT OF ORDINARY OF SAID STATE AND COUNTY:

208

"Now comes ROY W. HARRELL, petitioner in the above-styled cause, and amends his petition as follows:

1. The petitioner shows that subsequent to the filing of his petition to probate the Last Will and testament of Burrell F. Harrell, deceased, heretofore filed in this Honorable Court, petitioner learned that Sam Harrell, a brother of Burrell F. Harrell, who died about 1935 without issue of his body surviving him, made a declaration on or about the 10th of April 1925, to the Probate of Jefferson County, Alabama, adopting Margarette Thornton, a girl child about four years of age, said child being his stepchild, and changing the child's name to Margarette Harrell. Petitioner has been unable to determine whether the said Margarette Thornton Harrell is living or dead, and if living, her place of residence is unknown to your petitioner.

2. Petitioner amends the list of heirs at law of said deceased listed in the petition heretofore filed, by adding thereto the following person believed to be an heir at law of said deceased:

Name   Margarette Thornton Harrell
Address   Place of residence and address unknown
Age   Over 21
Relation niece by adoption

WHEREFORE, Petitioner prays that this amendment be allowed and ordered filed, that Margarette Thornton Harrell, whose place of residence is unknown and all singular heirs at law of Burrell F. Harrell, deceased, be cited to appear at the next term of this court to be held on the first Monday in February, 1966, to show cause if any they have, why said will should not be proven in Solemn Form and entered of the record as the Last Will and Testament of said deceased.

/s/ Paul L. Coulter.

Attorney for Petitioner

GEORGIA, TROUP COUNTY

Personally appeared before the undersigned who on oath states that the facts set forth in the foregoing amendment are true.

/s/ Roy W. Harrell

Sworn and subscribed before me, this 7th day of January, 1966.

/s/ Mrs. Trevah P. Ball
Notary Public

ORDER

GEORGIA, TROUP COUNTY.

AT CHAMBERS 1966

Upon motion made in open court on the first Monday in January, 1966, the hearing of the petition of Roy W. Harrell to probate the Last Will and Testament of Burrell F. Harrell, deceased, and that Letters Testamentary issue to petitioner was and is hereby ordered continued to and set for the first Monday in February, 1966.

Upon reading and considering the foregoing amendment, the same is allowed and order filed.

"It is further ordered that as Margarette Thornton Harrell is a non-resident, or unknown or legal residence in doubt, and that there may be other heirs at law of Burrell F. Harrell, deceased, who are non-residents, unknown or legal residence in doubt, and can only be served by publication, that Margarette Thornton Harrell and all singular the heirs at law of said deceased be cited and made a party by publication of notice of said proceedings in the LaGrange Daily News, a newspaper published in LaGrange, Georgia, in which Sheriff's Sales are advertised once a week for four weeks immediately prior to said Court.

/s/ P. T. Hipp
Ordinary

The dredging up of the person named Margarette Thornton Harrell appeared to be nefarious on its face so as to notify the Winstons that they should not intercede or interfere in any way. Was there some interracial aspect of their bringing up the issue of Sam's adopted daughter? This extraordinary action created suspicion, as Sam had no share in the first place, and of what value was it to the proceedings now taking place? The issues were never pursued and seemed really to have no bearing on the matters at hand.

In fact, Sam throughout the history of the family had received little notice. He was the "Baby Boy" and was doted upon by his mother and cherished by his sisters. When his mother accompanied his sisters to Auburn for their education at Alabama Polytechnic Institute (API), Sam was brought along. While he was there, he also completed his education at API, receiving his Electrical Engineering degree. He did not want to stay in the dormitory, as he wanted to avoid the hazing and such other "childish" inconveniences of not living at home. But like the man he was, he struck out on his own and started his own business, took on a partner, an unscrupulous lout, and a wife who was widely known as a floozy, with a daughter from previous dalliances. Hence, Margarette. Sam grew to love this young lady, adopted her and truly made her his own, loving her as if she were indeed of his own flesh and blood. Her mother, Margie, soon returned to the ways of profligacy, totally disrespecting her husband, to the displeasure of Sam's mother and sisters. They persuaded him to divorce her. He did and found himself unhappy because he so missed his beautiful little daughter. Margie soon returned with Margarette, Peggy, as Sam called her, begging forgiveness. Sam took her back primarily because of the daughter, the love of his life. Margie was unable to keep her promise to be a faithful and dutiful wife, and eventually they drifted apart again. Sam became unhappy and remained so for the rest of his relatively short life.

What was the extent of the effort put forth to locate Margarette to prove conclusively that she no longer existed? It appears that no hard and fast search was made to find her but perhaps a reasonable effort was made to establish the legal insufficiency of the adoption. Whatever legal search was made, it was sufficient to convince the judge that the adoption itself was faulty and therefore it was "annulled." Margarette was no longer the daughter of Samuel Harrell and therefore not entitled to a share in the family's inheritance. But legitimate or not, an "adoption" did take place, the act of designating Sam as her father who loved this little girl with all his heart. They were dealing with a human being – a child who had found a father to love her.

The Ordinary was aware of the makeup of the family because of a recently settled high profile condemnation case by the State against Burrell Harrell. LaGrange, although the county seat, still was a "small" town where everybody knew everybody else's business. This was the talk of the legal community of LaGrange and the outlying communities, and it was sizable considering that it was the county seat, and the proceedings were held in public. The Ordinary had suspicions of the thoroughness of the search for Margarette undertaken by Roy, and appended further conditions to the petition, seemingly, to give the Winstons one last opportunity to lay claim of "at law" status. Those conditions are repeated here:

"It is further ordered that as Margarette Thornton Harrell is a non-resident, or unknown or legal residence in doubt, and that there may be other heirs at law of Burrell F. Harrell, deceased, who are non-residents, unknown or legal residence in doubt,"

Not a soul came forward, even though the Winstons were fully aware of the proceedings throughout, either by word of mouth or information in the print media. Not a single one showed up at the Probate Court.

The other probable issue was who else was aware of a "second" or "new" Will and dated in 1959 which would have indeed been truly Burrell F. Harrell's "Last Will and Testament," a Will that, if filed, would have revoked the previous Will of 1941, not only he but also Roy W. Harrell, and John Thomas Winston, son of Burrell F. Harrell, had served as witnesses, to include Burrell's daughters as inheritors.

One of Burrell's well-meaning friends and other white acquaintances of the Winston-Harrell family and friends of the deceased gave advice to John Thomas as to how he or other family members might challenge the Will to be probated in February. Included in this advice was that race was not a factor in prohibiting inheritance, nor illegitimacy, nor common law marriage, per se, as Georgia recognized them all. Still none of the Winstons took any action in time. The easiest action for the family was to blame Alfred for his not having executed the conveyance of the 171.8 acres that made up the balance of the Rose Hill Place and wound up in this instance as the "goat" for yet another miscue, which doomed the Winstons to be inheritors of their father's assets. Other members of the Winston family who were around West Point at that time could have easily undertaken the task themselves. Absolutely no one came forward.

Roy, after the probate, set out immediately to identify all of the parcels that he controlled so that he could take further action, if necessary, to acquire the remainder of the Harrell lands not ceded to him or other "at-law" family members. Roy didn't shrink from this formidable task, knowing that with all of the Winstons' failures to seize beckoning opportunities to receive some of Uncle Burrell's properties, they would never ever pose any threat to him or his sons in the future. He couldn't believe how easy it was to wrap up the whole shebang. He was home free. Was everybody afraid of him, particularly the Winstons? He believed that none of them dare sue him because they feared that he would take everything they had through some legal stratagem or bluff, as again everybody seemed so naïve and timid. Such behavior whetted Roy's aggressive drive against the rest of the Harrell family, so much so that it had the appearance of vengeance because of their alleged disinheritance of his father, Thomas Gordon.

All available evidence shows that Roy's father, Tom, was not formally disinherited, but the net affect was the same because he did give up his entitlement to whatever he could inherit by signing an affidavit to that effect. It was not a collective action on the part of the family to deny him or his children their due. It was, however, that Miss Cordie, Tom's mother, had spent a small fortune seeing to it that Tom was beyond the reach of the law. Any caring mother with means would have done the same thing, no matter the infraction committed. Miss Cordie, after a while, did tally up her expenditures and other outlays and found them foreboding, so much so that they amounted to more than one seventh of the value of all of the properties; therefore, she reasoned that she had satisfied the equal division of her wealth, and Tom had already gotten his, leaving absolutely nothing to his family. The record shows that Tom, on December 27, 1901, relinquished:

"My entire interest in the estate of B.W. Harrell late of said county, deceased, as one of the heirs of the said B.W. Harrell, the interest herein

213

conveyed being all my right, title and interest, claim and demand on said Estate of whatever it may contain and where ever found."

This was noted that the consideration sought was "For value received." There was no other explanation thereon or alluded thereto. As this was twenty years before Tom's demise, what then was the issue? It was apparently that Tom owed his mother substantial sums of money from previous encounters with the authorities and creditors, and was unable to pay up, but children never pay their parents anyway, but in this instance, his mother demanded payment or provide something of value equal to his indebtedness, and therefore, he had to give up his rights to satisfy this debt not just to his mother, a no nonsense woman, but to the family's estate. She was the keeper – the Administrator.

The responsibility now to take care of his aunts fell squarely on Roy's shoulders. It was daunting. This was his Uncle Burrell's will as was his grandfather's (Burrell Whatley Harrell). All they had remaining of significant value was the land, except for Evans, who had accumulated a personal fortune in West Point Manufacturing Company investments. This was the land their mother, Cordelia Alpha Combs Harrell, had granted them in 1932, many acres of which were not farmed anymore and therefore not generating cash, so there was no cash, to speak of, to be distributed. Roy would, at the proper time, after having endeared himself to his Aunts, make an offer to buy or sell their land so that the proceeds could provide for their upkeep and health and welfare. When he made these offers in exchange for services, "the Family" considered such actions not only noble but also equally fair and reasonable. And they were. This pleased them. This understanding included, of course, the upkeep and maintenance of the homestead. No further hurdles remained, or it was so thought. In this way, Roy now had free hand to acquire, receive, distribute, sell and/or retain all inherited as well as newly acquired Harrell properties, formerly under the control of one Burrell Floyd Harrell, lands for himself and his family. This excluded lands, which were, conveyed to Cordelia Harrell Johnson's heirs, namely, her children John William Johnson, Jr., Marie Johnson Cunningham, and Evans Chester Johnson, sister and brothers.

There was still the issue of whether Uncle Burrell's true "Last Will and Testament," the unsigned Warranty Deed, the intended conveyance of 171.8 acres (Rose Hill) to his sons, should be passed on to them rather than Roy's retaining it for himself. There was also the question of disposing the 273.5 acres, on which now is the site of the Coca-Cola Bottling Plant of West Point, previously intended for John Thomas' inheritance. Should this property be Roy's, as it was owned solely by Uncle Burrell, and Roy's being the sole inheritor, or should it be split between the first cousins, John Will and Roy? Roy's point of contention was that all of it should be his because Uncle Burrell's Will clearly stated that he, Roy, would be the sole inheritor notwithstanding any unexecuted documents to the contrary. There was the issue of morality notwithstanding the tradition of honoring the wishes of the dead, whether or not they were signed, sealed, and/or delivered. This means that the properties should be deeded as the deceased intended, that is, Rose Hill be deeded to the boys, George Frank, Gaines Tyrone, James Floyd, and Alfred Gordon, as listed on the plat plan dated November 15, 1965, and that John Thomas receive the 273.5 acres on which sits the Coca-Cola Bottling Company's Plant even though no documents could be located because Uncle Burrell's intentions were well known. Neither of the latter actions ever took place. On balance, there was no compelling legal reason for this to take place. The moral integrity, if any, would be borne by the one(s) who would take title to the properties. Roy maintained that no such obligation existed; this was solely a matter of business, as the required actions did not take place in accordance with the law.

February 7, 1966 was the appointed time for the Last Will and Testament to be exhibited to the court. May had already ceded her share to Burrell; therefore it became part of Burrell's property. Evans had tried to cede her property to Roy and his family, but there were objections as it was contended that Tom's "disinheritance" had to remain in effect as it was for his demeanor and disposition that it happened in the first place. Bubber, John Will, Jr., representing his siblings, and their inheritance from their mother, Cordelia, rose to his feet as he was now entitled to the utmost of respect from the Harrell family due to his prestige as a prominent lawyer and an officer of the court. Bubber paid strict attention to the proceedings, as he was a party to or overseer of many of the legal actions before now, and it was in his best interest as well to see to it that everything was lawfully executed and all of the at-law relatives were treated fairly and equitably.

"It's about time all of this denial of Uncle Tom's family be stopped," John Will declared. "It is just plain wrong. From this day on, we must include Roy and his siblings and their issue as if Uncle Tom had a full share of the family's inheritance. They all sat there dumfounded that someone had the temerity to say openly what seemed to contravene Miss Cordie's dictates.

"This court is now in session, Judge P. T. Hipp, presiding", bellowed the bailiff. Roy W. Harrell, nephew of Burrell F. Harrell exhibited the will as follows:

GEORGIA, TROUP COUNTY

I, Burrell F. Harrell, of said County, being of sound and disposing mind and memory, do make this my last will and testament, hereby revoking any and all others that I have heretofore made.

ITEM ONE

It is my will and desire that my body be buried in a Christian-like manner, the place and details I leave to my family.

ITEM TWO

It is my will and desire that all my just debts be paid as soon as practicable after my death.

ITEM THREE

I will and bequeath and devise all of my property both real and personal, to my sister, Mrs. May Harrell Duncan, to be hers for and during her natural life and at her death the remainder to be distributed as hereinafter directed.

ITEM FOUR

I will and direct that my sister, Mrs. May Harrell Duncan, shall have the full right, power and authority to sell any portion of the property of which I may die seized and to use the proceeds thereof should it, in her judgment, be necessary that such be done.

ITEM FIVE

I, will, bequeath and devise the remainder of the property, after the death of my sister, Mrs. May Harrell Duncan, to my nephew, Roy Harrell, to be his in fee simple, directing however, that he retain the interest in the Harrell Plantation and that the plantation be kept together and that he, in turn, devise it to his child or children.

ITEM SIX

I hereby make and appoint Mrs. May Harrell Duncan and Roy Harrell, executors of this will. Should either be unable or unwilling for any reason to act, the other shall act with the full power and authority granted to the two. They and neither of them shall be required to make any inventory of my property and appraisement, or from giving any bond, the only requirement being that this will be probated, and they are further relieved from making any returns of their acts and doings to any court whatsoever.

This the ___ of November 1941. (The blank was filled in with the numeral "4" with November written over with the handwritten "DEC" for December

The Will was signed typically in Burrell's flowing cursive signature: "Burrell F. Harrell" *[see page 259].*

Declared, published, signed and sealed by Burrell F. Harrell, as his last will and testament, in the presence of the undersigned as witnesses, he first signing in our presence, and we, then, at this special instance and request, signing in his presence and in the presence of each other.

This the ___ day of November 1941. (Again Mr. Harrell inserted the numeral "4" at the blank and writing over "November" with "DEC" for: December)

Signatures for the following persons were affixed:

/s/ <u>Loeb C. Ketzky</u>

/s/ <u>Annie Jane Davis</u>

/s/ <u>Mrs. Otis Williams</u>

ORDER

TROUP COURT OF ORDINARY

Feb. 7, Term, 1966

It being shown to the court in the matter of BURRELL F. HARRELL, deceased, last Will and Testament, propounded by Roy W. Harrell, named as executor, that said deceased died a resident of said County, and that due and legal notice of the pending probation of said will in Solemn Form at this term of Court, has been duly served on all of the heirs at law, mentioned in said petition and of said deceased, all in accordance with the laws of this State and all other requirements of law having been complied with, and the said will having been proven in open Court by the witnesses thereto to be the Last Will and Testament of BURRELL F. HARRELL, deceased as alleged by the propounder:

It is ordered by this court that said Will be established as the Last Will and Testament of BURRELL F. HARRELL, and that the same be admitted to record, as proven in Solemn Form, and Letters of Testamentary issued to ROY W. HARRELL as Executor of the estate of said deceased upon his, taking the oath of office.

/s/ P. T. Hipp
Ordinary.

The oath of office was administered to Roy W. Harrell on the 10th of December 1965 by P. T. Hipp, Ordinary. It read as follows:

GEORGIA, TROUP COUNTY

I, do solemnly swear that his writing contains the true last Will of the within named BURRELL F. HARRELL deceased, so far as I know or believe, and that I will well and truly execute the same in accordance with the laws of the State. So help me God.

Sworn to and submitted before me, This 10th day of Dec. 1965.

/s/   Roy W. Harrell

/s/.........P. T. Hipp

The very same persons who witnessed the signing of the original will back in 1941 were again the same persons, 25 years later, who gave witness to the Affidavit to probate the Will, namely, as above. It seemed as if nothing had changed except the signatures of the witnesses tellingly reflected their more advanced ages.

Despite the Witnesses attesting to the integrity of the Will, the Winston family privately maintained that the original Will had been changed or tampered with and not by Mister Burrell; that notwithstanding, the Will was probated as being in order. To their great consternation, this was not the Will that Mister Burrell, Roy, Simon -- the new lawyer, and John Thomas had crafted. The protest was not formally submitted. Again, too little, too late.

The Will was presented as per the Letters of Testamentary – Solemn Form:

STATE OF GEORGIA

TROUP COUNTY

BY THE COURT OF ORDINARY OF SAID COUNTY.

As all Wills, this one revokes any and all other Wills and as such would have invalidated the so-called new Will as it had never been probated

219

and bona fide copies were not made available to the court. It was legally executed and without a flaw. Roy was home free once again.

The occasion was the reading of the will of Burrell Floyd Harrell. Roy had assembled the principal beneficiaries as enumerated in the Petition to Probate the Will in Solemn Form. They were Evans Harrell, Burrell's surviving sister, three issues of Cordelia, the youngest of Burrell's siblings, and those of brother Thomas (deceased) and a host of nephews and nieces.

The backdrop for the Will was the vast land estate of "Burrell F. Harrell" and "Mrs. C.A. Harrell" around 1930. Reviewing the Plan and Profile for Georgia State Highway 18, a layout of the Harrell properties shows that their holdings stretched several miles into the countryside on both the north and south sides of Highway 18. Those properties that were controlled solely by Mrs. C.A. Harrell, the Administrator and Burrell's mother, were listed as such. Those that were entirely Burrell's, inherited or acquired by other means, were listed as "B. F. Harrell" to include the "Rose Hill Place." A diagram is attached for the purpose of identifying the estates. The Will that was just probated was based on the properties owned by the Harrells in the late 1930s.

Surprisingly, the State Plan and Profile showed two colored owners of vast land acreage.

They were namely, Walter Caracter and Isaiah Palmore. Race of the colored landholders were identified as "(Col.)." Any discussion of these landholders is not germane to this book and noted here because of what appears to be an anomaly for the times.

The conveyance and distribution of the deceased's properties to the heirs at law were first ceded by Roy to his wife, Pearl Colville Harrell, who in turn redistributed specific properties to designated heirs at law. Because the children of Burrell F. Harrell were not designated as heirs at law in the Will of 1941, none received any of the probated property whatsoever. The acreage initially conveyed to the sons of B. F. Harrell remained separate from the Will's designation.

After there were no challenges to the will, Roy set out to create the necessary deeds to distribute the apportioned shares to the heirs at law.

There were rumors that John Thomas and Rosa Belle were going to sue to get their rightful share of the property. The rumor iterated that Roy had a meeting with both of them. Roy already had John Thomas' number because he didn't press to receive the full five acres promised for John Thomas' selling the frontage of his property on Georgia Highway 18 for the gas station. John Thomas knew from experience that whatever they settled on, Roy felt no obligation to honor it. The other Winstons stood by without any further actions taken despite the many pleas to seek their rightful share. Insofar as the Will was concerned, the daughters were still left nothing by Mr. Burrell. It was clear however, that in his last days, he wanted to grant the boys more parcels of land, the 171.8 acres, but Roy totally ignored all of that and nothing took place prior to his death. That part of the Rose Hill parcel of 171.8 acres intended for the Winston brothers was eventually ceded to ROY W. HARRELL, JR. and FRANK C. HARRELL to wit:

"A tract of land containing 48 acres, being that part of Land Lot 224 and Land Lot 179 lying south of the Old Columbus Road, now Georgia Highway No, 18, and east of Georgia Highway 103, better known as the "Rose Hill Place" in the 5th Land District of Troup County, Georgia...."

This was tantamount to rubbing salt in the wound. The Winstons were hoping or at least believed that in a weak moment, Roy would transfer that land to them. Nothing doing. There was nothing illegal about this nor any of the other transactions taken by Roy as he followed the rules relating to wills and the distribution of the land. It was just the American way of doing business – you take care of yourself and your kind first and last. But what good is an oath even swearing on the Bible if there is no force of good behind it? In the America of yore, oaths and Bibles were deep-seated precepts that one's honor was at stake, and that affected one's standing in his community. But then again, everything is relative in its degree of importance, meaning that you follow the dictates of your own conscience to gain and maintain your advantage or capture what you covet, the truth notwithstanding. One can only wonder whether Roy participated in or knew of any other Wills than the one signed by B. F. Harrell in December 1941, three days before Pearl Harbor, notwithstanding his reputedly being present when "the second Will" was drawn up.

Is it reasonable to believe that the content and substance of any Will would not change over a period of more than twenty years? But be that as it may, the system was designed to allow challenges to one's testimony, certifications, oaths, affidavits, or truthfulness of one's words. This suggests that these principles hold when one is dealing among equals and the well intentioned. It was therefore up to the Winstons and none other, to challenge the actions of Roy when their interests were at stake. It is naïve to think that any other party would come forward to challenge the probate of the Will. What protections are built in by the System to make sure that interests and rights of the uninitiated are not trampled upon by the unscrupulous?

Chapter 17. The Aftermath

The Winstons lost out big time by not coming forward. What was their problem? Did someone offer some one of them a deal not to pursue the challenge or did money change hands to thwart the continued processing of the new Will? All of the above were accusations made by some within the Winston Family itself against other family members. They thought that Roy was the culprit without any evidence whatsoever as not a mumbling word was sounded.

The Winstons and the townspeople knew Roy's demeanor as well as his business acumen. Roy could always turn a buck. He was a businessman. The problem was that the opportunities were not substantial enough to enable him to amass a fortune of the size he wanted. He was tough on all of his creditors, white or black. He would hound them to the bitter end to pay up on whatever they owed no matter how small the debt. "If you owe, you must pay," was his creed. On the other hand, nothing could stop him from trying to extract the maximum in dollars from any investment from a creditor. It was just simply good business.

Some years after Roy's coup, urban renewal came to West Point, Georgia at the behest of the Federal Government. A large area in the colored section of West Point was declared substandard and unfit for human habitation. The number of shacks that Roy and other whites had built in the thirties and forties fell under this determination. All such housing was slated for razing, to be replaced with well-designed, modern brick facilities to include running water, electricity, and inside toilets. This was a godsend for the coloreds. They would live a healthier and more prosperous life, so that they could give their best in their work for the businesses and white townspeople in West Point. This was the principal justification given for the project.

The Government, of course, had to acquire the properties from the owners, most of whom were white. Roy Harrell was the biggest owner and he was willing to sell for an attractive price. The Government negotiators found Roy a most competent and tough adversary.

"Mr. Harrell, the Government is obligated to pay a fair and reasonable price for the housing which you so generously provided for these poor, suffering people. According to the papers that you have submitted to us for review, it appears that you were able to build these houses for around $300.00 a piece. Other information you have given us shows that you insured these houses on the average of about $1000.00 apiece, yet you are asking us to pay you about $3,000.00 on the average for each. Just how do you justify such an increase?

"I am begging your pardon, Sir. Are you asking me to justify to you the value of housing which you want to buy when you are the one who is demanding that I sell it to you? This is puzzling to me. If you want to say that this is how much they have appreciated over the years, I don't care. Pay me on the average of $3000.00 per unit and we have a deal. Obviously, some are worth more than others, but that's my offer. You can take it or leave it. That's my price, buddy."

"Do you have an appraisal or some valuation to show that this is what they are worth?"

"It's my own appraisal. I don't need nobody telling me what something of mine is worth. I am a professional real estate man and have been in the business for a long time," Roy said. "That should be sufficient for you. If not, you can start your condemnation proceedings; it's as simple as that. I can't understand why you people go to such great lengths for such simple dealings. If you can't make that decision, then I am dealing with the wrong outfit. I have to go."

"We will get in touch with you Mr. Harrell, soon and you have a good day."

Everybody negotiates with the Government, even Roy.

The very next day, Roy telephoned the Government agent and suggested that he would like to negotiate the total cost of the property, however, he did follow the agent's suggestion that he get an independent appraiser. "There is a problem, however, the appraiser values the price of the units on the average of $3500.00. Y'all seem as though y'all are pretty good people and if y'all want to carry this thing forward, I'm willing to settle for an average of $3000.00 per unit. That is my final offer.

Roy got his price. He, for the very first time in his life, was really flush with cash. He would be able to treat all of his heirs to the lifestyle he had always dreamed of for himself and carrying out his full responsibilities towards his Aunts in the old Harrell mansion, except now it has vastly deteriorated. He cared as to how he would be remembered.

He found the remaining Aunts, Evans and Verne, not doing well at all. The Harrells were indeed long-lived people, of course, of pioneer stock, especially the women. The question was should they be kept at the mansion with help brought in, or should he arrange for them in private care facilities.

After the Aunts were moved to personal care facilities, Roy was not one to wait for things to develop; he carved the mansion up into two units and rented them out for a while. The tenants would only stay for a short time because of the deficiencies and the rent that they could afford. This was a "Heritage House," one that had to be remembered. Efforts to get it on the National Register failed. The cost of renovations and upkeep were just simply too high without Government support. It was abandoned. Nature assumed control of the house, and the elements ravaged it beyond recognition in a few short years. During this time, crack heads moved in and made "The Old Harrell House" their sanctuary. It was just a shadow of itself, and barely recognizable to those who would bother to glance in its direction. The West Point City Limits had been extended well into the countryside by this time. The City now having the authority to rid itself of hazards, decided to demolish the house under the supervision of the fire department. This vital landmark which once defined the life of a great family in that time is lost forever. If one had ever seen it, he would still be looking for it because it had always been there, a prominent landmark on its knoll. Nothing is in its place, and the knoll is now all grown over. Roy did not find it necessary to keep the pledge to maintain it; to do so was a poor business decision.

Why didn't the Winstons act? Some say that it was out of sheer fear of Roy's power over them. He now owned them. It was the colored man's abject fear of the white man. They were afraid of his power to punish them with impunity. Seemingly, the law was never on their side. Others say that they were not of the mind to do what was necessary, namely, to hire an attorney to file suit for redress of their grievances. Could the Winstons have believed that they would not have been able to find an attorney who would pursue their case fairly and with alacrity on their behalf? Just because there were only white attorneys in the county, would the Winstons be justified in the belief that all were or would be prejudiced against them because they were not white? Or could it be that cowardice or abject fear had beset them so much so that they failed to engage, because of likely repercussions and reprisals that in turn would jeopardize their mere being? Could it perhaps have been none of these, but the fact that Mr. Burrell had done everything for them, including their thinking, their speaking, their reason for being, their initiatives, if any, and on and on? Could it be that even their sense of responsibility of self was never truly established? He had protected them to the fullest without realizing himself that one day he would be gone and they would have to fend for themselves. They had been subjected to abject paternalism, and now with Big Daddy out of the picture, a whole new world stood before them for their conquering, but they found that they could not cope with it. Their situation was not much different from that of the slaves, who found themselves afloat with nowhere to turn after Emancipation. They had no confidence in the System's dealing fairly because it was still heavily biased against them. This was not fantasy. It was a good thing that Mr. Burrell gave them that land on which the boys built their houses; otherwise, they would have been "out in the cold," evicted, from the old home house as well as other areas of the farm where they were born and raised and farmed. There was nothing else in writing that was legally acceptable on which they could lay claim to their birthplace and perhaps even their birthright.

Miss Rosa came to realize that she had nowhere else to live, because Mr. Burrell left her nothing, not even her own home. Roy had dominion over all. He called all of the shots. He called all of Burrell's boys together for a "reality session." He told them in all of his benevolence, "I will allow your mother to continue to live in her home house." This was unusual for Roy. Suspicions arose immediately that he was going to charge her rent or devise some nefarious scheme to make inordinate demands of her. He said it was hers as long as she wanted to live there, but it had to be understood that Sug had to grant an easement to allow his mother a path to go to and from her house, because it had been cut off from the main highway by the sale of John Thomas' land to the owners of the gas station. Sug refused. He had been burned too many times by Roy's schemes – no dice.

"This is for your Mother, boy, you know that," first cousin Roy said. "You should be willing to do something for her. You should be ashamed of yourself."

"Mr. Roy," Gaines asked. "Can't you ever do anything nice for anybody? You have created all of these problems for us and now you're blaming us. I just don't understand."

"I don't know why you ask that, Foy. I'm sure you heard that I give free rent to everybody at Christmastime if and when they pay their rent on time throughout the year."

They all looked at each other and burst out laughing. "What a crock!" They had never heard of this nor anyone's ever getting a break from Mr. Roy.

Roy became somewhat annoyed because they were making fun of him. "You boys had better watch yourselves. I control your fate. But it's OK to have fun at my expense just this one time," he smiled generously.

"I am taking over the entire farm as of today. It is all mine per Uncle Burrell's Will and the probate court. You can't live in your Mother's house anymore. And Sug, you have to turn in that truck you've been riding around in."

"You can't do that," Sug exclaimed. "That's my own truck! Mr. Burrell bought it for me and he took out for it each week from my paycheck."

"But you still owe money on the truck. It has been some time since anything has been paid on it, so you are in arrears and by rights, I will seize it. Turn it in immediately. I have checked the books, and it says that Uncle Burrell paid for it; therefore, it belongs to the farm. Did you get any receipts? Since the farm belongs to me, so does the truck. If you want to continue to work here, turn it in! Plus you have been burning up too much gas with racing in "Hee Haw" style all over the farm."

"I haven't been paid since Miss May died," Sug pleaded. "That's nearly 6 months ago. I've got wages coming, and I can still continue to pay the balance for the truck. Can't we still talk about it? I own most of it out right anyhow."

"Nothing doing! Gimme the keys and what's more, you're fired!" Roy said.

"You can't do this! These were not the terms that Mr. Burrell and I made."

"You got papers that say that? Is there anybody else that can vouch for you?" Roy asked.

"No but these were . . . . ."

"Shelve it, you got no case," Roy said extending his hand for the keys.

Sug tossed the keys to Roy and walked away.

"Come back here!" Roy shouted. Sug kept on going.

Each of the boys owned trucks except for Gaines. Mr. Burrell gave each of them a truck but kept his name on the papers as to ownership. Each was waiting for his to be confiscated by Roy. It never happened. Roy eventually gave Sug his back.

They licked their wounds for a few days, and all had reconciled themselves to the fact that they were defeated. This would be where they would stay to the end of their days, and perhaps they could still make a go of it, somehow. They were simply pathetic, although John Thomas had a steady job at the Lanett Bleachery and Dye Works, part of the West Point Manufacturing Company. The pay was decent, he had a family, had built himself an attractive, sturdy and ample brick house for his family on the land once owned by his father but later under the control of Roy, but more important, he had managed to get Roy to deliver on the promise to exchange five acres of land, which turned out to be only an acre and a half. Most important was that he, John Thomas, held the deeds. John Thomas was thankful to get that, and decided it would do. He was not going to fight anymore. He always came out on the short end of the stick whenever dealing with the whites anyway. He just wanted to be left alone to raise his family. He was even offered a supervisory job at the Dye Works during his tenure, but he declined it even though it was offered in part because he was known to the management as one of "the boys in Burrell Harrell's colored family." If he had taken this job, he believed that he would have had difficulty not only with the whites but the blacks as well. He knew that the blacks would only accept whites as their bosses. With all that said and done, it was good enough for him to do a little farming on his own, as he was inured to the soil and this seemed to be his fate. He simply had had it.

James drifted between Mother and brothers, and finally wasted away in a sea of booze. The baby boy, Gaines, decided that he would become the entrepreneur; he would sell the property that Mr. Burrell conveyed to him to a commercial outfit. The family went to pieces.

"You can't do that!" exclaimed Rosa Belle, his oldest sister, almost 20 years his senior. "This is the land where we were born and raised. It is sacred to us! We must keep this together."

"If you want to buy it to keep things together, then I will sell it to you for less than I am getting from them," Gaines said.

"You're just being a smart ass, you know I have no money," she said.

"Anybody else?" Gaines asked. "No tickee, no washee. I won't keep it myself. I must and will sell." And he did.

The family had to reshuffle. Pandemonium reigned. John Thomas had already distanced himself from the family squabbles. When James up and died, he had almost finished building his house but left no will. A major crisis ensued. Because the other siblings were unable to come to terms on the disposition of James' property, John Thomas found it necessary to reenter the fray. James' heirs were John Thomas himself, George Frank (Sug), Gaines, Alfred, Rosa Belle, the eldest sister, Marguerite, Precious, Mary Bessie, and his Mother Rosa. John Thomas, after removing himself as an heir, proposed that each of the remaining heirs receive a one seventh share of James' property. Mercifully, all present agreed. Coordination took place with Mary Bessie and Precious by telephone as they lived in Michigan. The other properties for the boys conveyed by Mr. Burrell remained unaffected.

The only thing that was resolved was ownership, but there were insufficient funds among the local family members for any one of them to buy the other(s) out.

The following Affidavit describes the heirs to James' property:

AFFIDAVIT

    RE: Deed from John T. Winston, et al, heirs at law
              of James F. Winston, to John T. Winston, et al.
              Recorded in Deed Book 223, Page 247,
              Troup County Records.

GEORGIA, TROUP COUNTY

Personally appeared before the undersigned authority authorized to administer oaths come GRADY FULLER, who, after being duly sworn, deposes that he personally knew the late James F. Winston. Affiant deposes further that James F. Winston was 42 years of age, unmarried, and died intestate as a resident of Troup County, Georgia, leaving as his sole surviving heir at law, the following:

JOHN T. WINSTON, ALFRED GORDON WINSTON, GEORGE FRANK WINSTON, GAINES T. WINSTON, ROSA BELL WINSTON PARKER, ROSA WINSTON, MARGARET WINSTON ADAMS, PRECIOUS WINSTON BROOKS, MARY B. WINSTON FANNINGS.

Affiant deposes further that all of said heirs at law are sui juris and have sound mind.

        Grady A. Fuller, L.S.

Sworn to and subscribed to before me this 8th day of October, 1968.

        Martha Birdsong Jones
        Notary Public

Mary Bessie had been yearning to come back home as she had been away far too long. She had money due to her success in the restaurant business and properties she and Jim had come into and sold while living up North. But she had to convince Jim, as he was still pursuing his career and what's more, he was an "outsider" in her family. The nineties began as turbulently as the eighties. If Mary wanted him to come back to Georgia to live, there were a few things that had to be ironed out, such as, where were they going to live, in town or "on the farm" notwithstanding that there was no more farming. Jim felt that he could never live in a small town again because he was a guy from the big city up North now and had put down small town, southern ways. He needed to be assured that the civil rights campaigns of the fifties and sixties had made West Point and its surrounding areas including the Alabama side of the community much more friendly to blacks than he knew in the past. No one could give him that assurance because there was no appreciable organized civil rights movement in the area except for the Montgomery, Alabama civil rights activities headed by Martin Luther King, Junior, and they were carried out more than 75 miles away and about 40 years ago. That phase of the movement was over and had had little or no effect on West Point. Everyone who could have benefited from the civil rights activities had left the area for greener pastures a long time ago, and those who remained were accustomed to the ways in which they lived or had acquiesced even before the Civil Rights movement was declared a success. The schools had been desegregated, not integrated, but the great majority of whites had gone off to private or parochial schools to avoid racial mixing. Nobody really cared, the blacks voted now regularly but so what? Blacks were never truly banned from voting anyway in West Point – they just didn't vote. What difference did it or would it make? Civil Rights were a non-issue in West Point, even though there was the perceived curtailment of rights and privileges such as poor quality and separate schools and residential restrictions. Only Eddie B. Canady voted regularly.

Eddie B. was the most prosperous colored person around and a successful farmer of cotton, sugar cane, and corn. He had large land holdings, some overlooking the Chattahoochee River from a bluff, a large number of rental properties in both Georgia and Alabama, and a combination convenience store and gas station that many whites and blacks patronized. He was the black Roy Harrell, except that his tenants loved him. He even owned the largest dance hall in West Georgia. It operated every Friday and Saturday night, with the major big band orchestras of the day such as Jimmy Lunceford, Cootie James, Erskine Hawkins, and Count Basie. Their soloists were world renowned – including Ella Fitzgerald, Joe Williams, and Mildred Bailey; it was said that he rented rooms downstairs to anybody who wanted to cut a black oak. The dance hall was located on Georgia Highway 18, Tenth Street, or the main drag through the colored section of West Point. Eddie B. was well known and well liked and even his enemies were his friends. Furthermore, he did pay his poll taxes during the time they were required and always operated under the radar, never ever challenging the white establishment.

Jim Earnest knew all of this. His real problem was that he really didn't know how he was going to get along with Mary's brothers, particularly since Mr. Burrell had passed on. In spite of the family's internal problems, they always circled the wagons when outsiders moved in. Even though he was married to their sister, Jim was still considered an outsider of sorts. Jim learned quickly that all he had to do was to give the brothers a fifth of "seal whisky" on occasion and everything was "hunky dory."

Jim quickly overcame the family's veiled irritation, even though he and Mary had been married for 45 years. That irritation lasted for 45 years because Jim had a glistening black color and therein laid the heart of the matter -- color prejudice. Color prejudice was as pervasive among the "colored" as it was with the whites. It was no secret; it was just not talked about. Jim was definitely an asset to the family because he had experiences and skills that the brothers never had but needed to survive. Jim had gone to the University of Detroit and got himself one of those powerful degrees, the MBA -- Master of Business Administration, and became an important executive in the Federal Government at the Detroit Arsenal. He was a financial wizard with a presidential appointment. He analyzed their situation, and spearheaded the action to acquire all of the property that was conveyed by Mr. Burrell from the rest of the Winston family, females and all, and put it in the hands of his wife and himself. He asked Mary what she thought about the plan.

"Well, Mary said, "that certainly depends on what the issues are as you know as well as I do that we are not going to set the agenda for anybody around here.

"No, I won't get involved," Jim said. "All I want to do is be a figure in the community to see what good I can do. This requires me to switch my denomination from Baptist to Methodist, though Bethlehem Baptist will always be my church. We can sing in the choir together and join the various clubs, but I don't believe that I can ever be anything but a Baptist. We can get a youth movement going to include our children. If you want, we can even get the farm going again if there's a willingness on the part of your brothers; otherwise, we can sit in the swing on the front porch and drink Coca-Colas and eat soda crackers for the rest of our lives just like Miss Rosa and Mr. Burrell did for so long."

"Do you plan to run for office or something?"

"How did you guess? It's about time someone in the black community made himself felt at the polls because if they don't exercise their newly gained rights at the polls, the desired changes may never come. But there's nothing here. Why do people stay?" Blacks often referred to themselves in the third person as if the individual speaking didn't belong to the group. This could have been due to their being outsiders with no power to control their own destiny.

"The same reason we're coming back. You know, I've just inherited a fractional share of James' property. We can build our dream house out there in the 'burbs and live quite comfortably if not luxuriously, and live quite happily ever afterwards. We will have to figure out how we can preserve what's ours. We will have to band together to salvage what else is left. Let's buy. Let's buy everybody out. Nobody has lived there long enough to become attached to it. We can have the lots appraised and make an offer and see what comes of it."

Jim asked Mary to call John Thomas in to get the family together and involved to explain their proposal.

John Thomas had to remind them that he wanted nothing for himself, as he was satisfied with his holdings. The important thing was that each of the heirs at law would get money for his or her share, but each must forever let it go, as they would get paid for it. The amount of money quickly became the big issue. Well, how much was it worth was the question, and who knew? It was still a rural property, but after Gaines sold his 2.4 acres to the BP service station interests and the Quality Inn went up at the intersection of I-85 and Georgia Highway 18, there had to be some significant appreciation of the property values.

Mary Bessie entered the discussion by asking, "Just how much do you want for your piece?" addressing the question first to the eldest sister, Rosa Belle.

"Let's get an appraiser to come over and give us an estimate as to what the land's value is," she answered.

"But that will cost money and do we need to get any outsiders involved," Precious injected. "Why can't we agree among ourselves? We must not let anybody else know what we are doing." They all nodded in agreement for they were still a closely-knit family in spite of their constant quarrels.

"How about $2,500.00 apiece, is that too much?" Marguerite asked.

"Too much? That will hardly scratch the surface!" Precious exclaimed. "It should be at least $4,000.00 for each of us," She suggested.

"How much would you take, Rosa Belle?" Mary Bessie asked.

"I don't know, how about $5,000.00 for each of us," Rosa Belle suggested.

"I think that you should kick that around a little more, because I want all of you to be satisfied," said John Thomas. "Why don't y'all go into the other room and talk it over and when y'all have an answer, we can come back in and we should be able to arrive at a figure."

Mary, Jim, and John Thomas went to the sitting room to await the decision. Ardell and John Thomas' children were in the sitting room enjoying the TV. Ardell and Jim had never really talked to each other about their status in the family. She had a medium brown skin complexion but relative to the Winstons, she was black and also considered an outsider. This now was Jim's opportunity to enter the family as another "outsider" and just to compare notes and find ways of belonging. Ardell was reluctant to respond at first, as her relationship with John Thomas was good, and she wanted to keep it private. She felt that she had nothing to offer, as she had no real dealings with the rest of the family, including Miss Rosa. She for the most part was willing to raise her children apart from the rest of the family because they were a bit darker than the other grandchildren and did not expect that they would be received very well. This was enough for Jim to know how to navigate the waters as he was now going to make West Point his home again.

A few minutes had passed as the sisters discussed the settlement of their share of the property. Precious came to the door and said, "We are ready to continue if y'all are."

"So soon?" John Thomas said with some surprise.

"There was really nothing to it. We thought that $100,000.00 each would be more than enough. Those numbers you were throwing around in there were nothing but chump change. We cannot be bought cheap! We may be country bumpkins," Precious said, "but we are not stupid!"

"What!!" John Thomas, Jim, and Mary Bessie shouted altogether in sheer disbelief.

"Don't be so surprised. There's going to be a building boom all around here because of the Interstate. You know?" Precious said.

Then she burst out laughing. "Just fooling!" Then Rosa Belle and Marguerite came into the living room in loud laughter. "We gotcha! Didn't We? We'll settle for $5,000.00 apiece. That's our price. Otherwise the deal is off."

Mary Bessie, being the coy one, spoke up as Jim realized that it was best that he not say anything yet, as his position was still not quite secure in the family, "I imagine Doll persuaded you. (Doll was Marguerite.) Let us kick it around a bit ourselves to see if we can't work something out. I just want to sleep on it."

235

"Better yet, let's drink to it," said Rosa Belle. "No sense in dragging it out. It's $5,000.00, otherwise, we sell to somebody else," she was not bluffing. She really was the no nonsense type, just like her grandmother, Miss Cordie.

"Then I will break out the booze, "John Thomas said. "This moment is too good to let it get away from us. Let's come back to the living room and settle all of our differences." Ardell had the setups ready anticipating agreement.

This was a strange moment for the Winstons because things were almost never joyous. They were either getting shafted or they were shafting somebody including each other but not without good reason. "It ran in the family" was the general thinking.

It fell to John Thomas to sell their offer. He had to convince Mary and Jim that this was not a whole lot of land, and the best thing to do was to accept the offer; at least the property would remain in the family if that were a major issue. Jim remained studiously silent because this was now solely a Winston family matter. Jim nodded to Mary without John Thomas' noticing it.

"In that case, do it!" Mary said. "Son, you must explain to them that this is it. There's no coming back to the well for more. There will be no more where this is coming from."

The evening was wearing on. They were back together again. Mary said, "Jim and I accept your offer. We will get the paperwork going tomorrow. Son will take care of it."

"I knew that I was going to get stuck with the action but it's no real problem. I want all of y'all to remember, somebody else must step up and take some of the load off of my back. I won't always be around to be the patsy," John Thomas said. "This is what Mr. Burrell went through. This is what Mr. Roy went through. It's never ending. You people become so dependent and have no confidence in what you can do for yourselves. Get over it. It's time!"

The following Warranty Deed was drawn up, by the Richter law firm, to seal the deal, the same one that Mr. Burrell had used for years:

WARRANTY DEED

STATE OF GEORGIA

COUNTY OF TROUP

This indenture, made this 31st day of August, 1992, between JOHN T. WINSTON of the County of Troup, State of Georgia, Party of the First Part, and MARY B. WINSTON FANNINGS, Sr. of the County of Troup, State of Georgia, Parties of the Second Part.

Witnesseth, that the said Party of the First Part, for and in consideration of the sum of TEN ($10.00) DOLLARS AND OTHER VALUABLE CONSIDERATION, in hand paid at and before sealing and delivery of these presents, the receipt whereof is hereby acknowledged, has granted, bargained, sold, and conveyed and by these presents does grant, bargain, sell, and convey unto said Parties of the Second Part, their heirs and assigns, the following described property:

TRACT I

An undivided 1/7 interest in and to: All that tract or parcel of land lying and being in Troup County, Georgia, 2.4 acres. More or less, of land located in Land Lot No. 235 in the 5th Land District, Troup County, Georgia, and more fully described as follows, to wit: BEGIN at the intersection of the center line of Georgia State Highway No. 103 and No. 18 at Station No. 32 plus 96, according to a recent survey of said highway by the Georgia State Highway Engineers, and the west margin of land Lot 236 in the 5th Land District, Troup County, Georgia; thence measure in an Easterly direction along the center line of said Highway a distance of 2354.8 feet for a point; thence turn an angle of 90 degrees to the right and measure 90 feet to an iron pin for a point located on the South margin of the above mentioned Highway Right-of-Way; thence with a MB of South 67 degrees 16 minutes East along said Highway Right-of Way for 480 feet to an iron pin for a corner and Starting Point of the parcel to be described; thence, continue along said Right-of-Way feet to an iron pin for a corner; thence South 12 degrees 24 minutes East for 413 feet to an iron pin for a corner located in the center of a branch; thence in a Westerly direction along the center of said branch for 245 feet, more of less, to an iron pin for a corner; thence North 12 degrees 24 minutes East for 460 feet to an iron pin for a corner and STARTING POINT.

See Plat recorded in Plat Book 9, page 122.

This is the same tract as conveyed by B. F. Harrell to James F. Winston on 9/14/62 and recorded in Deed Book 157, Page 385, Troup County Records.

TRACT 2

An undivided 1/7 interest in and to: All that tract or parcel of land lying and being in Troup County, Georgia, 1.9 acres, more or less, of land located in Land Lot No. 235, a small portion being in Land Lot 224, in the 5th Land District, Troup County, Georgia, and more fully described as follows, to wit: BEGIN at the intersection of the center line of Georgia State Highway No. 103 and No. 18 at Station No. 32 plus 96, according to a recent survey of said Highway by the Georgia State Highway Engineers, and the West margin of Land Lot 236 in the 5th Land District, Troup County, Georgia; thence measure in an Easterly direction along the center line of said Highway a distance of 2354.8 feet for a point; thence turn an angle of 90 degrees to the right and measure 90 feet to an iron pin for a point located on the South margin of the above mentioned Highway Right-of-Way; thence with a MB of South 67 degrees 16 minutes East along said Highway Right-of Way for 720 feet to an iron pin for a corner and Starting Point of the parcel to be described; thence, continue along said Right-of-Way for 129.4 feet to an iron pin for a corner; thence 90 degrees to the left for 40 feet to an iron pin for a corner; thence 90 degrees to the right for 174 feet to an iron pin for a corner located at the head of the branch and the mouth of a storm drain under the above mentioned highway; thence in a South-Westerly and Westerly direction along the center of the said branch for 500 feet;, more of less, to an iron pin for a corner; thence North 12 degrees 24 minutes East for 413 feet to an iron pin for a corner and Starting Point

238

See Plat recorded in Plat Book 9, page 122.

This is the same tract as conveyed by B. F. Harrell to Alfred G. Winston on 9/14/62 and recorded in Deed Book 157, Page 385, Troup County Records.

It is the purpose of this deed to convey the entire interest in both Tract 1 and Tract 2 owned by Grantor to the Grantees herein in fee simple.

TO HAVE AND TO HOLD, The said bargained premises, together with all and singular the rights, members, and appurtenances thereof to the same being, belonging or in anywise appertaining, to the only proper use, benefit and behoof of MARY B. WINSTON FANNINGS and JIM E. FANNINGS, SR., the said Parties of the Second Part, their heirs and assigns, forever, in fee simple.

And the said Party of the First Part, for his heirs, executors and administrators, will warrant and forever defend the right and title to the above described property unto the said Parties of the Second Part, their heirs and assigns, against the claims of all persons whomsoever.

IN WITNESS WHEREOF, THE SAID OF THE first Part has set his hand and affixed his seal the day and year first above written.

/s/ (John T. Winston) (Seal)

Signed, sealed and delivered in the presence of:

/s/ Aubrey N. Ferrell

Witness

/s/ Christine Billings

Notary Public

Mary Bessie and Jim had been gone all of 45 years. Mister Burrell had been dead now for more than twenty years. So long was his absence that it was noted only occasionally. The farm was still being operated, but it was no longer profitable as many of the farm hands had moved on and the few left were not very productive. Roy was considering shutting down the farm altogether as they were only breaking even. It was more trouble to him than it was worth.

Because he had done so well in selling his houses to the urban renewal project, Roy was now able to work on consolidating his wealth and making strategic investments. He was bent on becoming the bona fide millionaire or see to it that his sons achieve it. The gross receipts for the houses exceeded a quarter-million dollars.

It was coming around to retirement time. There was a lot of unfinished business left. So Roy started to get his house in order. The first order of business was to get his and his wife's wills together. It is a beautiful piece of legal work – a masterpiece. It was devised by John Will Johnson, Jr., -- Cousin Bubber. Roy arranged for him and his bride to do the same, although it was known that his bride was the real mastermind in the house. She, Miss "Bebe," was tough and resolute. The template of her Will was identical to Roy's. Between the two of them, they would leave everything to the boys, Roy, Jr. and Colville, but would pay sufficiently large cash sums to their daughter. Gail relinquished her interests to any inheritable assets, similarly to her grandfather Thomas Gordon. Roy's aim was to cede every piece of property that he owned and all other assets to Pearl and she "in the event of" to Roy, Jr. and Colville so that when he passed on, there was absolutely nothing left – an estate that was completely devoid of any assets or worldly goods. His retirement package was sufficiently extensive that he needed no assist from anyone. He had succeeded in achieving his goal of total independence. He, in reality, owed no man a thing, not even the Winstons. He took nothing that was not legally his. He gave no quarter and expected none in return. He played by the rough and tumble rules book -- no holds barred. He had no friends – didn't want any, because friends need you. He was tired of being the caretaker for the extended family; although his role as the head of the family dictated that he remain in control till the bitter end. Although there was this illustrious Will, the important thing was that the deed was the instrument used to convey properties through his wife to their boys. He avoided the dreaded "death" taxes and was able to pay token fees in assessments. He profited from the mistakes of his Uncle Burrell, following the maxim that if you want to transfer assets, you should do it for the children before you pass on, and not be concerned that 'thy Will be done." He was a "free" man for the first time in his life. He could now spend blissful time with his bride of 48 years.

They, however, never moved out of their home house in West Point, where they had raised their children and had lived all of their married life, even though they had the wherewithal to do otherwise. They once had designs to move to the backwater property created by the damming of the Chattahoochee River, the West Point Lake, as a flood control measure to reduce the annual inundation of West Point and the surrounding areas in Alabama and Georgia. Instead they bought property for Roy, Jr. on the backwater. The shoreline and beaches at the lake are owned by the Federal Government; however, the property owners have access to the water's edge from their landings or from nearby public parks for swimming, picnicking, and fishing. It was created by the Corps of Engineers. West Point always took a beating from the river as far north as 20 miles and about five to the south. The flooding to the east was compounded by the overflow of the Long Cane Creek that regularly flooded the bottomlands of the Rose Hill Place. Colville chose to build on family or ancestral lands.

Epilogue

This book was initiated to tell the romantic story of love, romance, and sacrifice in an era that not only prohibited interracial relationships but also actively denied the enjoyment of their togetherness through intimidation and duress with the force of law. The common law union of Burrell Floyd Harrell and Rosa Rutledge Winston produced nine children who survived in a hostile environment being neither "Black nor White." Two of those children survive today on the same family lands, where their "second cousin," Frank Colville Harrell, lives just a mile up the road. The survivors are Mary and Precious, 78 and 85 years young, and each lives relatively modestly but comfortably. Their memories of the family and especially of "Mr. Burrell," the father, are mixed. They have resolved that "Mr. Burrell" was good to them although there were undercurrents that prevented his being an exemplary father himself. Unfortunately, they still have issues focused primarily on what should have been. To a degree, they have resolved their living such that they are no longer ashamed of who they are but can enjoy occasional visits from their children, grandchildren, nieces and nephews, and the freedom to practice their religious interests as they choose. Too, some members from the "other side" of the family may be visiting them and they will be welcome.

The descendants of Burrell Harrell and Rosa Winston, a brave woman who withstood the rigors of would-be scorn, are shown in the family tree and genealogical charts of Appendixes II and I. The descendants of his children are enjoying their retirements and pursuing professional careers in the land of opportunity like any other "privileged" American descended from European, African, and Arabian Forebears. They have succeeded in becoming successful doctors, lawyers, teachers, nurses, and business stalwarts, most having chosen to remain at home – in the South. They didn't have to leave home anymore to seek professional careers. Their own immediate descendants have equaled or far exceeded the accomplishments of their forebears.

The descendants of Burrell Whatley Harrell, one of whom was Burrell Floyd, are shown in Appendix I. Most notable are the educational accomplishments of the female members of the family, namely, May, Verne, Ethel De Vere, and Evans. They were teachers or school heads. Cordelia, the youngest, opted for marriage before completing her education, and shepherded her sons to greater heights as professionals, lawyers/bankers and educators. Thomas, Burrell Whatley's second son, met with a violent death but through his son, Roy, corralled the family's homestead and estate, thus extending the legacy of the Harrell family itself. Not least in the accomplishments of the family was the Mother, Cordelia Alpha Combs Harrell, who instilled educational values in most, and saw to it that the girls and the baby boy, Sam, the only one of the sons to graduate from college, would be sufficiently educated so as to lead contributory lives. She moved to the center of education in East Alabama, Auburn, as it is the alma mater of many of her grandchildren, their spouses as well as so many of their children.

The "Harrells" who stand as the "keepers" of the Harrell fortunes today are John Will Johnson, Jr., son of Cordelia, and Frank Colville Harrell, son of Roy, and grandson of Thomas Gordon. Colville is the principal beneficiary of his father's acumen and talents in garnering and retaining and extending the family's landholdings. He also retains the "Rose Hill Plantation" along with his brother Roy Jr. intended for his Uncle Burrell's children for perpetual safekeeping. He along with his spouse and issue occupy and control the still vast acreage, most of which was acquired by his Grand Uncle Burrell Floyd and Great Grandfather Burrell Whatley. The driveway to Colville's grand ranch house is exactly one-mile long, ending in a cul-de-sac at the front of a magnificently appointed edifice. The setting is cosmic, for the rear of the house overlooks a grand crystal-clear lake designed for his personal and family enjoyment.

The construction of Interstate Highway 85, through the Harrell property at Georgia State Road 18, has fulfilled the prophecy of hastening the economic demise of West Point. It is still a viable little city that retains the Headquarters of the now West Point-Stevens Manufacturing Company, still the pre-eminent purveyor of cotton products to the world. It is also the home of one of the largest construction and engineering companies in the southeast – The Batson-Cook Company. Except for the modest buildup around the interchange, there has been little change in the landscape at Rose Hill Plantation and the surrounding communities. The bulk of the economic activity has moved farther south into Alabama as feared by the Georgia politicians back when. Rose Hill's farming activity is gone but the shimmering leaves of the sweet gum trees still remain among those skyscraping Georgia pines as backdrop as far as one can see. On a clear day, it's forever.

But wait! West Point has not yet been vanquished by those points south in Alabama. The very lands that were just covered in this book have just been opened up to commercial development. The KIA Motor Corporation of Korea has contracted to construct an automobile plant with suppliers and subsidiaries on the premises. This land came to the attention of Korean industrialists when traveling from Atlanta to their Montgomery, Alabama plant where Hyundai automobiles are being built. The acquisition for the KIA plant and supporting industries was consummated in March of 2006 between the State of Georgia and the Government of Korea. Most of the region in and around the proposed sites are perked to benefit from this expansive industry to include communities in which Korean Nationals may want to sequester themselves in their new land of opportunity. This portends great economic and social challenges for West Point and the region. Colville Harrell indicated that when this deal is completed, the impact would be like winning the national lottery! This further portends the rebirth of West Point, Georgia and its surroundings. Mister Burrell lives!

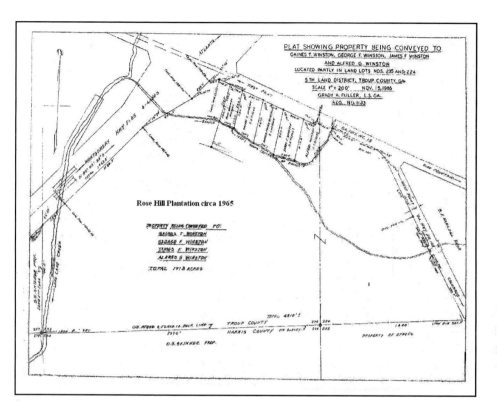

Rose Hill Plantation circa 1965

Note. This drawing shows the Homestead property of the Winstons at two weeks before their father's death. Note the lots marked off at the center top of the drawing. They are the properties, which were conveyed to the Sons in 1962. The rest of the land south of Route 18 was supposed to be conveyed to the sons in December1965.

245

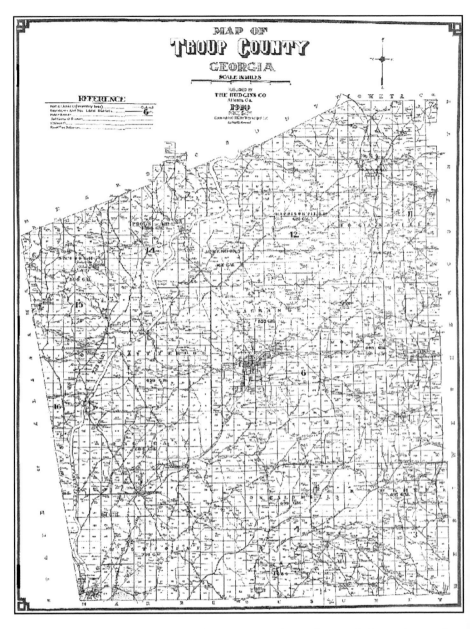

Troup County is situated on the western boundary of Georgia at the Alabama line. It has been the center of the textile industry in Georgia. Its principal cities are West Point and LaGrange, the county seat. West Point, seen at the lower left corner, is the location of the story. The Harrells owned significant acreage and were big time farmers.

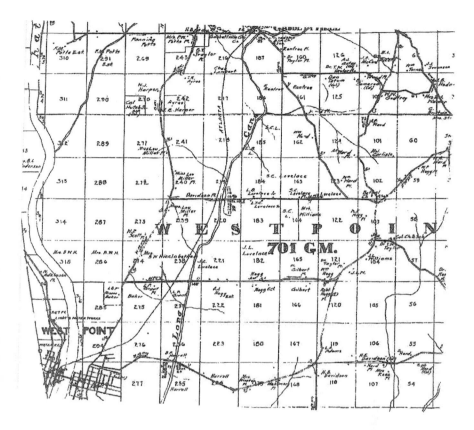

This excerpt from the preceding map shows the B.F. Harrell holdings in 1910. The Rose Hill Plantation occupies Land Lots 235 and 234 and into 175. Acquisitions by B. F. Harrell and later by Nephew Roy extended north and beyond. The intersection of I-85 (not shown) and Georgia State Highway 18 is at a point east of the Long Cane Creek extending through Land Lots 165 and beyond. KIA Corp. has purchased more than 600 acres to the west of the Interstate with plans of acquiring more toward the east.

APPENDIX I
Descendants of Abner Harrell

Generation No. 1

1. ABNER[1] HARRELL

Child of ABNER HARRELL is:
2.   i.   SAMUEL[2] HARRELL, b. 1774; d. 09 Jun 1843, Shawmut, Chambers County, AL.

Generation No. 2

2. SAMUEL[2] HARRELL *(ABNER[1])* was born 1774, and died 09 Jun 1843 in Shawmut, Chambers County, AL. He married SUSANNAH HEATH 1803 in Shawmut, Chambers County, AL. She was born 1782 in Virginia, and died 07 Nov 1860 in Shawmut, Chambers County, AL.

Child of SAMUEL HARRELL and SUSANNAH HEATH is:
3.   i.   ALFRED LEE[3] HARRELL, b. 07 Mar 1808, Troup County, Georgia; d. 15 Oct 1866, Cusseta, Chambers County, Alabama.

Generation No. 3

3. ALFRED LEE[3] HARRELL *(SAMUEL[2], ABNER[1])* was born 07 Mar 1808 in Troup County, Georgia, and died 15 Oct 1866 in Cusseta, Chambers County, Alabama. He married MAHALA T. WHATLEY 25 Aug 1835 in Chambers County, Alabama. She was born 01 Mar 1816 in Troup County, Georgia, and died 19 Feb 1895 in Cusseta, Chambers County, Alabama.

Child of ALFRED HARRELL and MAHALA WHATLEY is:
4.   i.   BURRELL WHATLEY[4] HARRELL, b. 17 May 1847, Cusseta, Chambers County, Alabama; d. 06 Jan 1901, West Point, Troup County, GA.

Generation No. 4

4. BURRELL WHATLEY[4] HARRELL *(ALFRED LEE[3], SAMUEL[2], ABNER[1])* was born 17 May 1847 in Cusseta, Chambers County, Alabama, and died 06 Jan 1901 in West Point, Troup County, GA. He married CORDELIA ALPHA COMBS 09 Oct 1869 in Cusseta, Chambers County, Alabama. She was born 25 Apr 1852 in Cusseta, Chambers County, Alabama, and died 17 May 1941 in West Point, Troup County, GA.

Children of BURRELL HARRELL and CORDELIA COMBS are:
      i.   MAY JIMMIE[5] HARRELL, b. 1870, West Point, Troup County, GA; d. 1965, West Point, Troup County, GA; m. DUNCAN.

248

5.   ii.   ALFRED LEE HARRELL, b. 02 Feb 1873, West Point, Troup County, GA; d. 24 Feb 1947, West Point, Troup County, GA.

6.   iii. THOMAS GORDON HARRELL, b. 01 Jul 1876, West Point, Troup County, GA; d. 28 Mar 1920, West Point, Troup County, GA.

          iv. ROBERT CLAUDE HARRELL, b. 29 Oct 1878.

          v.   INA VERNE HARRELL, b. 1881, West Point, Troup County, GA; d. West Point, Troup County, GA; m. IKE COLE; d. Columbus, Muscogee Cty, GA.

7.   vi. BURRELL FLOYD HARRELL, b. 08 May 1884, West Point, Troup County, GA; d. 01 Dec 1965, West Point, Troup County, GA.

8.   vii. ETHEL DEVERE HARRELL, b. 26 Mar 1886, West Point, Troup County, GA; d. Dec 1970, Pittsburgh, Allegheny Cty, PA.

         viii. E. O. EVANS HARRELL, b. 1889, West Point, Troup County, GA; d. Nov 1973, Lanett, Chambers County, AL.

9.   ix. SAMUEL CHEATHAM HARRELL, b. 1892, West Point, Troup County, GA; d. 18 Jul 1930, Birmingham, AL.

10.   x.   CORDELIA COMBS HARRELL, b. 1896, West Point, Troup County, GA; d. 1958, Langdale, Chambers Cty, AL.

Generation No. 5

5. ALFRED LEE[5] HARRELL *(BURRELL WHATLEY[4], ALFRED LEE[3], SAMUEL[2], ABNER[1])* was born 02 Feb 1873 in West Point, Troup County, GA, and died 24 Feb 1947 in West Point, Troup County, GA. He married SARAH THORNTON in West Point, Troup County, GA. She was born 23 Oct 1893 in West Point, Troup County, GA, and died 04 Aug 1967 in West Point, Troup County, GA.

Children of ALFRED HARRELL and SARAH THORNTON are:

         i.   FRANCES[6] HARRELL.

         ii. ALFRED LEE HARRELL, JR., m. MARY.

6. THOMAS GORDON[5] HARRELL *(BURRELL WHATLEY[4], ALFRED LEE[3], SAMUEL[2], ABNER[1])* was born 01 Jul 1876 in West Point, Troup County, GA, and died 28 Mar 1920 in West Point, Troup County, GA. He married LURA WALLACE 09 Jul 1901, daughter of JOHN WALLACE and MYRTIE STRICKLAND. She was born 1879 in Greenville, Meriwether County, Georgia, and died 1960 in West Point, Troup County, GA.

Children of THOMAS HARRELL and LURA WALLACE are:

11.   i.   ROY WALLACE[6] HARRELL, b. 01 Jul 1903, West Point, Troup County, GA; d. 1986, West Point, Troup County, GA.

         ii. HUGH HARRELL.

         iii. THOMAS WILLARD HARRELL.

7. BURRELL FLOYD[5] HARRELL *(BURRELL WHATLEY[4], ALFRED LEE[3], SAMUEL[2], ABNER[1])* was born 08 May 1884 in West Point, Troup County, GA, and died 01 Dec 1965 in West Point, Troup County, GA. He met ROSA WINSTON-DAVIDSON 1910 in West Point, Troup County, GA. She was born 17 May 1890 in West Point, Troup County, GA, and died 16 Jun 1977 in West Point, Troup County, GA.

Children of BURRELL HARRELL and ROSA WINSTON-DAVIDSON are:

12.   i.   MRS. ROSA BELLE[6] WINSTON-HARRELL, b. 18 May 1911, West Point, Troup County, GA; d. 24 May 2003, West Point, Troup County, GA.

         ii.   GEORGE FRANK WINSTON-HARRELL, b. 16 Jul 1916, West Point, Troup County, GA; d. 25 Jun 1970, West Point, Troup County, GA.

13.   iii.   MARGUERITE GLORIA WINSTON-HARRELL, b. 22 Sep 1919, West Point, Troup County, GA; d. 24 Aug 1991, West Point, Troup County, GA.

14.   iv.   PRECIOUS MYRA WINSTON-HARRELL, b. 28 Jan 1922, West Point, Troup County, GA.

15.   v.   JOHN THOMAS WINSTON-HARRELL, b. 24 Apr 1923, West Point, Troup County, GA; d. 04 Sep 2002, West Point, Troup County, GA.

         vi.   ALFRED GORDON WINSTON-HARRELL, b. 19 Aug 1924, West Point, Troup County, GA; d. 10 Oct 1969, West Point, Troup County, GA.

         vii.   JAMES FLOYD WINSTON-HARRELL, b. 04 Mar 1926, West Point, Troup County, GA; d. 09 Sep 1968, West Point, Troup County, GA.

16.   viii.   MARY BESSIE WINSTON-HARRELL, b. 16 Sep 1928, West Point, Troup County, GA.

         ix.   GAINES TYRONE WINSTON-HARRELL, b. 14 Jul 1930, West Point, Troup County, GA; d. 12 Jan 1991, West Point, Troup County, GA.

8. ETHEL DEVERE[5] HARRELL (*BURRELL WHATLEY[4], ALFRED LEE[3], SAMUEL[2], ABNER[1]*) was born 26 Mar 1886 in West Point, Troup County, GA, and died Dec 1970 in Pittsburgh, Allegheny Cty, PA. She married LONSON MONSON WHITTEN 02 Oct 1906 in West Point, Troup County, GA. He was born 31 Mar 1886 in South Bend, St. Joseph Cty, IN, and died 21 May 1951 in Sarasota, FL.

Children of ETHEL HARRELL and LONSON WHITTEN are:

17.   i.   OLIVE VERNE[6] WHITTEN, b. 19 Nov 1907, West Point, Troup County, GA; d. 13 Aug 1975, Auburn, Lee County, AL.

         ii.   CORDELIA WHITTEN, b. 16 Dec 1911.

         iii.   MAY HARRELL WHITTEN, b. 31 Jan 1915.

9. SAMUEL CHEATHAM[5] HARRELL (*BURRELL WHATLEY[4], ALFRED LEE[3], SAMUEL[2], ABNER[1]*) was born 1892 in West Point, Troup County, GA, and died 18 Jul 1930 in Birmingham, AL. He married MARGIE THORNTON 1924 in Birmingham, AL. She was born in Birmingham, Jefferson Cty, AL, and died Unknown in unknown.

Child of SAMUEL HARRELL and MARGIE THORNTON is:

         i.   MARGARETTE "PEGGY"[6] THORNTON-HARRELL, b. 1919, Birmingham, Jefferson Cty, AL; d. Unknown; Adopted child.

10. CORDELIA COMBS[5] HARRELL (*BURRELL WHATLEY[4], ALFRED LEE[3], SAMUEL[2], ABNER[1]*) was born 1896 in West Point, Troup County, GA, and died 1958 in Langdale, Chambers Cty, AL. She married JOHN WILLIAM JOHNSON in Langdale, AL.

Children of CORDELIA HARRELL and JOHN JOHNSON are:

         i.   MARIE HARRELL[6] JOHNSON, b. 09 Nov 1918.

         ii.   JOHN WILLIAM "BUBBER" JOHNSON, JR., b. 19 Jul 1920.

iii. EVANS COMBS JOHNSON, b. 09 Nov 1922.

11. ROY WALLACE[6] HARRELL *(THOMAS GORDON[5], BURRELL WHATLEY[4], ALFRED LEE[3], SAMUEL[2], ABNER[1])* was born 01 Jul 1903 in West Point, Troup County, GA, and died 1986 in West Point, Troup County, GA. He married PEARL "BEBE" COLVILLE 17 Nov 1928 in McMinnville, TN, daughter of FRANK COLVILLE and MAY RICE. She was born 19 Jun 1904 in McMinnville, TN, and died 20 Feb 2005 in LaGrange, Troup County, GA.

Children of ROY HARRELL and PEARL COLVILLE are:

    i.   ROY WALLACE[7] HARRELL, JR., b. 31 Dec 1930, West Point, Troup County, GA; m. JULIE SHEPPARD, West Point, Troup County, GA.

    ii.   FRANK COLVILLE HARRELL, b. 16 Dec 1934, West Point, Troup County, GA; m. VIVIAN DORIS HARPER, 31 Aug 1956, West Point, Troup County, GA.

    iii. GAIL HARRELL, b. 1936.

12. MRS. ROSA BELLE[6] WINSTON-HARRELL *(BURRELL FLOYD[5] HARRELL, BURRELL WHATLEY[4], ALFRED LEE[3], SAMUEL[2], ABNER[1])* was born 18 May 1911 in West Point, Troup County, GA, and died 24 May 2003 in West Point, Troup County, GA. She married WALTER PARKER 1934 in West Point, Troup County, GA. He was born 1906 in West Point, Troup County, GA, and died 13 Dec 1965 in West Point, Troup County, GA.

Children of ROSA WINSTON-HARRELL and WALTER PARKER are:

18.   i.   PEARSON[7] PARKER, b. 20 Aug 1934, West Point, Troup County, GA.

19.   ii.   EDGAR PARKER, b. 16 Aug 1936, West Point, Troup County, GA.

20.   iii. ROSALIND PARKER, b. 1938, West Point, Troup County, GA; d. 1966, West Point, Troup County, GA.

21.   iv. GREGG PARKER, b. 1942, West Point, Troup County, GA.

    v.   EMILY ROSE PARKER, b. 31 Oct 1944, West Point, Troup County, GA; m. JOHN REED.

13. MARGUERITE GLORIA[6] WINSTON-HARRELL *(BURRELL FLOYD[5] HARRELL, BURRELL WHATLEY[4], ALFRED LEE[3], SAMUEL[2], ABNER[1])* was born 22 Sep 1919 in West Point, Troup County, GA, and died 24 Aug 1991 in West Point, Troup County, GA. She married RAYMOND ADAMS, SENIOR May 1940 in Marietta, Cobb,GA. He was born 24 Nov 1908 in Green County, GA, and died Jul 1991 in Atlanta, Fulton County, GA.

Children of MARGUERITE WINSTON-HARRELL and RAYMOND ADAMS are:

22.   i.   BRENDA[7] ADAMS, b. 02 Aug 1943, Atlanta, Fulton County, GA.

23.   ii.   PAMELA ADAMS, b. 02 May 1948, Atlanta, Fulton County, GA; d. 22 May 1969, Atlanta, Fulton County, GA.

    iii. RAYMOND ADAMS, JR., b. 07 Dec 1941, Atlanta, Fulton County, GA; d. 22 May 1969, Atlanta, Fulton County, GA.

14. PRECIOUS MYRA[6] WINSTON-HARRELL *(BURRELL FLOYD[5] HARRELL, BURRELL WHATLEY[4], ALFRED LEE[3], SAMUEL[2], ABNER[1])* was born 28 Jan 1922 in West Point, Troup County, GA. She married EDDIE BROOKS 30 May 1954 in Detroit, Michigan. He was born 11 May 1919 in Gabbettville, Troup County, GA, and died 19 Aug 2001 in West Point, Troup County, GA.

Children of PRECIOUS WINSTON-HARRELL and EDDIE BROOKS are:

    i.   THOMAS FLOYD[7] BROOKS, b. 12 Dec 1947.

   ii.   HARRELL WINSTON BROOKS, b. 01 Feb 1957.

15. JOHN THOMAS[6] WINSTON-HARRELL *(BURRELL FLOYD[5] HARRELL, BURRELL WHATLEY[4], ALFRED LEE[3], SAMUEL[2], ABNER[1])* was born 24 Apr 1923 in West Point, Troup County, GA, and died 04 Sep 2002 in West Point, Troup County, GA. He met (1) MOZELL GILLIAM. She was born 07 Oct 1917 in West Point, Troup County, GA, and died in West Point, Troup County, GA. He married (2) ARDELL DAVIDSON 19 Feb 1952 in West Point, Troup County, GA. She was born 07 Nov 1931 in West Point, Troup County, GA.

Children of JOHN WINSTON-HARRELL and MOZELL GILLIAM are:

    i.   DONALD[7] GILLIAM-WINSTON-HARRELL, b. 11 Jan 1941, West Point, Troup County, GA.

   ii.   GAYNELL GILLIAM-WINSTON-HARRELL, b. 09 Oct 1942, West Point, Troup County, GA.

Children of JOHN WINSTON-HARRELL and ARDELL DAVIDSON are:

   iii.   THOMAS DELL[7] WINSTON-HARRELL, b. 06 Jun 1952.

   iv.   WILLIAM CARL WINSTON-HARRELL, b. 23 Nov 1953.

    v.   VICTOR MORRIS WINSTON-HARRELL, b. 17 Jul 1955.

   vi.   TERRI ANN WINSTON-HARRELL, b. 23 Mar 1957.

   vii.   DEXTER CURT WINSTON-HARRELL, b. 05 May 1959, West Point, Troup County, GA; d. 1964, West Point, Troup County, GA.

   viii.   VALERIE JAN WINSTON-HARRELL, b. 26 Jan 1962.

16. MARY BESSIE[6] WINSTON-HARRELL *(BURRELL FLOYD[5] HARRELL, BURRELL WHATLEY[4], ALFRED LEE[3], SAMUEL[2], ABNER[1])* was born 16 Sep 1928 in West Point, Troup County, GA. She married JIM ERNEST FANNINGS 13 Sep 1947 in West Point, Troup County, GA. He was born 17 Mar 1927 in West Point, Troup County, GA, and died 23 Dec 1993 in West Point, Troup County, GA.

Children of MARY WINSTON-HARRELL and JIM FANNINGS are:

    i.   BEVERLY EVE[7] FANNINGS, b. 24 Dec 1948, West Point, Troup County, GA; d. May 2004, Columbus, Muscogee Cty, GA; m. JAMES EARL MAYO, 1998; d. Jan 2003.

   ii.   JIM ERNEST FANNINGS, JR., b. 22 Sep 1951.

17. OLIVE VERNE[6] WHITTEN *(ETHEL DEVERE[5] HARRELL, BURRELL WHATLEY[4], ALFRED LEE[3], SAMUEL[2], ABNER[1])* was born 19 Nov 1907 in West Point, Troup County, GA, and died 13 Aug 1975 in Auburn, Lee County, AL. She married JAMES NICHOLAS FICHTER 02 Apr 1907 in Alva, FL. He was born 02 Apr 1900 in Vero Beach, FL, and died 31 Jan 1965 in Punta Gorda, FL.

Children of OLIVE WHITTEN and JAMES FICHTER are:
24.   i.   ETHEL JEANNETTE[7] FICHTER, b. 30 Dec 1932, Alva, FL.
        ii. ROBERT WHITTEN FICHTER, b. 30 Dec 1939, Fort Myers, Florida; m. NANCY SMITH, 01 May 1985.
       iii. CORDELIA WHITTEN FICHTER, m. VIRGIL WAYNE BARKER.

Generation No. 7

18. PEARSON[7] PARKER *(ROSA BELLE[6] WINSTON-HARRELL, BURRELL FLOYD[5] HARRELL, BURRELL WHATLEY[4], ALFRED LEE[3], SAMUEL[2], ABNER[1])* was born 20 Aug 1934 in West Point, Troup County, GA. He married BERNICE WILLIS 11 May 1959 in LaGrange, Troup County, GA. She was born 04 Apr 1937 in Albany, Georgia.

Children of PEARSON PARKER and BERNICE WILLIS are:
      i.   PEARSON[8] PARKER, JR., b. 03 Aug 1960.
      ii. BERNARD PARKER, b. 13 Sep 1961.
     iii. SUSIE ROSE PARKER, b. 15 Feb 1967.

19. EDGAR[7] PARKER *(ROSA BELLE[6] WINSTON-HARRELL, BURRELL FLOYD[5] HARRELL, BURRELL WHATLEY[4], ALFRED LEE[3], SAMUEL[2], ABNER[1])* was born 16 Aug 1936 in West Point, Troup County, GA. He married MONA.

Children of EDGAR PARKER and MONA are:
      i.   EDGAR[8] PARKER, JR..
      ii. PHILLIP TODD PARKER.

20. ROSALIND[7] PARKER *(ROSA BELLE[6] WINSTON-HARRELL, BURRELL FLOYD[5] HARRELL, BURRELL WHATLEY[4], ALFRED LEE[3], SAMUEL[2], ABNER[1])* was born 1938 in West Point, Troup County, GA, and died 1966 in West Point, Troup County, GA. She met BURRESS.

Child of ROSALIND PARKER and BURRESS is:
      i.   ANDREA[8] PARKER-BURRESS, b. 1965.

21. GREGG[7] PARKER *(ROSA BELLE[6] WINSTON-HARRELL, BURRELL FLOYD[5] HARRELL, BURRELL WHATLEY[4], ALFRED LEE[3], SAMUEL[2], ABNER[1])* was born 1942 in West Point, Troup County, GA. He married MERITA.

Children of GREGG PARKER and MERITA are:
      i.   WALTER[8] PARKER.

ii. MONICA PARKER.
iii. PARKE PARKER.

22. BRENDA[7] ADAMS *(MARGUERITE GLORIA[6] WINSTON-HARRELL, BURRELL FLOYD[5] HARRELL, BURRELL WHATLEY[4], ALFRED LEE[3], SAMUEL[2], ABNER[1])* was born 02 Aug 1943 in Atlanta, Fulton County, GA. She married (1) FREDDIE EUGENE MYRICK Jan 1964 in Atlanta, Fulton County, GA. He was born 1941 in Warrenton, Georgia, and died 1980 in Warren, Georgia. She married (2) COYLE WISE 02 Feb 1966 in Atlanta, GA. He was born 31 Jan 1939 in Atlanta, Fulton County, GA, and died 18 Dec 1975 in Atlanta, Fulton County, GA.

Child of BRENDA ADAMS and FREDDIE MYRICK is:
    i. DERRICK ANTHONY[8] MYRICK, b. 13 Dec 1964.

Children of BRENDA ADAMS and COYLE WISE are:
    ii. TERRENCE COYLE[8] WISE, b. 31 Mar 1967.
    iii. CARLOS RODRIGUEZ WISE, b. 28 Nov 1968.
    iv. ALEJANDRO MIGUEL WISE, b. 21 Sep 1970.

23. PAMELA[7] ADAMS *(MARGUERITE GLORIA[6] WINSTON-HARRELL, BURRELL FLOYD[5] HARRELL, BURRELL WHATLEY[4], ALFRED LEE[3], SAMUEL[2], ABNER[1])* was born 02 May 1948 in Atlanta, Fulton County, GA, and died 22 May 1969 in Atlanta, Fulton County, GA. She married WILLIE CURTIS in Atlanta, Fulton County, GA.

Child of PAMELA ADAMS and WILLIE CURTIS is:
    i. CHERYL LYNN[8] CURTIS.

24. ETHEL JEANNETTE[7] FICHTER *(OLIVE VERNE[6] WHITTEN, ETHEL DEVERE[5] HARRELL, BURRELL WHATLEY[4], ALFRED LEE[3], SAMUEL[2], ABNER[1])* was born 30 Dec 1932 in Alva, FL. She married JOHN WRIGHT BLOW 31 Jan 1955.

Children of ETHEL FICHTER and JOHN BLOW are:
    i. MARGARET VERNE[8] BLOW, b. 03 Nov 1960.
    ii. ELIZABETH LOVETT BLOW, b. 18 Oct 1963.
    iii. SUSAN LUCRETIA BLOW, b. 02 Jun 1965.

APPENDIX II

Descendants of Burrell Floyd Harrell

Generation No. 1

1. BURRELL FLOYD[5] HARRELL *(BURRELL WHATLEY[4], ALFRED LEE[3], SAMUEL[2], ABNER[1])* was born 08 May 1884 in West Point, Troup County, GA, and died 01 Dec 1965 in West Point, Troup County, GA. He met ROSA WINSTON-DAVIDSON 1910 in West Point, Troup County, GA. She was born 17 May 1890 in West Point, Troup County, GA, and died 16 Jun 1977 in West Point, Troup County, GA.

Children of BURRELL HARRELL and ROSA WINSTON-DAVIDSON are:

2.	i.	MRS. ROSA BELLE[6] WINSTON-HARRELL, b. 18 May 1911, West Point, Troup County, GA; d. 24 May 2003, West Point, Troup County, GA.
	ii.	GEORGE FRANK WINSTON-HARRELL, b. 16 Jul 1916, West Point, Troup County, GA; d. 25 Jun 1970, West Point, Troup County, GA.
3.	iii.	MARGUERITE GLORIA WINSTON-HARRELL, b. 22 Sep 1919, West Point, Troup County, GA; d. 24 Aug 1991, West Point, Troup County, GA.
4.	iv.	PRECIOUS MYRA WINSTON-HARRELL, b. 28 Jan 1922, West Point, Troup County, GA.
5.	v.	JOHN THOMAS WINSTON-HARRELL, b. 24 Apr 1923, West Point, Troup County, GA; d. 04 Sep 2002, West Point, Troup County, GA.
	vi.	ALFRED GORDON WINSTON-HARRELL, b. 19 Aug 1924, West Point, Troup County, GA; d. 10 Oct 1969, West Point, Troup County, GA.
	vii.	JAMES FLOYD WINSTON-HARRELL, b. 04 Mar 1926, West Point, Troup County, GA; d. 09 Sep 1968, West Point, Troup County, GA.
6.	viii.	MARY BESSIE WINSTON-HARRELL, b. 16 Sep 1928, West Point, Troup County, GA.
	ix.	GAINES TYRONE WINSTON-HARRELL, b. 14 Jul 1930, West Point, Troup County, GA; d. 12 Jan 1991, West Point, Troup County, GA.

Generation No. 2

2. MRS. ROSA BELLE[6] WINSTON-HARRELL *(BURRELL FLOYD[5] HARRELL, BURRELL WHATLEY[4], ALFRED LEE[3], SAMUEL[2], ABNER[1])* was born 18 May 1911 in West Point, Troup County, GA, and died 24 May 2003 in West Point, Troup County, GA. She married WALTER PARKER 1934 in West Point, Troup County, GA. He was born 1906 in West Point, Troup County, GA, and died 13 Dec 1965 in West Point, Troup County, GA.

Children of ROSA WINSTON-HARRELL and WALTER PARKER are:

7.	i.	PEARSON[7] PARKER, b. 20 Aug 1934, West Point, Troup County, GA.
8.	ii.	EDGAR PARKER, b. 16 Aug 1936, West Point, Troup County, GA.
9.	iii.	ROSALIND PARKER, b. 1938, West Point, Troup County, GA; d. 1966, West Point, Troup County, GA.
10.	iv.	GREGG PARKER, b. 1942, West Point, Troup County, GA.
	v.	EMILY ROSE PARKER, b. 31 Oct 1944, West Point, Troup County, GA; m. JOHN REED.

255

3. MARGUERITE GLORIA[6] WINSTON-HARRELL *(BURRELL FLOYD[5] HARRELL, BURRELL WHATLEY[4], ALFRED LEE[3], SAMUEL[2], ABNER[1])* was born 22 Sep 1919 in West Point, Troup County, GA, and died 24 Aug 1991 in West Point, Troup County, GA. She married RAYMOND ADAMS, SENIOR May 1940 in Marietta, Cobb,GA. He was born 24 Nov 1908 in Green County, GA, and died Jul 1991 in Atlanta, Fulton County, GA.

Children of MARGUERITE WINSTON-HARRELL and RAYMOND ADAMS are:

11.　　　i.　BRENDA[7] ADAMS, b. 02 Aug 1943, Atlanta, Fulton County, GA.
12.　　　ii.　PAMELA ADAMS, b. 02 May 1948, Atlanta, Fulton County, GA; d. 22 May 1969, Atlanta, Fulton County, GA.
　　　　iii.　RAYMOND ADAMS, JR., b. 07 Dec 1941, Atlanta, Fulton County, GA; d. 22 May 1969, Atlanta, Fulton County, GA.

4. PRECIOUS MYRA[6] WINSTON-HARRELL *(BURRELL FLOYD[5] HARRELL, BURRELL WHATLEY[4], ALFRED LEE[3], SAMUEL[2], ABNER[1])* was born 28 Jan 1922 in West Point, Troup County, GA. She married EDDIE BROOKS 30 May 1954 in Detroit, Michigan. He was born 11 May 1919 in Gabbettville, Troup County, GA, and died 19 Aug 2001 in West Point, Troup County, GA.

Children of PRECIOUS WINSTON-HARRELL and EDDIE BROOKS are:

　　　　i.　THOMAS FLOYD[7] BROOKS, b. 12 Dec 1947.
　　　　ii.　HARRELL WINSTON BROOKS, b. 01 Feb 1957.

5. JOHN THOMAS[6] WINSTON-HARRELL *(BURRELL FLOYD[5] HARRELL, BURRELL WHATLEY[4], ALFRED LEE[3], SAMUEL[2], ABNER[1])* was born 24 Apr 1923 in West Point, Troup County, GA, and died 04 Sep 2002 in West Point, Troup County, GA. He met (1) MOZELL GILLIAM. She was born 07 Oct 1917 in West Point, Troup County, GA, and died in West Point, Troup County, GA. He married (2) ARDELL DAVIDSON 19 Feb 1952 in West Point, Troup County, GA. She was born 07 Nov 1931 in West Point, Troup County, GA.

Children of JOHN WINSTON-HARRELL and MOZELL GILLIAM are:

　　　　i.　DONALD[7] GILLIAM-WINSTON-HARRELL, b. 11 Jan 1941, West Point, Troup County, GA.
　　　　ii.　GAYNELL GILLIAM-WINSTON-HARRELL, b. 09 Oct 1942, West Point, Troup County, GA.

Children of JOHN WINSTON-HARRELL and ARDELL DAVIDSON are:

　　　　iii.　THOMAS DELL[7] WINSTON-HARRELL, b. 06 Jun 1952.
　　　　iv.　WILLIAM CARL WINSTON-HARRELL, b. 23 Nov 1953.
　　　　v.　VICTOR MORRIS WINSTON-HARRELL, b. 17 Jul 1955.
　　　　vi.　TERRI ANN WINSTON-HARRELL, b. 23 Mar 1957.
　　　　vii.　DEXTER CURT WINSTON-HARRELL, b. 05 May 1959, West Point, Troup County, GA; d. 1964, West Point, Troup County, GA.
　　　　viii.　VALERIE JAN WINSTON-HARRELL, b. 26 Jan 1962.

6. MARY BESSIE[6] WINSTON-HARRELL *(BURRELL FLOYD[5] HARRELL, BURRELL WHATLEY[4], ALFRED LEE[3], SAMUEL[2], ABNER[1])* was born 16 Sep 1928 in West Point, Troup County, GA. She married JIM ERNEST FANNINGS 13 Sep 1947 in West Point, Troup County, GA. He was born 17 Mar 1927 in West Point, Troup County, GA, and died 23 Dec 1993 in West Point, Troup County, GA.

Children of MARY WINSTON-HARRELL and JIM FANNINGS are:
    i.   BEVERLY EVE[7] FANNINGS, b. 24 Dec 1948, West Point, Troup County, GA; d. May 2004, Columbus, Muscogee Cty, GA; m. JAMES EARL MAYO, 1998; d. Jan 2003.
   ii.   JIM ERNEST FANNINGS, JR., b. 22 Sep 1951.

Generation No. 3

7. PEARSON[7] PARKER *(ROSA BELLE[6] WINSTON-HARRELL, BURRELL FLOYD[5] HARRELL, BURRELL WHATLEY[4], ALFRED LEE[3], SAMUEL[2], ABNER[1])* was born 20 Aug 1934 in West Point, Troup County, GA. He married BERNICE WILLIS 11 May 1959 in LaGrange, Troup County, GA. She was born 04 Apr 1937 in Albany, Georgia.

Children of PEARSON PARKER and BERNICE WILLIS are:
    i.   PEARSON[8] PARKER, JR., b. 03 Aug 1960.
   ii.   BERNARD PARKER, b. 13 Sep 1961.
  iii.   SUSIE ROSE PARKER, b. 15 Feb 1967.

8. EDGAR[7] PARKER *(ROSA BELLE[6] WINSTON-HARRELL, BURRELL FLOYD[5] HARRELL, BURRELL WHATLEY[4], ALFRED LEE[3], SAMUEL[2], ABNER[1])* was born 16 Aug 1936 in West Point, Troup County, GA. He married MONA.

Children of EDGAR PARKER and MONA are:
    i.   EDGAR[8] PARKER, JR..
   ii.   PHILLIP TODD PARKER.

9. ROSALIND[7] PARKER *(ROSA BELLE[6] WINSTON-HARRELL, BURRELL FLOYD[5] HARRELL, BURRELL WHATLEY[4], ALFRED LEE[3], SAMUEL[2], ABNER[1])* was born 1938 in West Point, Troup County, GA, and died 1966 in West Point, Troup County, GA. She met BURRESS.

Child of ROSALIND PARKER and BURRESS is:
    i.   ANDREA[8] PARKER-BURRESS, b. 1965.

10. GREGG[7] PARKER *(ROSA BELLE[6] WINSTON-HARRELL, BURRELL FLOYD[5] HARRELL, BURRELL WHATLEY[4], ALFRED LEE[3], SAMUEL[2], ABNER[1])* was born 1942 in West Point, Troup County, GA. He married MERITA.

Children of GREGG PARKER and MERITA are:

      i.   WALTER[8] PARKER.
     ii.   MONICA PARKER.
   iii.   PARKE PARKER.

11. BRENDA[7] ADAMS *(MARGUERITE GLORIA[6] WINSTON-HARRELL, BURRELL FLOYD[5] HARRELL, BURRELL WHATLEY[4], ALFRED LEE[3], SAMUEL[2], ABNER[1])* was born 02 Aug 1943 in Atlanta, Fulton County, GA. She married (1) FREDDIE EUGENE MYRICK Jan 1964 in Atlanta, Fulton County, GA. He was born 1941 in Warrenton, Georgia, and died 1980 in Warren, Georgia. She married (2) COYLE WISE 02 Feb 1966 in Atlanta, GA. He was born 31 Jan 1939 in Atlanta, Fulton County, GA, and died 18 Dec 1975 in Atlanta, Fulton County, GA.

Child of BRENDA ADAMS and FREDDIE MYRICK is:
      i.   DERRICK ANTHONY[8] MYRICK, b. 13 Dec 1964.

Children of BRENDA ADAMS and COYLE WISE are:
     ii.   TERRENCE COYLE[8] WISE, b. 31 Mar 1967.
   iii.   CARLOS RODRIGUEZ WISE, b. 28 Nov 1968.
   iv.   ALEJANDRO MIGUEL WISE, b. 21 Sep 1970.

12. PAMELA[7] ADAMS *(MARGUERITE GLORIA[6] WINSTON-HARRELL, BURRELL FLOYD[5] HARRELL, BURRELL WHATLEY[4], ALFRED LEE[3], SAMUEL[2], ABNER[1])* was born 02 May 1948 in Atlanta, Fulton County, GA, and died 22 May 1969 in Atlanta, Fulton County, GA. She married WILLIE CURTIS in Atlanta, Fulton County, GA.

Child of PAMELA ADAMS and WILLIE CURTIS is:
      i.   CHERYL LYNN[8] CURTIS.

Burrell Floyd Harrell's signature

About the Author

James (Jim) Schell is a retired Federal Government and Industry  Executive now performing in his fourth career. His experience ranges from teaching to creating publications in technology and doctrinal domains, to service as a Director in Industry as well as winning a Presidential Appointment as Senior Executive, Director of Tactical Computer Systems and Software Engineering Centers, US Army.

He has written three unpublished books of the memoir genre, *Aunt Nora --The Lives and Times of a Wise Woman; Moi;* and *Talk,* various short stories, numerous technical papers, a travel log, *Trekking through France,* and two children's books, *Beepy* and *JATO.*

He is a graduate of Morehouse College in Mathematics and Physics, has studied graduate level Anthropology, and Genetics at California State University, Northridge. He pens articles occasionally for The Boulé Journal, Sigma Pi Phi Fraternity, Inc., Alpha Pi Boulé.

He is married to the former **Doris E. Hunter.** Both were born in West Point, Georgia, graduates of Tenth Street High School and now live in Ocean Hills, California. They are the parents of five adult children and seven grandchildren.

Index

ISBN 978-1-4276-0692-1; Biography, Interracial socialization, Genetics, Genealogy, History; $19.65